The Memoirs of Maurice Paléologue at the Russian Court of Nicholas II

Volume 1
July 20, 1914 – March 31, 1915

by

Maurice Paléologue

ISBN-10: 1725115352
ISBN-13: 978-1725115354

"The Memoirs of Maurice Paléologue at the Russian Court of Nicholas II, Volume 1 – July 20, 1914 – March 31, 1915' is based on Maurice Paléologue's 'An Ambassador's Memoirs, Volume 1,' first published by Plon in 1922, first published in English in 1923, and later republished by Hutchinson in 1973. The text was translated from the original French by F.A. Holt.

The current version of this book is published by Winter Palace Publishing after a full re-editing of the text, including modernization of some of the language.

Chapter 1

Monday, July 20, 1914

I left St. Petersburg at ten o'clock this morning on the Admiralty yacht and went to Peterhof. Sazonov, the Minister for Foreign Affairs, Isvolsky, the Russian Ambassador to France, and General de Laguiche, my military attaché, accompanied me. All four of us had been invited by the Tsar to lunch on the imperial yacht before going to meet the President of the Republic at Kronstadt. The staff of my Embassy, the Russian ministers and Court functionaries will go by rail direct to Peterhof.

The weather was cloudy. Our vessel steamed at high speed between low banks towards the Gulf of Finland. Suddenly a fresh breeze from the open sea brought us a heavy shower, but as suddenly the sun burst forth in his splendor. A few pearl-gray clouds, through which the sun s rays darted, hung here and there in the sky like sashes shot with gold. As far as the eye could reach, in a limpid flood of light the estuary of the Neva spread the immense sheet of its greenish, viscous, changing waters which always remind me of Venice.

At half-past eleven, we stopped in the little harbor of Peterhof where The Alexandria, the Tsar's favorite yacht, was lying under steam.

Nicholas II, in the uniform of an admiral, arrived at the quay almost at once. We transferred to The Alexandria.

Luncheon was served immediately. We had at least an hour-and-three-quarters before us until the arrival of the France, but the Tsar likes to linger over his meals. There are always long intervals between the courses in which he chats and smokes cigarettes.

I was on his right, Sazonov on his left, and Count Fredericks, Minister of the Court, was opposite us.

After a few commonplaces, the Tsar told me of his pleasure at receiving the President of the French Republic.

"We shall have weighty matters to discuss," he said. "I'm sure we shall agree on all points .But there's one question which is very much in my mind – our understanding with England. We must get her to come into our alliance. It would be such a guarantee of peace!"

"Yes, Sire," I replied. "The Triple Entente cannot be too strong if it is to keep the peace."

"I've been told that you yourself are uneasy about Germany's intentions."

"Uneasy? Yes, Sire, I am uneasy, although at the moment I have no particular reason to anticipate a war in the immediate future. But the Emperor William and his Government have let Germany get into a state of mind such that if some dispute arose – in Morocco, the East, anywhere – they could neither give way nor compromise. A success is essential at any price and to obtain it they'll risk some adventure."

The Tsar reflected a moment.

"I can't believe the Emperor wants war. If you knew him as I do! If you knew how much theatricality there is in his posing!"

"Perhaps I am doing the Emperor Wilhelm too much honor in thinking him capable of willing, or simply accepting, the consequences of his acts. But if war threatened, would he and could he prevent it? No, Sire, I don't think so, honestly I don't."

The Tsar sat silent and puffed at his cigarette. Then he said in a resolute voice, "It's all the more important for us to be able to count on England in an emergency. Unless she has gone out of her mind altogether, Germany will never attack Russia, France and England combined."

Coffee had just arrived when the French squadron was signaled. The Tsar made me go up on the bridge with him.

It was a magnificent spectacle. In a quivering, silvery light The France slowly surged forward over the turquoise and emerald waves, leaving a long white furrow behind her. Then she stopped majestically. The mighty warship, which has brought the head of the French State, is well worthy of her name. She was indeed France coming to Russia. I felt my heart beating.

For a few minutes there was a prodigious din in the harbor; the guns of the ships and the shore batteries firing, the crews cheering, the 'Marseillaise' answering the Russian national anthem, the cheers of thousands of spectators who had come from St. Petersburg on pleasure boats, and so forth.

At length the President of the Republic stepped on board The Alexandria. The Tsar received him at the gangway.

As soon as the presentations were over, the imperial yacht steered for Peterhof. Seated in the stern, the Tsar and the President immediately entered into conversation, I should perhaps say a discussion, for it was obvious that they were talking business, firing questions at each other and arguing. As was proper, it was Poincaré who had the initiative. Before long he was doing all the talking, The Tsar simply nodded acquiescence, but his whole appearance showed his sincere approval. It radiated confidence and sympathy.

Before long we were at Peterhof. Through its magnificent trees and sparkling fountains, Catherine II's favorite residence appeared above a long terrace from which a foaming cascade poured its majestic waters.

At a sharp trot our carriages ascended the drive leading to the palace entrance. At every bend we had a fleeting glimpse of some fresh vista, a line of statues, fountains or terraces. Though the detail is somewhat meretricious, one scents something of the keen and delicious atmosphere of Versailles in the balmy, sunlit air.

At half-past seven, there was a banquet in the Empress Elizabeth room.

Thanks to the brilliance of the uniforms, superb dresses, elaborate liveries, magnificent furnishings and fittings – in short the whole panoply of pomp and power – the spectacle was such as no court in the world can rival. I shall long remember the dazzling display of jewels on the women's shoulders. It was simply a fantastic shower of diamonds, pearls, rubies, sapphires, emeralds, topaz, beryls – a blaze of fire and flame.

Amid this fairy milieu, Poincaré's black coat was a drab touch, but the wide, sky-blue ribbon of St. Andrew across his breast increased his importance in the eyes of the Russians. And then it was soon seen that the Tsar was listening to him with the closest and most sympathetic attention.

During dinner I kept an eye on the Tsaritza Alexandra Feodorovna, opposite whom I was sitting. Although long ceremonies are a very great trial to her, she was anxious to be present this evening to do honor to the President of the Allied Republic. She was a beautiful sight with her low brocade gown and a diamond tiara on her head. Her forty-two years have left her face and figure still pleasant to look upon.

After the first course she entered into conversation with Poincaré who was on her right. Before long, however, her smile became set and the veins stood out in her cheeks. She bit her lips every minute. Her labored breathing made the network of diamonds sparkle on her bosom. Until the end of dinner, which was very long, the poor woman was obviously struggling with hysteria.

Her features suddenly relaxed when the Tsar rose to propose his toast. The imperial speech was received in a composed silence, for it was the reply which was most eagerly awaited.

Poincaré spoke without notes instead of reading his speech as the Tsar had done. Never had his diction been more clear, lucid and pointed. What he said was only the stale and formal official verbiage, but in his mouth the words acquired a remarkable wealth of meaning and authority. The effect was quite marked on that audience, brought up as it was in the traditions of despotism and the discipline of courts. I'm sure that of those decorated functionaries, more than one thought, "That's how an autocrat should talk."

After dinner, the Tsar held a levee. The general eagerness to be presented to Poincaré showed he had been a success. Even the German clique, the ultra-reactionary group, sought the honor of an introduction to the President.

At eleven o'clock, a procession was formed. The Tsar conducted the President of the Republic to his room. There Poincaré kept me in conversation a few minutes. We exchanged impressions, and very good they were.

When I returned to St. Petersburg by rail at a quarter to one in the morning, I heard that this afternoon the principal factories went on strike for no reason and on a signal from no one knows where. There have been collisions with the police at several points. My informant knows the working-class quarters well and tells me that the movement has been instigated by German agents.

Tuesday, July 21, 1914

The President of the Republic has spent to-day visiting St. Petersburg.

Before leaving Peterhof he was in conference with the Tsar. They discussed variously all the questions on the diplomatic agenda at the moment: the strained relations between Greece and Turkey; the intrigues of the Bulgarian Government in the Balkans; the Prince of Wied's arrival in Albania; the application of the Anglo-Russian Agreements in Persia; the political orientation of the Scandinavian States, etc. They concluded their review with the problem of the Austro-Serbian dispute, a problem which becomes more worrying every day owing to the arrogant and mysterious attitude of Austria.

Poincaré has insisted with great force that the only way of saving the peace of the world is an open discussion between all the Great Powers, taking care that one group is not opposed to another.

"It's the method that served us so well in 1913," he said. "Let's try it again!"

Nicholas II entirely agreed.

At half-past one, I attended the President at the imperial quay near to Nicholas Bridge. The Naval Minister, the Prefect of Police, the Commander of the Fortress and the municipal authorities were there to receive him.

In accordance with the old Slav rites, Count Ivan Tolstoy, the Mayor of the capital, offered him bread and salt. Then we mounted our carriages to visit the Fortress of Saints Peter and Paul, which is the Bastille and the St. Denis of the Romanovs. As tradition decrees, the President laid a wreath on the tomb of Alexander III, father of the alliance.

Escorted by the Guard Cossacks, whose scarlet tunics flamed in the sunshine, our carriages passed along the Neva at a smart trot.

A few days ago, when I was settling with Sazonov the final details of the President's visit, he had said to me with a smile, "The Guard Cossacks have been told to escort the President. You see what fine figures they'll cut! They're splendid fellows, fearful fellows. Besides, they're dressed in red. I rather think your President of the Council, Monsieur Viviani, does not dislike that color."

I had replied, "No, he doesn't dislike it, but his artistic eye doesn't enjoy it thoroughly, except when it's next to white and blue."

In their scarlet tunics these long-haired, bearded and bristly Cossacks are certainly a formidable sight. When our carriages disappeared with them through the gateway of the fortress, a spectator with a turn for irony, or a lover of historical antitheses might well have asked whether it was not to the State Prison that they were conducting these two certified and avowed "revolutionaries," President Poincaré and President of the Council Viviani, not to mention myself, their accomplice. The moral contradiction in terms, the tacit paradox in the background of the Franco-Russian Alliance, has never struck me more forcibly.

At three o'clock, the President received the deputations of the French colonies in St. Petersburg and throughout Russia. Some of them had come from Moscow, Kharkov, Odessa, Kiev, Rostov, Tiflis. In presenting them to Poincaré, I could say with perfect sincerity, "Their eagerness to come and greet you in no way surprises me. Every day I see practical proofs of the fervent and pious love of the French colonies in

Russia for their distant homeland. In no province of our old France, Monsieur le Président, will you find better Frenchmen than those here before you."

At four o'clock, the procession was reformed to take the President to the Winter Palace where a diplomatic levee was to be held. We received an enthusiastic welcome all along the route. The police had arranged it all. At every street corner a group of poor wretches cheered loudly under the eye of a policeman.

At the Winter Palace, it was a full-dress occasion and etiquette required that the ambassadors should be introduced one by one to the President, who had Viviani on his left. It was my function to present my foreign colleagues.

The first to enter was the German Ambassador, Count Pourtalès, doyen of the Corps Diplomatique. The President received him with the greatest affability. He asked him about the French origin of his family, his wife's relationship to the Castellanes, a motor tour which the Count and Countess were proposing to make through Provence and particularly Castellane, etc. Not a word of politics.

I next presented my Japanese colleague, Baron Motono, whom Poincaré knew in Paris in the old days. Their conversation was short but not without importance. In a few words the principle of the accession of Japan to the Triple Entente was formulated and virtually agreed.

After Motono, I introduced my English colleague, Sir George Buchanan. Poincaré assured him that the Tsar was determined to show himself most conciliatory in the Persian question and added that the British Government must ultimately realize the necessity of transforming the Triple Entente into a Triple Alliance.

His conversations with the ambassadors of Italy and Spain were merely superficial.

At last there appeared my Austro-Hungarian colleague, Count Szapary, a typical Hungarian nobleman, dressed to perfection. For two months he has been away from St. Petersburg at the bedside of his invalid wife and son. He came back unexpectedly yesterday. I inferred from his sudden return that the Austro-Serbian difference is getting more acute; there is going to be a rupture and the ambassador must be at his post to play his part in the dispute and take his share of responsibility.

I told Poincaré what I thought and he replied, "I'll try and clear up this business."

After a few words of sympathy on the assassination of the Archduke Franz Ferdinand, the President asked Szapary, "Have you any news of Serbia?"

"The judicial enquiry is proceeding," Szapary replied coldly.

Poincaré continued, "Of course I'm anxious about the results of this enquiry, Monsieur l'Ambassadeur. I can remember two previous enquiries which did not improve your relations with Serbia. Don't you remember the Friedjung affair and the Prochaska affair?"

Szapary replied in a dry tone, "Monsieur le Président, we cannot suffer a foreign government to allow plots against our sovereignty to be hatched on its territory!"

In a more than conciliatory tone Poincaré endeavored to point out that in the present state of public feeling in Europe, every government should be twice as cautious as usual.

"With a little good will this Serbian business is easy to settle. But it can just as easily become acute. Serbia has some very warm friends in the Russian people. And Russia has an ally in France. There are plenty of complications to be feared!"

Then he thanked the ambassador for his call. Szapary bowed and went out without a word.

When we three were alone again Poincaré said, "I'm not satisfied with this conversation. The ambassador had obviously been instructed to say nothing. Austria has a coup de théâtre in store for us. Sazonov must be firm and we must back him up. "

We then went to the next room where the ministers of the minor powers were in line in order of seniority. As he was pressed for time, Poincaré passed swiftly down the line shaking hands with each minister in turn. Their disappointment could be read in their faces. Each was hoping he would make some substantial and veiled observation on which he could make a long report to his government. The President only stopped to speak to the Serbian minister, Spalaikovitch, for whom he had a few words of sympathy.

At six o'clock, there was a visit to the French Hospital where the President laid the first stone of a public dispensary.

At eight o'clock there was a banquet at the Embassy. Ninety-six covers. The Embassy has been entirely renovated and looks very fine. The Garde-Meuble National has let me have a splendid series of gobelins, including Natoire's Triumph of Mark Antony and the Triumph of Mardocheus, superb decoration for my banqueting hall. Last, but not least, the Embassy was carpeted with roses and orchids.

The guests arrived, each more resplendent than the last. Their selection has put me on the rack owing to all the rivalries and jealousies life at Court involves. The question of seating has been an even more difficult problem, but I've received such excellent assistance from my secretaries that dinner and the evening passed off without a hitch.

Promptly at eleven o'clock, the President withdrew. I accompanied him to the City Hall where the Petersburg Duma was giving a soirée to the officers of the French squadron. It is the first time that the head of a foreign state has honored a Municipal Council's reception with his presence, so his reception was exceedingly warm.

At midnight, the President returned to Peterhof by water.

The violent demonstrations continued today in the industrial quarters of St. Petersburg. This evening the Prefect of Police assured me that the agitation had been stopped and that work will resume tomorrow. He has also confirmed the fact that among the arrested leaders several notorious agents in the German espionage service have been identified. From the point of view of the Alliance the incident gives one food for thought.

Wednesday, July 22, 1914

At midday, the Tsar gave a luncheon in Peterhof Palace to the President of the Republic and the officers of the French squadron. No ladies were present, not even the Tsaritsa. We sat down at small tables for ten to twelve covers. It was very hot outside but cool, sweet breezes wafted through the open windows from the leafy shade and fountains and cascades of the park.

I was at the same table as the Tsar and the President, with Viviani, Admiral Le Bris – commanding the French squadron, Goremykin – President of the Council, Count Fredericks – Minister of the Court, Sazonov and Isvolsky. I was on Viviani's left and he had Count Fredericks on his right.

Count Fredericks, who will soon be seventy-seven, is the very personification of court life. Of all the subjects of the Tsar, none has received more honors and titles. He is Minister of the Imperial Court and household, aide-de-camp to the Tsar, cavalry general, member of the Council of Empire, Chancellor of the Imperial Orders, Head of his Majesty's Cabinet and military establishment, etc. He has passed the whole of his long life in palaces and ceremonies, in carriages and processions, under gold lace and decorations.

In virtue of his functions he takes precedence over the highest dignitaries of the empire and he knows all the secrets of the imperial family. In the Tsar's name, he dispenses all the favors and gifts, all the reproofs and punishments. The grand dukes and grand duchesses overwhelm him with their attentions, for he it is who controls their households, hushes up their scandals, and pays their debts.

For all the difficulties of his task he is not known to have an enemy, such is his charm of manner and tact. He was also one of the handsomest men of his generation, one of the finest horsemen, and his successes with women were past counting. He has kept his lithe figure, his fine drooping moustache, and his charming manners. From a physical and moral point of view, he is the ideal type for his office, the supreme arbiter of the rites and precedence, conventions and traditions, manners and etiquette.

At half-past three, we left by the imperial train for the camp at Krasnoe Selo.

A blazing sun lit up the vast plain, a tawny and undulating plain bounded on the horizon by wooded hills. While the Tsar, the Tsaritsa, the President of the Republic, the grand dukes, the grand duchesses, and the entire imperial staff were inspecting the troops, I waited for them with the ministers and civil functionaries on a mound on which tents had been pitched. The élite of Petersburg society were crowded into some stands. The light attire of the women, their white hats and parasols, made the stands look like azalea beds.

Before long the imperial party arrived. In a four-horse *calèche* was the Tsaritsa, with the President of the Republic on her right and her two elder daughters opposite her. The Tsar was galloping by the side of the carriage, followed by a brilliant escort of the grand dukes and aides-de-camp.

They all dismounted and assembled on the low hill dominating the plain. The troops, without arms, were drawn up in serried ranks as far as the eye could reach before the row of tents. The front line ran along the very foot of the hill.

The sun was dropping towards the horizon in a sky of purple and gold. On a sign from the Tsar, an artillery salvo signaled evening prayer. The bands played a hymn. Everyone uncovered their heads. A non-commissioned officer recited the Our Father in a loud voice. All those men, thousands upon thousands, prayed for the Tsar and Holy Russia. The silence and composure of that multitude in that great plain, the magic poetry of the hour, the vision of the alliance which sanctified everything, gave the ceremony a touching majesty.

From the camps, we returned to the village of Krasnoe Selo, where Grand Duke Nicholas Nicholaievitch, Commander of the Imperial Guard, G.O.C. of the St. Petersburg military area, and subsequently Commander-in-Chief of the Russian armies, gave a dinner to the President of the Republic and the sovereigns. Three long tables were set in half-open tents around a garden which was in full flower. The beds had just been watered and from them the fresh scent of flowers – a delicious change after the baking day – rose into the warm air.

I was one of the first to arrive. Grand Duchess Anastasia and her sister, Grand Duchess Militza, gave me a boisterous welcome.

The two Montenegrins burst out into conversation, talking both at once.

"Do you realize that we're passing through historic days, fateful days? At the review tomorrow, the bands will play nothing but the Marche Lorraine and Sambre et Meuse. I've had a telegram in pre-arranged code from my father to-day. He tells me we shall have war before the end of the month. What a hero my father is! .He's worthy of 'The Iliad'! Just look at this little box I always take about with me. It's got some Lorraine soil in it, real Lorraine soil I picked up over the frontier when I was in France with my husband two years ago. Look there, at the table of honor – it's covered with thistles. I didn't want to have any other flowers there. They're Lorraine thistles, don't you see? I gathered several plants on the annexed territory, brought them here and had the seeds sown in my garden. Militza, you talk to the ambassador. Tell him all today means to us while I go and receive the Tsar."

At dinner, I was on the left of Grand Duchess Anastasia, and the rhapsody continued, interspersed with prophecies.

"There's going to be war. There'll be nothing left of Austria. You're going to get back Alsace and Lorraine. Our armies will meet in Berlin. Germany will be destroyed ..." Then suddenly, "I must restrain myself. The Emperor has his eye on me."

Under the Tsar's stern gaze, the Montenegrin sybil suddenly lapsed into silence.

Thursday, July 23, 1914

Review at Krasnoe Selo this morning. Sixty thousand men took part. A magnificent pageant of might and majesty. The infantry marched past to the strains of the Marche de Sambre et Meuse and the Marche Lorraine.

What a wealth of suggestion there was in this military machine set in motion by the Tsar of all the Russias before the President of the allied republic, himself a son of Lorraine!

The Tsar was mounted at the foot of the mound upon which was the imperial tent. Poincaré was seated on the Tsaritsa's right in front of the tent. The few glances he exchanged with me showed me that our thoughts were the same.

This evening we had a farewell dinner on The France. The moment it was over, the French squadron was to prepare to leave for Stockholm.

The Tsaritsa had made a point of coming with the Tsar. All the grand dukes and grand duchesses were there.

About seven o'clock, a momentary squall did some slight damage to the floral decorations of the deck, but the table looked very fine all the same. It had indeed a kind of terrifying grandeur, with the four gigantic 30 mm. guns raising their huge muzzles above the heads of the guests. The sky was soon clear again; a light breeze kissed the waves; the moon rose above the horizon.

Conversation between the Tsar and the President never ceased.

In the distance Grand Duchess Anastasia raised her champagne glass towards me more than once, indicating with a sweep of her arm the warlike tackle all about us.

As the second entrée was about to be served, a servant brought me a note from Viviani scribbled on a menu.

"Be quick and prepare a communiqué for the press."

Admiral Grigorovitch, Naval Minister, who was next to me, whispered in my ear, "It seems to me you're not left in peace for a minute!"

I took my own and my neighbor's menus and hastily drew up a note for the Havas Agency, using the neutral and empty phraseology suitable for documents of this kind. But to end up, I alluded to Serbia in the following terms:

> *The two governments have discovered that their views and intentions for the maintenance of the European balance of power, especially in the Balkan Peninsula, are absolutely identical.*

I sent my note to Viviani, who read it and then shook his head at me across the table.

At length the toasts were reached. Poincaré delivered his concluding phrase like a trumpet call, "The two countries have the same ideal of peace in strength, honor and self-respect."

These last words, words that had to be heard really to be appreciated, were followed by thunderous applause. Grand Duke Nicholas, Grand Duchess Anastasia and Grand Duke Nicholas Michaïlovitch turned flaming eyes upon me.

As we were rising from the table Viviani came up to me.

"I don't much like the last sentence of your note. I think it involves us a little too much in Russia's Balkan policy. Wouldn't it be better to leave it out?"

"But you can't publish an official report of your voyage and pretend not to know that there are serious differences, a threat of open conflict between Austria and Serbia," I replied. "It might even be thought that you were engaged in some scheme here which you dare not mention."

"That's true. Well, give me another draft."

A few minutes later I brought him this version:

> *The visit which the President of the Republic has just paid to H.M. the Emperor of Russia has given the two friendly and allied governments an opportunity of discovering that they are in entire agreement in their views on the various problems which concern for peace and the balance of power in Europe has laid before the Powers, particularly in the East.*

"Excellent!" said Viviani.

We immediately went on to discuss the matter with the President of the Republic, the Tsar, Sazonov and Isvolsky. All four unreservedly approved the new draft and I sent it at once to the Havas Agency.

The time for departure was approaching. The Tsar told Poincaré he would like to continue the discussion a few minutes longer.

"Suppose we go on the bridge, Monsieur le President?" he proposed. "It will be quieter."

Thus I found myself alone with the Tsaritsa, who asked me to take a chair on her left. The poor lady seemed worn out.

With a forced smile she said in a tired tone, "I'm glad I came tonight. I was afraid there would be a storm. The decorations on the boat are magnificent. The President will have lovely weather for his voyage." But suddenly she put her hands to her ears. Then with a pained and pleading glance, she timidly pointed to the ship's band quite near to us which had just started on a furious allegro with a full battery of brass and big drums. "Couldn't you ...?" she murmured.

I guessed the cause of her trouble and signaled sharply to the conductor who did not understand why but stopped his band at once.

"Thank you, thank you!" sighed the Tsaritsa.

The young Grand Duchess Olga, who was sitting at the other end of the ship with the rest of the imperial family and the members of the French mission, had been observing us for some minutes with an anxious eye. She suddenly rose, glided towards her mother with graceful ease and whispered two or three words in her ear.

Then addressing me, she continued, "The Empress is rather tired, but she asks you to stay with her, Monsieur l'Ambassadeur, and to go on talking to her."

I resumed our conversation as she went off with quick, light steps. At that very moment the moon appeared in an archipelago of flaky, slow-moving clouds. The whole Gulf of

Finland was lit up. My subject was found for me. I enlarged on the charm of sea voyages. The Tsaritsa listened to me in silence, her gaze vacant and strained, her cheeks livid, her lips motionless and swollen.

After ten minutes or so, which seemed to me an eternity, the Tsar and the President of the Republic came down from the bridge.

It was eleven o'clock. Preparations for the departure were in progress. The guard shouldered arms. Sharp commands rang out. The Alexandria's launch greeted The France. The farewells were said to the strains of the Russian national anthem and the 'Marseillaise.' The Tsar spoke very warmly to the President of the Republic. I myself said goodbye to Poincaré, who kindly asked me to call on him in Paris in a fortnight's time.

As I was bowing to the Tsar at the top of the gangway, he said to me, "Will you come with me, Monsieur l'Ambassadeur? We can talk undisturbed on my yacht. You'll be taken straight back to Petersburg."

From The France we transferred to The Alexandria. Only the imperial family accompanied their majesties. The ministers, functionaries, military staff and my personal staff returned directly to Petersburg in an Admiralty yacht.

It was a splendid night. The milky way stretched, a pure band of silver, into unending space. Not a breath of wind. The France and her escorting division sped rapidly towards the west, leaving behind them long ribbons of foam which glistened in the moonlight like silvery streams.

When the imperial suite was on board Admiral Nilov came to the Tsar for orders and the latter said to me, "It's a wonderful night. Suppose we go for a sail."

The Alexandria steered for the coast of Finland.

The Tsar made me sit behind him in the stern of the yacht and told me of the conversation he had just had with Poincaré.

"I'm delighted with my talk with the President. We see absolutely eye-to-eye. I am no less peace-loving than he is, and he is no less determined than I to do everything necessary to prevent the cause of peace being compromised. He fears some Austro-German maneuver against Serbia and thinks we should reply with the united front of a common diplomatic policy. I think the same. We must show ourselves firm and united in our efforts to find possible solutions and the necessary adjustments. The more difficult the situation becomes, the more important will unity and firmness become."

"That policy seems to me the essence of wisdom' I'm afraid we shall have to resort to it before long," I said.

"You are still uneasy?"

"Yes, Sire."

"Have you any fresh reason for your apprehension?"

"I have at least one, the unexpected return of my colleague Szapary, and the air of cold and hostile reserve he adopted towards the President of the Republic the day before yesterday. Germany and Austria are preparing a shock for us."

"What can they want? A diplomatic success at the expense of Serbia? To score a point off the Triple Entente? No, no. Notwithstanding appearances, Emperor Wilhelm is too cautious to launch his country on some wild adventure, and Emperor Franz Joseph's only wish is to die in peace."

For a minute the Tsar sat in silence, lost in thought as if he were following up some vague line of thought. Then he rose and paced the deck.

Around us, the grand dukes were standing waiting for the moment to approach their master, who grudgingly dispensed a few commonplaces among them. He called them up in turn and seemed to show them an unrestrained frankness, an affectionate familiarity, as if he wanted them to forget that he usually kept them at a distance and made it a rule never to talk politics with them.

Grand Duke Nicholas Nicholaievitch, Grand Duke Nicholas Michaïlovitch, Grand Duke Paul Alexandrovitch and Grand Duchess Marie Pavlovna came up to me, congratulating themselves and me on the fact that the presidential visit had been so supreme a success. In the court code that meant that the sovereign was satisfied.

The Grand Duchesses Anastasia and Militza, 'the two Montenegrins,' got me in a corner:

"What a glorious speech the President made. It was just what wanted saying, just what we've been awaiting for so long! Peace in strength, honor and self-respect. Remember those words, Monsieur l'Ambassadeur. They will mark a date in the history of the world."

At a quarter to one, The Alexandria dropped anchor in Peterhof bay, and after leaving the Tsar and Tsaritsa, I transferred to the escort yacht, Strela, and was taken to Petersburg, which I reached at half-past two in the morning.

As we sailed up the Neva, I was thinking of the eager prophecy of the Montenegrin sybils.

Chapter 2

Friday, July 24, 1914

Tired from these four days of continuous high pressure, I was hoping for a little rest and had told my servant to let me sleep through this morning. At seven o'clock, however, the ringing of the telephone woke me with a start and I was informed that Austria had presented an ultimatum to Serbia yesterday evening.

As I was half-asleep, the news at first produced a curious impression of amazement and authority. The occurrence seemed to me unreal and yet definite, imaginary but authentic. I seemed to be continuing my conversation of yesterday with the Tsar, putting forward my theories and conjectures. At the same time I had a sensation, a potent, positive and compelling sensation, that I was in the presence of a *fait accompli*.

During the morning, details of what had happened in Belgrade began to come in.

At half-past twelve, Sazonov and Buchanan came to the Embassy to confer on the situation. Our discussion was interrupted by lunch but we resumed immediately afterwards. Taking my stand on the toasts exchanged between the Tsar and the President, the declarations of the two foreign ministers, and the communiqué to the Havas Agency yesterday, I had no hesitation in advocating a policy of firmness.

"But suppose that policy is bound to lead to war?" said Sazonov.

"It will only lead to war if the Germanic powers have already made up their minds to resort to force to secure the hegemony of the East. Firmness does not exclude conciliation. But it is essential for the other side to be prepared to negotiate and compromise. You know my own views as to Germany's designs. The Austrian ultimatum seems to me to provoke the dangerous crisis I have anticipated for a long time. Henceforth we must recognize that war may break out at any moment. That prospect must govern all our diplomatic action."

Buchanan assumed that his government would desire to remain neutral and was therefore apprehensive that France and Russia would be crushed by the Triple Alliance.

Sazonov protested, "At the present juncture, England's neutrality would be tantamount to her suicide!"

"I'm certain of that," Sir George replied sadly, "but I'm afraid public opinion with us is still far from realizing what our national interests so imperiously require."

I emphasized the decisive part England could play in quenching Germany's warlike ardor, citing the view Tsar Nicholas expressed to me four days ago. "Unless Germany has lost her reason altogether, she will never dare to attack Russia, France and England combined." Thus it was urgently necessary for the British Government to announce its adhesion to our cause, which was the cause of peace.

Sazonov warmly advocated the same course.

Buchanan promised to make strong representations to Sir Edward Grey in favor of the policy of resistance to German arrogance.

At three o'clock, Sazonov left us to go to Ielaguin Island to which Goremykin, the President of the Council, had summoned the ministers.

At eight o'clock in the evening, I went to the Foreign Office where Sazonov was closeted with my German colleague.

A few minutes later, I saw Pourtalès come out, his face purple and his eyes flashing. The discussion must have been lively. He furtively shook my hand as I entered the minister's room.

Sazonov was still agitated over the dispute in which he had just been engaged. He has quick, nervous movements and his voice is dry and jerky.

"What's happened? " I asked.

"As I anticipated," he replied, "Germany wholeheartedly supports the Austrian cause. Not the slightest suggestion of conciliation. So I told Pourtalès quite bluntly that we should not leave Serbia to settle her differences with Austria alone. Our talk ended in a very acrimonious tone."

"Really?"

"Yes. Can you imagine what he had the audacity to tell me? He reproached me, me and all other Russians, with disliking Austria and having no scruples about troubling the last years of her aged Emperor. I retorted, 'No, of course we don't like Austria. Why should we like her? She has never done us anything but harm. As for her aged Emperor, he owes it to us that he still has his crown on his head. Just remember how he showed his gratitude in 1855, 1878 and 1908. What! Reproach us with not liking Austria! That's a bit too much!' "

"It's a bad business, Minister," I said. "If conversations between Petersburg and Berlin are to continue in this strain, they won't last long. Very soon we shall see Emperor Wilhelm rise in his shining armor. Please be calm. Exhaust every possibility of compromise. Don't forget that my government is a government based on public opinion and can only support you effectively if it has public opinion behind it. And think of English opinion also."

"I shall do everything possible to avoid war. But like you, I am very uneasy about the turn events are taking."

"Can I give my government an assurance that you have not yet ordered any military preparations?"

"None whatsoever. All we have decided is privately to withdraw the eighty million rubles we have on deposit in the German banks." He added that he would endeavor to obtain from Count Berchtold an extension of the time fixed for the Serbian reply in the ultimatum so that the powers might have an opportunity of forming an opinion on the legal aspect of the dispute and finding some peaceful solution.

The Russian ministers are to meet again to-morrow, with the Tsar presiding. I recommended to Sazonov the greatest caution as to the advice he is to give.

Our conversation was enough to soothe his nerves and he continued with calm deliberation, "You needn't fear. Besides, you know the Tsar's caution. Berchtold has put himself in the wrong. It's our business to make him solely responsible for everything that comes. I even consider that if the Vienna cabinet resorts to action, the Serbians ought to let their territory be invaded and confine themselves to denouncing Austria's infamy to the civilized world."

Saturday, July 25, 1914

Yesterday, the German ambassadors in Paris and London read to the French and British governments a note to the effect that the Austro-Serbian dispute must be settled by Vienna and Belgrade alone.

The note ended thus:

> *The German Government is extremely anxious that the conflict shall be localized, as any intervention by a third power may, by the natural operation of alliances, have incalculable consequences.*

The policy of threats is already beginning

At three o'clock in the afternoon, Sazonov received me with Buchanan. He told us that an extraordinary council was held this morning at Krasnoe Selo, with the Tsar presiding, and that His Majesty has decided in principle to mobilize the thirteen army corps which are ultimately earmarked for operations against Austria-Hungary. Then he turned to

Buchanan very gravely and pleaded with all his might that England should hesitate no longer to range herself on the side of Russia and France in a crisis in which the stake is not merely the European balance of power but the very liberties of Europe itself.

I backed up Sazonov and concluded with an argument *ad hominem,* pointing to the portrait of the great Chancellor Gortchakov which adorns the room in which we were talking:

"In July, 1870, on this very spot, my dear Sir George, Prince Gortchakov said to your father, who was warning him of the danger of German ambition, 'There's nothing to worry Russia in the increase of German power.' Don't let England make the same mistake today which cost Russia so dear then."

"You know you're preaching to the converted," said Buchanan with a weary smile.

Public feeling is rising every hour. The following note has been communicated to the Press:

> *The Imperial Government is closely following the development of the Austro-Serbian conflict which cannot leave Russia indifferent.*

Almost simultaneously, Pourtalès informed Sazonov that, as Austria's ally, she naturally supported the legitimate claims of the Vienna cabinet against Serbia.

Sazonov, on his part, has advised the Serbian government immediately to invite the mediation of the British Government.

At seven o'clock this evening, I went to the Warsaw station to say goodbye to Isvolsky, who is returning to his post in extreme haste. There was a great bustle on the platforms. The trains were packed with officers and men. This looked like mobilization. We rapidly exchanged impressions and came to the same conclusion.

"It's war this time."

When I returned to the embassy, I was informed that the Tsar had just ordered the measures preliminary to mobilization in the military areas of Kiev, Odessa, Kazan and Moscow. Further, the cities and Governments of St. Petersburg and Moscow have been declared in a state of siege. Lastly, the camp at Krasnoe Selo has been broken up, and from this evening the troops are being sent back to their usual garrisons.

At half-past eight, my military attaché, General de Laguiche, was summoned to Krasnoe Selo to confer with Grand Duke Nicholas Nicholaievitch and General Sukhomlinov, the War Minister.

Sunday, July 26, 1914

When I went to see Sazonov this afternoon, my impressions were better.

He had just received my Austro-Hungarian colleague, Count Szapary, and had asked him for a frank and honest explanation.

Then, article by article, he read through the text of the ultimatum presented to Belgrade, bringing out the impossible, ridiculous and insulting character of the principal clauses, all this in a most friendly tone.

"The intention behind this document is legitimate enough, if your only object is to protect your territory against the plots of Serbian anarchists. But its form is indefensible," he declared, concluding with some warmth, "Withdraw your ultimatum, modify the wording, and I'll guarantee the result."

Szapary seemed moved, even half-persuaded by this language, but he would not commit himself as to the views of his government.

This evening Sazonov is therefore proposing to Berchtold to open direct conversations between Petersburg and Vienna with a view to cooperation in the changes to be made in the ultimatum.

I congratulated Sazonov on having given the conversation such a happy turn.

He replied, "I shall not depart from this attitude. I shall negotiate to the very last moment." Then, passing his hand across his eyes as if some terrible vision was flashing through his mind, he asked me in a trembling voice, "Honestly, between ourselves, do you think we can still save peace?"

"If we had only Austria to deal with," I replied, "I should be hopeful. But there is Germany. She has promised her ally a great personal triumph. She is convinced that we dare not resist her to the bitter end, and that the Triple Alliance will give way, as it has always given way. But this time we cannot give way, on pain of ceasing to exist. We shall not avert war."

"Oh my dear Ambassador," he said, "it's terrible to think of what's to come."

Monday, July 27, 1914

In official circles the day has been calm. Diplomacy methodically pursues its ordained course.

Overwhelmed with telegrams and callers, my head in a whirl, I went out before dinner for a walk on the islands, leaving my car in the shady and solitary avenue alongside the Ielaguin Palace.

The hour fostered reflection. A soft silken light filtered through the thick, glistening foliage of the great oaks. Not a breath of air stirred in the branches, but every now and then I could smell the damp odors which seem the fresh breath of plants and streams.

My reflections were utterly pessimistic. Whatever I did to fight them, they always brought me back to one conclusion, that there would be a war. The hour for discussion and diplomatic artifices had gone. Compared with the underlying and remote causes that have produced the present crisis, the incidents of the last few days were nothing. Individual initiative existed no longer. There was no longer any human will capable of withstanding the automatic mechanism of the forces let loose. We diplomats had lost all influence over the course of events. All we could do was to try and forecast them and insist on our governments regulating their action accordingly.

Judging by the agency telegrams, public spirit in France would appear to be high: No neurotic outbursts; no war fever; a calm, strong confidence; perfect national solidarity. And to think that this is the same country that but a short time back was in ecstasies over the scandals of the Caillaux trial and wallowing in the outpourings of the law courts.

Throughout Russia, public feeling is becoming exasperated. Sazonov is trying hard and is still successful in restraining the press, but he is obliged to give the journalists a sop to assuage their hunger, and has had to tell them, "If you want, go for Austria, but be moderate towards Germany."

Tuesday, July 28, 1914

At three o'clock this afternoon, I went to the Foreign Office.

Buchanan was in conference with Sazonov. The German Ambassador was waiting his turn to be received.

I addressed him quite frankly.

"So you've decided to calm down your ally at last? You're the only one of us in a position to make Austria listen to wisdom."

He protested at once in a jerky voice. "But it's here that they ought to calm down and stop egging on Serbia!"

"I assure you, on my honor, that the Russian Government is perfectly calm and ready for any conciliatory solution. But don't ask it to let Serbia be crushed. It would be to ask the impossible."

"We cannot abandon our ally," he darted at me in a dry tone.

"Let me speak freely to you, my dear colleague. This is a grave moment and I think we respect each other enough to have the right to speak our minds without reserve. If the Austro-Serbian differences are not resolved within twenty-four hours, or two days at most, it means war, a general war, a catastrophe such as the world has never known. This calamity may still be averted as the Russian Government is peace-loving, the British Government is peace-loving, and your Government itself claims to be peace-loving."

At these words, Pourtalès burst out, "Yes, indeed, I call God to witness! Germany is peace-loving. For forty-three years we have preserved the peace of Europe. For forty-three years we have pledged our honor not to abuse our strength. And it is we who are now accused of desiring to precipitate war. History will prove that we have right on our side and our conscience has nothing to reproach us for."

"Have we already got as far as finding it necessary to invoke the verdict of history?" I asked. "Is there then no chance of safety?"

Pourtalès' agitation was such that he could speak no more. His hands trembled. His eyes were a mist of tears.

Quivering with anger he repeated, "We cannot, we will not abandon our ally. No, we will not abandon her!"

At this point the British Ambassador came out of Sazonov's room and Pourtalès rushed in, looking fierce, without even shaking Buchanan's hand as he passed.

"What a state he's in!" Sir George said to me. "The situation is worse. I don't doubt that Russia will go through with it. She is thoroughly in earnest. I have just been begging Sazonov not to consent to any military measure which Germany could call provocative. The German Government must be saddled with all the responsibility and all the initiative. English opinion will accept the idea of intervening in the war only if Germany is indubitably the aggressor. Please talk to Sazonov to that effect."

"That's what I'm always telling him."

At that moment the Austro-Hungarian Ambassador arrived. He looked pale. His stiff aloofness towards us was in contrast to his usual easy and courteous affability.

Buchanan and I tried to get him to talk.

"Have you had any better news from Vienna?" I asked. "Can you ease our minds a bit?"

"No, I know nothing more. The machine is in motion." Without volunteering any further explanation he repeated his apocalyptical metaphor. "The machine's in motion."

Realizing it was no use pressing, I went out with Buchanan. As a matter of fact, I did not want to see the minister until he had received Pourtalès and Szapary.

A quarter of an hour later I sent in my name to Sazonov. He was pale and agitated.

"I think things are very bad," he said, "very bad. It is quite clear now that Austria is refusing to treat with us, and Germany is secretly egging her on."

"So you haven't managed to get anything out of Pourtalès?"

"Nothing except that Germany cannot abandon Austria. But am I asking her to abandon Austria? All I ask is simply that she should help me to solve this critical problem by peaceful means. As a matter of fact, Pourtalès had lost his self-control. He didn't know what to say. He stammered and looked scared. Why that fear? You and I are not like that. We haven't lost our *sang froid* or self-control."

"Pourtalès is agitated because no doubt he feels personally involved. I'm afraid he has helped to drive his government into this terrible adventure by asserting that Russia would not face the music, and that if she did not yield, which was unthinkable, France would renounce the Russian Alliance. Now he sees the abyss into which he has hurled his country."

"You're quite certain of that?"

"Practically certain. Only yesterday, Pourtalès assured the Dutch Minister and the Belgian Chargé d'Affaires that Russia would give way and it would be a great triumph for the Triple Alliance. I have this from the best source."

Sazonov heaved a despondent sigh and sat silent.

I continued. "The die is cast so far as Berlin and Vienna are concerned. It's London we must think of now. I do ask you to resort to no military measures on the German front, and even to be very cautious on the Russian front until Germany has definitely shown her hand. The least imprudence on your part will cost us England's help."

"That's my opinion too, but our General Staff is getting restless and even now I am having great difficulty in holding it in."

These last words worried me and an idea came into my head

"However great the danger may be, and however remote the chance of salvation, you and I ought to leave nothing undone in the cause of peace. I do want you to realize that I am in a position which is unprecedented for an ambassador. The head of the State and the head of the Government are at sea. I can only communicate with them at intervals and through very uncertain channels. As their knowledge of the situation is incomplete, they cannot send me any instructions. The ministry in Paris is without its chief, and its means of communication with the President of the Republic and the President of the Council, are as irregular and defective as mine. My responsibility is thus enormous and that's why I ask you to pledge yourself henceforth to accept all the proposals France and England may make to you to save peace."

"But it's impossible! How can you expect me to accept beforehand proposals of which I know neither the object nor the terms?"

"I have just said that we must even attempt the impossible to save the cause of peace, so I must insist upon my request."

After a brief hesitation he replied.

"All right! I accept. I regard your undertaking as official and I'm going to wire it to Paris."

"You can do so."

"Thank you. You've taken a great weight off my mind."

Wednesday, July 29, 1914

I think we have reached the last scene of the prologue to the drama.

Yesterday evening, the Austro-Hungarian Government ordered the general mobilization of their army. The Vienna cabinet is thus refusing the suggestion of direct communication proposed by the Russian Government.

About three o'clock this afternoon, Pourtalès came to tell Sazonov that if Russia did not stop her military preparations at once, Germany also would mobilize her army.

Sazonov replied that the preparations of the Russian General Staff were the result of the uncompromising obstinacy of the Vienna cabinet and the fact that eight Austro-Hungarian army corps were already on a war footing.

At eleven o'clock tonight, Nicholas Alexandrovitch Basily, Deputy Director of the Chancellery of the Foreign Office, appeared at my embassy. He came to tell me that the imperious language used by the German Ambassador this afternoon has persuaded the Russian Government to order this very night the mobilization of the thirteen corps earmarked for operations against Austria-Hungary, and secretly to commence general mobilization.

These last words made me jump.

"Isn't it possible for them to confine themselves, provisionally at any rate, to a partial mobilization?"

"No, the question has just been gone into thoroughly by a council of our highest military officers. They have come to the conclusion that in existing circumstances the Russian Government has no choice between partial and general mobilization, as, from the technical point of view, a partial mobilization could be carried out only at the price of dislocating the entire machinery of general mobilization. So, if today we stopped at mobilizing the thirteen corps destined for operations against Austria, and tomorrow Germany decided to give her ally military support, we should be powerless to defend ourselves on the frontiers of Poland and East Prussia. Besides, isn't it as much in France's interest as our own that we should be able to intervene promptly against Germany?"

"Those are strong arguments, but I still think that your General Staff should take no step without conducting previous discussions with the French General Staff. Please tell M. Sazonov from me that I should like his most serious consideration of this matter, and a reply in the course of the night."

Thursday, July 30, 1914

Basily had hardly got back to the Foreign Office before Sazonov rang me to ask me to send him my First Secretary, Chambrun, "to receive a very urgent communication." At the same time, my Military Attaché, General de Laguiche, was summoned by the General Staff.

It was 11:45 p.m.

Tsar Nicholas had received a personal telegram from Emperor Wilhelm this evening, persuading him to decide to suspend general mobilization, as Emperor Wilhelm had told him "that he is doing everything in his power to bring about a direct understanding between Austria and Russia."

The Tsar has come to his decision on his own authority and in spite of the opposition of his generals, who have once more insisted upon the difficulties, or rather the dangers, of a partial mobilization.

I have therefore informed Paris of the mobilization only of the thirteen Russian corps destined for eventual operations against Austria.

We awoke this morning to find the papers announcing that, yesterday evening, the Austro-Hungarian army opened up an attack on Serbia with the bombardment of Belgrade.

The news has quickly spread among the public and produced intense excitement. I have been called from all quarters to ask if I have any detailed information on the matter, whether France has made up her mind to support Russia, and so forth.

Excited groups were arguing in the streets and below my window. On the Neva quay, four *moujiks*, who were unloading wood, stopped their work to listen to their employer who read the paper to them. Then all five made long speeches with solemn gestures and indignation writ large all over their faces. They crossed themselves when the discussion came to an end.

At two o'clock this afternoon, Pourtalès went to the Foreign Office. Sazonov received him at once, and from his first words I guessed that Germany would refuse to urge restraint on Vienna in order to save the peace.

The very attitude of Pourtalès was only too eloquent. He seemed a lost man, for he realizes now the consequences of the uncompromising policy of which he has been the instrument, if not actually the author. He sees the inevitable catastrophe and is collapsing under the weight of his responsibility.

"For Heaven's sake," he said to Sazonov, "make me some proposal I can recommend to my government. It's my last hope."

Sazonov at once put forward the following ingenious formula: If Austria will recognize that the Austro-Serbian question has assumed the character of a European question and declare her readiness to delete from her ultimatum the points which encroach upon the sovereign rights of Serbia, Russia undertakes to stop her military preparations.

Still in a state of collapse, Pourtalès staggered from the room, stammering feebly and his eyes staring.

An hour later, Sazonov was ushered into the Peterhof Palace to make his report to the Tsar. He found his sovereign sorely moved by a telegram Emperor Wilhelm had sent him during the night, its tone almost menacing:

> If Russia mobilizes against Austria-Hungary, the role of mediator, which I have undertaken at your urgent request, will be compromised, if not made impossible. The whole weight of the decision to be taken now rests on your shoulders and you will have to bear the responsibility for war or peace.

Sazonov read and re-read this telegram, and shrugged his shoulders in despair.

"We shall not escape war now," he declared. "Germany is obviously evading the role of mediator we asked her to undertake, and all she is after is to gain time to complete her military preparations in secret. Under these circumstances, I don't think Your Majesty can postpone the order for general mobilization any longer."

The Tsar was deadly pale and replied in a choking voice.

"Just think of the responsibility you're advising me to assume. Remember it's a question of sending thousands and thousands of men to their deaths."

Sazonov replied, "Neither Your Majesty's conscience nor mine will have anything to be reproached with if war breaks out. Your Majesty and the Government will have done everything to spare the world this terrible situation. But now I feel certain that diplomacy has finished its work. We must henceforth think of the safety of the empire. If Your Majesty orders a stop to our preliminary mobilization, all you will do is to dislocate our military organization and disconcert our allies. The war will break out just the same at Germany's appointed time and will catch us in hopeless confusion. "

After a moment's reflection, the Tsar said in a firm voice, "Sergei Dimitrievitch, call the Chief of Staff and tell him I order general mobilization."

Sazonov went down to the hall of the palace where the telephone cabinet was and transmitted the imperial order to General Janushkevitch.

It was exactly four o'clock.

The battleship France, with the President of the Republic and the President of the Council on board, arrived yesterday at Dunkirk, without calling at Copenhagen and Christiania as had been arranged.

At six p.m., I received a telegram dispatched from Paris this morning and signed by President of the Council Viviani. After once more emphasizing the. pacific intentions of the French Government and imposing caution on the Russian Government, Viviani added, "France is determined to meet all the obligations of the alliance."

I went to tell Sazonov, who replied very simply, "I was sure of France."

Friday, July 31, 1914

The mobilization decree was issued at dawn. Enthusiasm is general in the city, in the working-class districts as much as in the rich and aristocratic quarters. I am told there is cheering in the Winter Palace Square and in front of Our Lady of Kazan.

Tsar Nicholas and Emperor Wilhelm are continuing their telegraphic dialogue. This morning the Tsar telegraphed to the Kaiser:

> It is technically impossible for me to suspend my military preparations. But as long as conversations with Austria are not broken off, my troops will refrain from taking the offensive anywhere. I give you my word of honor on that.

To which the Emperor William has replied:

> I have gone to the utmost limits of the possible in my efforts to save peace. It is not I who will bear the responsibility for the terrible disaster which now threatens the civilized world. You and you alone can still avert it. My friendship for you and your Empire, which my grandfather bequeathed to me on his deathbed, is still sacred to me and I have been loyal to Russia when she was in trouble, notably during your last war. Even now you can still save the peace of Europe by stopping your military measures.

Sazonov, always on the look out to win over English opinion and anxious to do everything possible up to the last moment to avert war, has accepted without discussion certain changes Sir Edward Grey asked him to make in the proposal put forward to the Berlin Cabinet yesterday.

The new draft runs:

> *If Austria agrees to stop the march of her armies on Serbian territory, and, recognizing that the Austro-Serbian conflict has assumed the character of a question interesting all Europe, allows the Great Powers to examine what satisfaction Serbia could give the Austro-Hungarian Government without prejudice to her rights as a sovereign state and her independence, Russia guarantees to maintain her waiting attitude.*

.At three o'clock in the afternoon, Pourtalès requested an audience of the Tsar, who asked him to come to Peterhof at once.

Received with the greatest kindliness, Pourtalès confined himself to enlarging on the theme set out in the Kaiser's last telegram.

"Germany has always been Russia's best friend. Let Emperor Nicholas revoke his military measures and the peace of the world will be saved."

The Tsar replied by emphasizing the possibilities for conciliation, which Sazonov's proposal, as revised by Sir Edward Grey, still offers for an honorable settlement of the dispute.

At eleven o'clock in the evening, Pourtalès presented himself at the Foreign Office. He was received immediately, and announced to Sazonov that if, within twelve hours, Russia did not suspend her mobilization, on both the German and Austro-Hungarian frontiers, the whole German army would be mobilized. Then, with a glance at the clock which showed twenty-five minutes past eleven, he added, "The time will expire at midday tomorrow." Without giving Sazonov time to make a single remark, he continued in a trembling, hurried voice, "Agree to demobilize! Agree to demobilize! Agree to demobilize!"

To which Sazonov, quite unruffled, replied, "I can only confirm what His Majesty the Emperor has told you. As long as the conversations with Austria continue, as long as there's any chance of averting the war, we shall not attack. But it's technically impossible for us to demobilize without dislocating our entire military organization. It is a point the soundness of which your General Staff itself could not deny."

Pourtalès left, scared out of his wits.

Saturday, August 1, 1914

During yesterday, Emperor Wilhelm proclaimed Germany to be "in danger of war." The announcement of the *Kriegsgefahrzustand* means the immediate calling up of the reservists and the closing of the frontiers. If it is not the official mobilization, it is at any rate the prelude and opening move.

On receiving this news, the Tsar telegraphed to the Kaiser:

> *I understand that you are compelled to mobilize, but I should like to have the same guarantee from you that I gave you myself, that these measures do not mean war and that we shall continue our negotiations to save the general peace so dear to our hearts. With God's help, our long and tried friendship should be able to prevent bloodshed. I confidently await a reply from you.*

The time given by the ultimatum expired at midday today, but it was not before seven this evening that Pourtalès appeared at the Foreign Office.

His eyes were swollen and he was very red in the face and choking with emotion as he solemnly handed Sazonov a declaration of war, which concluded with this theatrical and mendacious phrase:

> *His Majesty the Emperor, my august sovereign, in the name of the empire accepts the challenge and considers himself in a state of war with Russia.*

Sazonov replied, "This is a criminal act of yours. The curses of the nations will be upon you."

Then, reading aloud the declaration of war, he was amazed to see between brackets two versions, a matter of slight importance in itself. For instance, after the words

'Russia having refused to acknowledge ...' there was '(not having considered there was any obligation to reply to).' And later on, after the words 'Russia having shown by their refusal ...' there was '(by this attitude).'

It is probable that these two different versions have been suggested from Berlin, and that owing either to inadvertence or haste on the part of the copyist, they have both been inserted in the official text.

Pourtalès was so overcome that he could not explain this curious form which will forever set the brand of ridicule upon the historic document which was to be the origin of so many evils.

When he had finished reading, Sazonov repeated, "This is a criminal act!"

"We are defending our honour!" Pourtalès insisted.

"Your honour was not involved," Sazonov replied. "You could have prevented the war by one word. You didn't want to. In all my efforts to save peace, I haven't had the slightest help from you. But there's a divine justice."

Pourtalès repeated in a dull voice, with a look of desperation, "That's true. There's a divine justice, a divine justice!"

He went on muttering a few incomprehensible words and staggered towards the window, which is on the right of the door, opposite the Winter Palace. There he leaned against the embrasure and burst into tears.

Sazonov, trying to calm him, tapped him on the shoulders.

Pourtalès stammered, "So this is the result of my mission." Finally he rushed to the door, which he could hardly open with his trembling fingers, and went out murmuring, "Goodbye! Goodbye!"

A few minutes later, I went to Sazonov who described the scene. He also told me that Buchanan had just requested an audience of the Tsar to hand him a personal telegram from his sovereign. In this telegram, King George makes a supreme appeal to the peace-loving nature of the Tsar and begs him to continue his efforts for conciliation. The step has no object now that Pourtalès has handed in the declaration of war, but the Tsar will receive Buchanan at eleven tonight in any case.

Sunday, August 2, 1914

General mobilization of the French army. The order reached me by telegraph at two o'clock this morning.

So the die is cast! The part played by reason in the government of nations is so small that it has only taken a week to let loose world madness. I do not know, history will judge the diplomatic operation in which I have just been concerned with Sazonov and Buchanan, but all three of us have a right to claim that we have conscientiously done everything in our power to save the peace of the world without, however, sacrificing to it those two other and still more precious possessions, the independence and honor of our countries.

During this decisive week the work of my embassy has been very hard. Night has been as busy as day. My staff has been models of industry and self-control. All of them – my counsellor, Doucet, my military attachés, General de Laguiche and Major Wehrlin, and my secretaries, Chambrun, Gentil, Dulong and Robirn – have given me help as active and intelligent as it has been spontaneous and devoted.

At three o'clock this afternoon, I went to the Winter Palace where the Tsar was to issue a proclamation to his people, as ancient rites decree. As the representative of the allied power, I was the only foreigner admitted to this ceremony.

It was a majestic spectacle. Five or six thousand people were assembled in the huge St. George's gallery which runs along the Neva quay. The whole court was in full formal dress and all the officers of the garrison were in field dress. In the center of the room an altar was placed, and on it was the miraculous icon of the Virgin of Kazan, brought from the national sanctuary on the Nevsky Prospekt, which had to do without it for a few hours. In 1812, Field Marshal Prince Kutusov, before leaving to join the army at Smolensk, spent a long time in prayer before this sacred image.

In a tense, religious silence, the imperial cortège crossed the gallery and took up station on the left of the altar.

The Tsar asked me to stand opposite him as he desired, so he said, "to do public homage in this way to the loyalty of his French ally."

Mass began at once, to the accompaniment of the noble and sympathetic chants of the orthodox liturgy. Nicholas II prayed with a holy fervor that gave his pale face a movingly mystical expression. The Tsaritsa Alexandra Feodorovna stood by him, gazing fixedly, her chest thrust forward, head high, lips crimson, eyes glassy. Every now and then she closed her eyes and then her livid face reminded one of a death mask.

After the final prayer, the court chaplain read the Tsar's manifesto to his people, a simple recital of the events which have made war inevitable, an eloquent appeal to all the national energies, an invocation to the Most High, and so forth. Then the Tsar went up to the altar and raised his right hand towards the gospel that was being held out to him, even more grave and composed, as if he were about to receive the sacrament.

In a slow, low voice which dwelt on every word, he made the following declaration.

"Officers of my guard, here present, I greet you are representatives of my whole army and give it my blessing. I solemnly swear that I will never make peace so long as one of the enemy is on the soil of the fatherland."

A wild outburst of cheering was the answer to this declaration, which was copied from the oath taken by the Emperor Alexander I in 1812. For nearly ten minutes there was a frantic tumult in the gallery and it was soon intensified by the cheers of the crowd massed along the Neva.

Suddenly Grand Duke Nicholas, Commander-in-Chief of the Russian armies, hurled himself upon me with his usual impetuosity and embraced me till I was half crushed. At this the cheers redoubled, and above all the din rose shouts of *"Vive la France! Vive la France!"*

Through the cheering crowd, I had great difficulty in clearing a way behind the sovereigns and reaching the door.

Ultimately I got to Winter Palace Square, where an enormous crowd had congregated with flags, banners, icons, and portraits of the Tsar.

The Emperor appeared on the balcony. The entire crowd at once knelt and sang the Russian national anthem. To those thousands of men on their knees at that moment the Tsar was really the autocrat appointed of God, the military, political and religious leader of his people, the absolute master of their bodies and souls.

As I was returning to the embassy, my eyes full of this grandiose spectacle, I could not help thinking of that sinister January 22, 1905, on which the working masses of St. Petersburg, led by the priest Gapon, and preceded as now by the sacred images, were assembled, as they were assembled today, before the Winter Palace to plead with "their Father, the Tsar," and pitilessly shot down.

Chapter 3

Monday, August 3, 1914

The Minister for the Interior, Nicholas Alexeivitch Maklakov, tells me that general mobilization is in progress in perfect order in the whole territory of the empire amid a great outburst of patriotism.

I had no doubts on that score; the most I feared was local incidents.

B….., one of my informants, who moves in advanced circles, said to me, "No strike or disorder is to be anticipated at this moment. The national enthusiasm is too strong. In all the factories and workshops, the leaders of the Socialist Party have therefore advocated resignation to military duty. Besides, they're convinced that this war will lead to the triumph of the proletariat."

"The triumph of the proletariat, even in case of victory?"

"Yes, because the war will effect a fusion of all the social classes. It will bring together the peasant, the workman and the student. It will once more reveal the scandal of our bureaucracy, and that will compel the Government to reckon with public opinion. Lastly, it will introduce a liberal and even democratic element – the lieutenants of the reserve – into the aristocratic officer caste. This element played an important political part even during the Manchurian War. The military revolts of 1905 would not have been possible without it."

"Our first business is to win," I cautioned. "We shall see what comes afterwards."

The President of the Duma, Michael Vladimirovitch Rodzianko, has also spoken to me in very reassuring terms, for the present.

"The war," he said, "has suddenly put an end to all our domestic strife. Throughout the Duma, the one thought is of fighting Germany. The Russian people has not known such a wave of patriotism since 1812."

Grand Duke Nicholas Nicholaievitch has been appointed Commander-in-Chief provisionally, as the Tsar reserves the right to assume personal command of his armies at a more convenient season. This appointment has led to a very lively discussion in the council His Majesty held with his ministers. His Majesty wanted to put himself at the head of his troops at once. Goremykin, Krivoshein, Admiral Grigorovitch, and particularly Sazonov respectfully insisted that he should not risk compromising his prestige and authority for a war which promises to be a very severe and dangerous struggle, and at the outset of which anything might happen.

"It's to be expected," said Sazonov, "that we may be forced to retreat during the first few weeks. Your Majesty ought not to be exposed to the criticism such a retreat would be bound to give rise to in the nation, and even in the army."

The Tsar, in protest, referred to the example of his ancestor, Alexander I in 1805 and 1812.

Sazonov judiciously replied, "If your Majesty would graciously read the memoirs and correspondence of that period, you would see how your august ancestor was criticized and blamed for taking command of the operations in person. You would also see how many evils might have been avoided if he had remained in his capital to control affairs from the head."

Ultimately the Tsar adopted this advice.

General Sukhomlinov, Minister for War, who has long coveted the august post of Commander-in-Chief, is furious at finding himself passed over in favor of Grand Duke Nicholas. Unhappily, he's the sort of man who wants his revenge.

Tuesday, August 4, 1914

Yesterday, Germany declared war on France. General mobilization is in active progress throughout the empire, and without the least incident. As a matter of fact, the relevant troops are five or six hours ahead of schedule in covering the ground.

Sazonov, whose virtue of disinterestedness and integrity I have often appreciated, has of late shown himself in a light which raises him even higher in my eyes. In the present crisis, he sees not only a political problem to be solved, but also, and in fact primarily, a moral problem in which religion itself is involved. The whole working of his mind is governed by the secret promptings of his conscience and his faith.

Several times he has said to me, "This action of Austria and Germany is as wicked as absurd. There's not a single element of morality about it. It outrages all the divine laws."

Seeing him utterly worn out this morning, with dark rings around his fevered eyes, I asked him how he managed to get through such an enormous amount of work with his delicate health.

His reply was, "God sustains me."

Every day, processions, with flags and icons, have passed under the embassy windows, to a chorus of "Vive la France! Vive la France!"

Very mixed crowds they are, too: workmen, priests, *moujiks,* students, male and female, servants, shop assistants, etc. Their enthusiasm seems genuine, but how far are the police responsible for these numerous demonstrations which take place at such regular intervals?

I put this question to myself at ten o'clock this evening when I was told that a mob had attacked the German Embassy and sacked it from top to bottom.

The German Embassy is a colossal edifice in the most important square of the city, between the Cathedral of St. Isaac and the Marie Palace. It has a heavy façade in Finnish granite, massive architraves, cyclopean masonry. On the roof, two enormous bronze horses, with giants holding their bridles, all but bring down the whole building. Hideous as a work of art, it is nonetheless a powerful piece of symbolism. With its coarse and blatant eloquence, it emphasizes Germany's claim to domination in Russia.

The mob has invaded the building, smashed the windows, torn down the tapestries, ripped up the pictures, thrown all the furniture (including the Renaissance marbles and bronzes which formed Pourtalès' admirable private collection) out of the windows. By way of conclusion, the marauders hurled the equestrian group on the façade down into the street. The sack lasted more than an hour under the tolerant eye of the police.

Has this act of vandalism any symbolic meaning? Can it be said to presage the ruin of German influence in Russia?

My Austro-Hungarian colleague, Count Szapary, is still in Petersburg and cannot understand why his government is apparently in so little hurry to break off relations with the Russian Government.

Wednesday, August 5, 1914

Today at Notre-Dame de France, the French colony in St. Petersburg held a solemn mass to pray for the divine blessing on our armies.

At five o'clock this morning, Buchanan rang me up to say that during the night he had received a telegram from the Foreign Office announcing England's participation in the war. I had therefore given orders that the British flag was to be added to the French and Russian flags which draped the high altar.

In the church I had my usual place in the right transept. Buchanan arrived almost simultaneously.

"My ally! My dear ally!" he said with great emotion.

In the center of the front row, two chairs were placed, one for Prince Bielosselsky – the Emperor's first aide-de-camp, representing His Majesty – and the other for General Krupensky – Grand Duke Nicholas's aide-de-camp – representing the Commander-in-Chief.

In the left transept were all the Russian ministers, with perhaps a hundred officials, officers etc. behind them.

A silence and composure filled the whole church.

I could see the same expression of happy surprise on the face of everyone who entered. The Union Jack over the altar told them all that England was henceforth our ally.

The flags of the three nations blend very eloquently. Composed of the same colors – blue, white and red – they are a very picturesque and striking expression of the interdependence of the three nations of the coalition.

At the end of mass the choir sang in turn:

Domine salvam fac Rempublicam ...
Domine, salvam fac Imperatorem Nicolaum
Domine, salvam fac Regem Brittannicum ...

When mass was over, Sazonov told me that the Tsar would like to see me in the afternoon at Peterhof.

I reached the little Alexandria Cottage about three o'clock, and was immediately ushered into His Majesty's study.

As etiquette decreed, I was in full dress, but the usual ceremonial requirements had been simplified. A Master of Ceremonies conducted me from Petersburg to Peterhof, an aide-de-camp announced me, and there was the inevitable courier of the imperial household in 18th century costume.

The Tsar's study on the first floor gets its light from wide windows from which the Gulf of Finland can be seen stretching away to the horizon. The furniture consists solely of two tables, piled high with papers, a settee, six leather chairs, and a few engravings of military subjects.

The Tsar, in field uniform, received me, standing.

"I wanted to assure you," he said, "of all my gratitude, all my admiration for your country. In showing herself so faithful an ally, France has given the world an immortal example of patriotism and loyalty. Please convey my very warmest thanks to the Government of the Republic."

He uttered the last sentence in a penetrating voice which trembled a little. His emotion was obvious.

I replied, "The Government of the Republic will greatly appreciate the thanks it deserves from Your Majesty for the promptitude and resolution with which it has accepted its obligations as an ally when once it recognized that the cause of peace was irreparably lost. It did not hesitate an instant, and from that moment onwards, my only task has been to convey assurances of support and solidarity to your ministers."

"I know, I know! I have always trusted France's word."

Then we talked about the struggle that now faced us. The Tsar thinks it will be very severe, protracted and perilous.

"We must arm ourselves with courage and patience. Speaking for myself, I shall fight to the bitter end. To win victory, I shall sacrifice my last ruble and my last soldier. As long as a single one of the enemy is on Russian or French soil, I shall never sign a peace treaty."

It was in a very calm and firm tone that the Tsar made this solemn declaration. In his voice, and still more in his expression, there was a curious hotchpot of resolution and placidity, a kind of ruthless determination and passivity, dreaminess and precision, as if he were not expressing his own will but rather obeying some external power, some decree of Providence or destiny.

Less tutored than he in the creed of fatalism, I summoned up all the vigor at my command to represent the terrible danger France would have to face in the first phase of the war.

"The French army will have to face the formidable onset of twenty-five German corps. I therefore beg Your Majesty to order your troops to take the offensive immediately. If they do not do so, there is a risk that the French army will be crushed, then the whole German mass will turn *en bloc* against Russia."

The Tsar replied, emphasizing each word, "The moment mobilization is complete, I shall order an advance. My troops are most enthusiastic. The attack will be pressed with the greatest vigor. No doubt you know that Grand Duke Nicholas is extraordinarily forceful."

The Tsar then asked me about various military technical matters, the effectives of the German army, the joint plans of the French and Russian General Staffs, the assistance of the English army and fleet, the eventual attitude of Turkey and Italy, and so on – all of them questions on which he seemed to me very well informed.

The audience had lasted an hour when the Tsar suddenly lapsed into silence. He seemed embarrassed and looked at me gravely in a somewhat gauche manner, with his hands half-held out. All at once he took me in his arms:

"Monsieur l'Ambassadeur, let me embrace in you my dear and glorious France!"

From the modest Alexandria Cottage, I went to the sumptuous Znamenka Palace, Grand Duke Nicholas's residence, which is nearby. The Commander-in-Chief received me in his enormous study where maps were spread out on all the tables. He came towards me with his quick, firm stride, and just as three days ago at the Winter Palace, squeezed the life out of me.

"God and Joan of Arc are with us!" he exclaimed. "We shall win! Isn't it providential that this war is for such a noble cause, that our two nations have responded so enthusiastically to the decree of mobilization, and the circumstances are so propitious?"

I did my best to rise to this note of military and mystic grandiloquence, the naive form of which did not prevent me from realizing its generous inspiration. But I refrained from invoking Joan of Arc. At the moment it is our business not to 'hunt the English out of France,' but to get them there, and as soon as possible.

Without feeling my way, I broached the question that was most serious of all.

"How soon will you order the offensive, Monseigneur?"

"I shall order the offensive as soon as the operation is feasible. Then I shall attack with all our might. Perhaps I shan't even wait till the concentration of all my corps is complete. As soon as I feel myself strong enough, I shall attack. It will probably be August 14."

He then explained to me his general plan of operations. There was be a group of armies operating on the Prussian front; a group of armies operating on the Galician front; a mass in Poland with the task of bearing down on Berlin as soon as the southern armies have succeeded in holding up and fixing the enemy.

His whole being exhaled a fierce energy as he stood thus, unveiling his plans, his finger on the map. His incisive, measured speech, flashing eyes, and quick, nervous movements, hard, steel-trap mouth, and gigantic stature, personify the imperious and impetuous audacity which was the dominant characteristic of the great Russian strategists such as Suvorov and Skobelev. But there is something else about Nicholas Nicholaievitch, something irascible, despotic and implacable, which places him in the true line of the Muscovite *voivodes* of the fifteenth and sixteenth centuries. And does he not share with them their child-like devotion, their superstitious credulity, their taste for the crude and vigorous life? Whatever there may be in this historical relationship, I can certainly say that the Grand Duke is a man of high spirit and that the supreme command of the Russian armies could not be confided to stronger or more loyal hands.

Towards the end of our conversation, he said, "Please convey to General Joffre my heartiest compliments and the assurances of my unshakable confidence in victory. Tell him that, side-by-side with my own Commander in Chief's flag, I shall carry the flag he gave me when I was at the French maneuvers two years ago." He shook my hand vigorously and led me to the door. "And now," he cried, "into God's hands!"

At half-past five, I rejoined the imperial train which brought me back to Petersburg.

A German army entered Belgian territory this evening.

Thursday, August 6, 1914

This morning, my Austro-Hungarian colleague, Szapary, handed Sazonov a declaration of war. This declaration alleged two reasons: (1) the attitude adopted by the Russian Government in the Austro-Serbian dispute; (2) the fact that according to a communication from Berlin, Russia had taken it upon herself to commence hostilities against Germany.

The Germans are entering western Poland. Since the day before yesterday they have occupied Kalish, Czenstschowa and Bendin. This swift advance shows how wise the Russian General Staff were in 1910 in withdrawing their frontier garrisons and creating a zone of concentration a hundred kilometers further east, a step which met with vigorous criticism in France at the time.

At midday, I left for Tsarskoe Selo where I was to lunch with Grand Duke Paul Alexandrovitch and his morganatic wife, Countess von Hohenfelsen, with whom I have been very friendly for many years.

During the whole run, my car was catching up and passing infantry regiments on the march with their field equipment. Each regiment was followed by an interminable string of vehicles, ammunition wagons, baggage carts, Army Service Corps lorries, ambulances, field kitchens, *telegas, lineikas*, peasants' carts etc. The vehicles followed each other in any sort of order. Sometimes they cut across the fields in a jumbled and picturesque confusion, which reminded one of an Asiatic horde. The infantrymen looked fine, though their march was hampered by rain and mud. Many women had joined the column to accompany their husbands to the first halt for the last goodbye. Several had children in their arms.

One of them made a very touching impression on me. She was very young and had a delicate face and fine neck, a red and white scarf tied round her fair hair, a blue cotton *sarafane* drawn in at the waist by a leather belt, and she was pressing a baby to her breast. She was striding out as well as she could to keep pace with the man at the rear of the file, a fine fellow, tanned and muscular. They did not exchange a word but gazed fixedly at each other with loving, haggard eyes. Three times in succession I saw the young mother offer the baby to the soldier for a kiss.

Grand Duke Paul and Countess von Hohenfelsen had invited only one guest in addition to myself, Michael Stakhovitch, Member of the Council of Empire for the *zemstvo* of Orel, one of the Russians who are particularly infused with French ideas. Thus I found myself in an atmosphere of warm and intimate sympathy.

As I entered, they all greeted me with a loud, *"Vive la France."* In the simple and straightforward manner which is all his own, the Grand Duke expressed his admiration for the burst of generous enthusiasm with which the French nation had rushed to help its ally.

"I know your Government did not hesitate a moment to support us when Germany forced us to defend ourselves. That alone is splendid. But it is extraordinary, nay sublime, that the whole nation at once realized its duty as an ally and that there has not been the slightest reluctance or protest in any class of society or any political party"

Stakhovitch chimed in.

"Yes, quite sublime. Of course, France today is only following her historical tradition. She has always been the land of the sublime."

I agreed, speaking with some emphasis.

"That's perfectly true. The French nation has frequently been accused of skepticism and frivolity, but unquestionably no nation has so often thrown itself into a conflict for purely disinterested motives, or sacrificed itself for the cause of idealism."

Then I gave my guests an account of the long series of events that have marked the last two weeks. For their part, they told me a large number of facts and episodes that furnish proof of the unanimous determination of all the Russians to save Serbia and beat Germany.

"No one in Russia would hear of us allowing the little Serbian nation to be crushed," said Stakhovitch.

I then asked him what were the views on the war of the members of the Extreme Right in the Council of Empire and the Duma, that large and influential party which, through the mouth of Prince Mestchersky, Stcheglovitov, Baron Rosen,

Purichkievitch and Markov, has always advocated an understanding with German imperialism.

He assured me that that doctrine, which has always been inspired mainly by considerations of domestic policy, had been utterly ruined by the attack upon Serbia, and added, "The war now under way is a duel to the death between Slavism and Germanism. There is not a Russian who does not know it."

On rising from the table I only gave myself time to smoke a cigarette and then left for Petersburg.

Near Pulkovo I passed a regiment of light infantry of the Guard which was leaving for the frontier. Its commander, a general, recognized the French Ambassador's car from the livery of my servant and sent one of his officers to ask me to get out so that he could parade his men before me.

I got out and went up to the General who leaned down from his horse to embrace me.

At a sharp word of command, the regiment halted, the ranks closed and dressed, and the band went to the head of the column.

While these preliminaries were in progress the General yelled at me, "We'll destroy these filthy Prussians! There must be no more Prussia, no more Germany! Wilhelm will be sent to St. Helena!" The march-past began. The men looked proud and well set-up. As each company passed the General rose in his stirrups and gave the order, "*Franzovski Pasol!* The French Ambassador! Hurrah!"

The men cheered frantically, "Hurrah! Hurrah!"

When the last file had passed, the General leaned down to embrace me again and said in a grave tone, "I'm very pleased to have met you, Monsieur l'Ambassadeur. All my men share my feeling that it's a good augury to have met France at the beginning of our journey." Then he galloped off to join the head of the column, and as I was getting back into my car, he bellowed his war cry, "Wilhelm will be sent to St. Helena! Wilhelm will be sent to St. Helena!"

At four o'clock, I had a long conversation with my Italian colleague, Marquis Carlotti di Riparbella. I was at some pains to show him that the present crisis offers his country an unhoped-for opportunity of realizing its national aspirations.

"Whatever my personal convictions may be, I'm not presumptuous enough to guarantee that the armies and fleets of the Triple Entente will be victorious. But I have a clear right, especially after my conversation with the Tsar yesterday, to assure you of the spirit which animates the three powers and their implacable determination to crush Germany. All three are at one in their resolution to put an end to German tyranny. The problem being stated thus, you can judge for yourself on which side are the chances of success and draw the inevitable inferences."

We left together and I went to the Ministry for Foreign Affairs, where I had a multitude of questions to settle wth regard to the blockade, repatriation, telegraphic correspondence, press, police and so on, not to mention diplomatic questions.

Sazonov tells me he sent for Diamandy, the Rumanian Minister, to ask for the immediate help of the Rumanian army against Austria. In exchange, he offers the Bucharest Cabinet the right to annex all Austro-Hungarian territory now inhabited by a Rumanian population, i.e. the larger part of Transylvania and the western Bukovina. In addition the Triple Entente powers will guarantee Rumania the integrity of her territory.

Lastly Sazonov has telegraphed to the Russian Minister at Sofia to ask him to secure the benevolent neutrality of Bulgaria in return for the promise of certain districts to be detached from Serbian Macedonia if Serbia acquires direct access to the Adriatic Sea.

Friday, August 7, 1914

Yesterday the Germans entered Liège, but some of the forts are still resisting.

Sazonov is proposing to the French and British Governments to enter into immediate negotiations at Tokio for the accession of Japan to our alliance. The allied powers would recognize the Japanese Government's right to annex the German territory of Kiaochau. Russia and Japan would mutually guarantee the integrity of each other's Asiatic possessions.

This evening I dined at the Yacht Club on the Morskaia. In this eminently conservative body I found confirmation of what Stakhovitch told me yesterday as to the feeling of the Extreme Right towards Germany. The very men who last week were protesting most loudly that it was necessary to strengthen orthodox Tsarism by a close alliance with Prussian autocracy, are now swearing that the bombardment of Belgrade is an intolerable insult to the whole Slav world and showing themselves as warlike as any. Others say nothing or confine themselves to the remark that Germany and Austria have dealt a mortal blow to the monarchical principle in Europe.

Before returning to the Embassy I called in at the Ministry for Foreign Affairs as Sazonov wanted to see me.

"I'm rather perturbed," he said, "by some news I've had from Constantinople. I'm very much afraid that Germany and Austria are engaged in a scheme there against us."

"Whatever is it?"

"I'm afraid that the Austro-Hungarian fleet is going to take refuge in the Sea of Marmora. You can imagine the result."

Saturday, August 8, 1914

Yesterday a French army entered Belgium on its way to support the Belgian army. Is the fate of France once more to be decided between the Sambre and the Meuse?

To-day there was a sitting of the Council of Empire and the Duma. After August 2, the Tsar announced his intention of convoking an extraordinary session of the legislature "so that I may be in perfect union with my people." This convocation would have been regarded as perfectly natural and necessary in any other country but here it has been interpreted as a manifestation of 'constitutionalism.' In liberal circles the Tsar is regarded all the more kindly, for it is not forgotten that the President of the Council (Goremykin), the Minister of the Interior (Maklakov), the Minister of Justice (Stcheglovitov), and the Procurator of the Holy Synod (Sabler), regard the Duma as the lowest and most negligible organ of state. I sat with Sir George Buchanan in the front row of the diplomatic gallery.

The session opened with a moving speech by the President, Rodzianko. His eloquent and sonorous oratory roused the assembly to great enthusiasm.

Next, the aged Goremykin tottered to the tribune. Forcing out his words with difficulty in a feeble voice, which seemed every now and then to be exhausted and about to expire, he declared that "Russia did not desire the war, that the Imperial Government had done everything possible to save the cause of peace, clinging even to the slightest chance of damming the deluge of blood which threatens to engulf the world." He concluded by saying that Russia could not shrink from the challenge thrown down to her by the German powers, and in any case "if we had yielded, our humiliation would not have changed the course of affairs." In emphasizing these last words his voice became a little stronger and his feeble old eyes flamed up for a moment. It might be said that this skeptical old man, laden with labors, honors and experience, found a malicious pleasure in proclaiming his disillusioned fatalism.

Sazonov followed him to the tribune. He was pale and nervous. From the very outset he cleared his conscience. "When history brings the day of unbiased judgment, I am convinced it will justify us." He vigorously reminded his audience that "it was not Russian policy that imperiled the peace of the world," and that if Germany had so desired, she could "with one word, one authoritative word," have stopped Austria in her bellicose tracks. Then, in warm tones, he exalted "magnanimous France, chivalrous France, which has risen to our side in the defense of right and justice."

At these words all the deputies rose, turned towards me, and gave round after round of cheers for France. All the same, I observed that the cheers were not very enthusiastic on the benches occupied by the Left. The liberal parties have never forgiven us for prolonging the life of Tsarism with our financial subsidies.

The cheering broke out afresh when Sazonov said that England also had recognized the moral impossibility of remaining indifferent to the outrage on Serbia. His peroration accurately translated the thought that has inspired all our actions and reflections in the last weeks. "We will not accept the yoke of Germany and her ally in Europe."

He descended from the tribune to the accompaniment of further cheers.

After the sitting was suspended, all the party leaders furnished proof of their patriotism by declaring their readiness to make any sacrifice to save Russia and the Slav peoples from German hegemony. When the President put the propositions asked for by the Government to the vote, the Socialist Party announced that it would abstain from voting, being unwilling to accept any responsibility for the policy of Tsarism, but it exhorted the democracy of Russia to defend its native soil against foreign invasion. "Workmen and peasants, summon up all your energies to defend our country. We will free it afterwards!" Except for the abstention of the Socialists, the military propositions have been voted for without a single dissentient voice.

When I left the Tauride Palace with Buchanan, our cars had some difficulty in making their way through the crowd that swarmed around us and warmly cheered us.

My impression of this session is satisfactory: The Russian people did not want the war and has even been surprised by the war, but it is firmly resolved to face the effort it requires. On the other hand, the Government and the ruling classes realize that the fate of Russia is henceforth indissolubly associated with the destinies of France and England. This second point is no less important than the first.

Sunday, August 9, 1914

Yesterday the French Troops entered Mulhausen.

Grand Duke Nicholas, who has not yet transferred his headquarters to the army front, sent me his Chief of Staff, General Janushkevitch, to tell me that mobilization has been all but completed under the best auspices and that the concentration is quite according to schedule. He added that, as the Government had every confidence in the maintenance of order in St. Petersburg, the troops in the capital and its suburbs were now to be sent to the front.

We then talked about the operations in prospect. General Janushkevitch confirmed, (1) that the Vilna Army will take the offensive in the direction of Königsberg; (2) that the Warsaw Army will at once be thrown on to the left bank of the Vistula to guard the flanks of the Vilna Army; (3) that a general offensive will begin on August 14.

At half-past six I took my car to Tsarskoe Selo to dine with Grand Duchess Marie Pavlovna.

The Grand Duchess was accompanied by her eldest son and daughter-in-law – Grand Duke Cyril Vladimirovitch and Grand Duchess Victoria Feodorovna; her son-in-law and her daughter – Prince Nicholas of Greece and Grand Duchess Helena Vladimirovna; and her maids-of-honor and some close friends.

The table was set in the garden in a tent three sides of which were open. The air was pure and soft. From the rose beds a balmy odor filled the air. The sun, which was high in the sky notwithstanding the late hour, shed a soft light and scattered diaphanous shadows around us.

Conversation was general, frank and warm. Of course, the only subject was the war, but one topic came up continuously – the distribution of the higher commands and the composition of their staff. Some criticized the appointments already made. Others tried to guess the appointments the Tsar had still to make. All the rivalries of the court and the drawing rooms betrayed themselves in the various suggestions. Every now and then I thought I was living through a chapter of Tolstoy's 'War and Peace.'

When dinner was over, Grand Duchess Marie Pavlovna took me to the bottom of the garden and made me sit by her on a seat.

"Now we can talk without restraint," she said. "I have a feeling that the Emperor and Russia are playing for a supreme stake. This is not a political war as so many others have been. It is a duel between Slavism and Germanism. One of the two must succumb. I have seen many people over last few days. My ambulances and hospital trains have brought me into contact with folk of all social circles and classes. I can assure you that no one has any illusions about the serious nature of the struggle on which we have embarked. From the Tsar down to the humblest *moujik*, all are determined to do their duty unflinchingly. We shall not shrink from any sacrifice. If our beginning is unfortunate, which God forbid, you'll soon see the miracles of 1812 again."

"It is probable that we shall have great difficulties at the outset. We must expect anything, even a disaster. All I ask of Russia is to hold fast."

"She will hold. Don't doubt it."

To induce the Grand Duchess to speak her mind on a more delicate subject, I congratulated her on the high courage she was showing, for I was bound to assume that her firm-mindedness was not divorced from a terrible inward wrench.

"I'm glad I can speak freely with you. Many a time over the last few days have I turned the searchlight on my conscience. I have seen into the very depths of my soul. But neither in my heart nor my mind have I found anything that is not utterly devoted to my Russian fatherland. And I have thanked God for that. Is it because the first inhabitants of Mecklenburg and their first rulers, my ancestors, were Slavs? It may be so, but I rather think that it is my forty years' residence in Russia – all the happiness I have known here, all the dreams that have come to me, all the affection and kindness I have received – that has given me a wholly Russian soul. I am only a Mecklenburger on one point, in my hatred for Emperor Wilhelm. He represents what I have been taught from my childhood to detest the most, the tyranny of the Hohenzollerns. Yes, it is the Hohenzollerns who have perverted, demoralized, degraded and humiliated Germany, and gradually destroyed in her all elements of idealism and generosity, refinement and charity."

She thus gave vent to her anger in a long diatribe that made me feel all the sentiments of inveterate hatred, of mute and tenacious detestation, that the small and once independent states of Germany have for the despotic House of Prussia.

About ten o'clock, I took my leave of the Grand Duchess, as a mass of work awaited me at the embassy.

The night was clear and warm. The moon, a wan and ghostly moon, drew silver scarves here and there across the great. featureless plain. In the west, where the Gulf of Finland lies, the horizon was veiled in coppery wreaths.

When I got back at half-past eleven, a bundle of telegrams that had arrived during the evening were brought to me.

It was nearly 2 a.m. when I got into bed.

Too tired to sleep, I took a book, one of the few books one can open in this hour of universal agitation and historical convulsion – the Bible. Once more I read the Revelation and stopped at this passage:

> *And there went out another horse that was red: and power was given to him that sat thereon to take peace from the earth, and that they should kill one another: and there was given unto him a great sword. And I looked and beheld a pale horse: and his name that sat on him was Death, and Hell followed with him. And power was given unto them over the fourth part of the earth, to kill with sword, and with hunger, and with death, and with the beasts of the earth.*

Today it is men who will play the part of the 'beasts of the earth.'

Monday, August 10, 1914

Sazonov is pressing the Italian Government to join our alliance and is proposing a compact based on the following terms:

> *(1) The Italian army and fleet will immediately attack the Austro-Hungarian army and fleet;*

(2) after the war, Trent and the ports of Trieste and Valona will be annexed by Italy.

From Sofia, our impressions are not reassuring. Tsar Ferdinand is capable of any infamy or crime when his vanity or his hatreds are at stake. I certainly know of three countries that are the object of his implacable hatred – Serbia, Rumania and Russia.

I said as much to Sazonov but he interrupted me.

"What? Tsar Ferdinand has a grudge against Russia! Whatever for?"

"In the first place, he accuses the Russian Government of having taken Serbia's side, and even Rumania's, in 1913. Then there are his old grudges which are innumerable."

"But what grudges? We have always loaded him with favors. When he came here in 1910, the Tsar treated him with the same honor and respect as if he had been the sovereign of a great kingdom. What more could we have done?"

"Why, it's that visit of 1910 that is one of his bitterest complaints. Just after he got back to Sofia, he summoned me to the palace and said, 'My dear Minister, I've sent for you because I want your help in disentangling the impressions I have brought with me from St. Petersburg. The truth is I haven't succeeded in finding out which they hate most: my people, my work or myself.' "

"He must be mad!"

"It's not too strong a word. Undoubtedly this individual shows signs of nervous degeneracy and psychic disturbances:

impulses, hallucinations, idées fixes, melancholia, megalomania, a dread of persecution. They only make him all the more dangerous, for he brings consummate skill and an uncommonly astute mind to the service of his ambitions and hatreds."

"I don't know how much would be left of his cleverness if the perfidy were eliminated from it. However that may be, we cannot keep too watchful an eye on his doings. I thought I ought to let him know that if he intrigues with Austria against Serbia, Russia will definitely withdraw her friendship from the Bulgarian people. Savinsky, our minister at Sofia, is very shrewd. He will carry out his task with all the tact desirable."

"That's not enough. There are other arguments that appeal very strongly to the clique of Bulgarian politicians. We should have recourse to them without delay."

"I think so, too. We'll discuss this again."

The war appears to have created an extraordinary wave of patriotism among the Russian people.

The information, both official and private, that reaches me from every part of Russia is always the same. In Moscow, Yaroslav, Kazan, Simbirsk, Tula, Kiev, Kharkov, Odessa, Rostov, Samara, Tiflis, Orenburg, Tomsk, Irkutsk, in fact everywhere, there are the same popular demonstrations, the same grave and religious enthusiasm, the same impulse to rally around the Tsar, the same faith in victory, the same exaltation of the national conscience. No opposition, no dissentient voice. The bad days of 1905 seem to have gone from the memory of all. The collective soul of Holy Russia has never manifested itself so forcibly since 1812.

Tuesday, August 11, 1914

The French troops that had occupied Mulhausen with such gay boldness have been obliged to evacuate it.

The popular hatred of the Germans continues to manifest itself throughout Russia in deeds of violence, causing much material damage. The supremacy Germany had won in every department of Russian economic life, a supremacy which was usually tantamount to a monopoly, justifies only too thoroughly this brutal reaction of national sentiment. It is difficult to give an exact figure for the number of German subjects in Russia, but it would not be far wrong to fix it at 170,000, compared with 120,000 Austro-Hungarians, 10,000 French, and 8,000 English. The table of imports is even more eloquent. During the last year, German goods were imported to the value of 643,000,000 rubles, whereas English imports totaled 170,000,000 only, French imports 56,000,000, and Austro-Hungarian imports 35,000,000.

To the elements of German influence in Russia must be added a whole population of German immigrants, speaking the German language, retaining German traditions, and counting not less than 2,000,000 souls, settled in the Baltic Provinces, the Ukraine and the valley of the lower Volga.

Lastly and above all, there are the "Baltic Barons," who have gradually cornered all the high court appointments and the best posts in the army and the administrative and diplomatic services. For one hundred and fifty years, the feudal castes of the Baltic Provinces has supplied Tsarism with its most devoted servants and its most formidable reactionary weapon. It was the Baltic nobility that ensured the triumph of autocratic absolutism by crushing the insurrection of December 1825. It is the Baltic nobility again that has always directed the work of repression whenever the liberal or revolutionary spirit has awakened from its slumbers. It is the Baltic nobility that more than anything else has contributed to making the Russian state into a great police bureaucracy in which the machinery of Tartar despotism and the methods of Prussian despotism are combined in a strange amalgam. It is the Baltic nobility that is the main framework of the régime.

To realize the aversion in which the "Baltic Barons" are held by the real Russians, I have only to listen to E….. the Director of Ceremonies, with whom I am on terms of confidence, and whose uncompromising nationalism amuses me. He came to see me yesterday about some routine matter and displayed even more than his usual fire in railing against the Germans at court – Count Fredericks, the Minister of the Imperial Household; Baron Korff, Grand Master of the Ceremonies; General von Grünewaldt, Grand Equerry; Count Benckendorff, Grand Marshal; and the whole tribe of Megendorffs, Budbergs, Heydens, Stackelbergs, Nieroths, Kotzebues, Knorrings etc. who encumber the imperial palaces.

Emphasizing his words with an expressive gesture he wound up with, "After the war, we'll wring the necks of the Baltic Barons."

"But when you've wrung their necks, are you quite sure you won't regret it?" I inquired.

"What? What do you mean? Do you really think we Russians aren't capable of governing ourselves?"

"I'm sure you're perfectly capable, but it's dangerous to remove the tie beam of a structure without having another handy to take its place."

Wednesday, August 12, 1914

While military forces are mobilizing, all the social organizations are equipping themselves for war. As usual, the signal is given by Moscow, the true center of national life and the place where the spirit of enterprise is more awake and developed than anywhere else. A congress of all the *zemstvos* and municipalities of Russia is about to be held there to co-ordinate the multifarious branches of social activity for the purposes of the war: Red Cross work, relief for the poorer classes, distribution of manpower, production of food, medicaments, clothing etc. The idea behind the movement is to help the Government in the fulfilment of the complex tasks that its bureaucracy, which is idle, corrupt and blind to the needs of the people, is incapable of performing itself. It is devoutly to be hoped that the *tchinovniks*, with their usual suspicion, will not oppose this fine, spontaneous impulse as a matter of routine.

In the Nevsky Prospekt, the Liteiny and the Sadovaia, I have passed regiments every day on their way to the Warsaw station. These fine and well-equipped men made an excellent impression upon me with their grave and determined air and firm, rhythmic step. As I looked at them, I reflected that a large number of them were already marked out for death. But what will be the feelings of those who return? What notions, reflections and clamors, what new spirit or new soul will they bring back with them to their own firesides?

Every great war has brought the Russian people a deep domestic crisis. The War of Liberation of 1812 prepared that silent work of emancipation that all but swept away Tsarism in December 1825. The unfortunate Crimean War resulted in the abolition of serfdom and necessitated the 'Great Reforms' of 1860. The Balkan War of 1877-1878, with its costly victories, was followed by the explosion of nihilist terrorism. The ill-omened Russo-Japanese War ended in the revolutionary outbreaks of 1905. What will follow the present war?

The Russian nation is so heterogeneous in its ethnic and moral composition, it is formed of elements so incongruous and anachronistic, it has always developed in such defiance of logic, through such a maze of clashes, shocks and inconsistencies, that its historic evolution utterly defies prophecy.

This evening I dined with Madame P…. and Countess R…., whose husbands have just left for the front. They themselves are about to join a frontline ambulance in Galicia as Red

Cross sisters. On the strength of various letters they have received from the provinces and the country, they assured me that mobilization has proceeded everywhere in a stimulating atmosphere of national pride and heroism.

We talked about the terrible test that modern weapons of war impose on the moral of the combatants. Never before have human nerves been subjected to such a strain.

Madame P…. said to me, "In that respect, I'll guarantee the Russian soldier. He has no equal in remaining unshaken in the presence of death."

Countess R…., however, who is usually so mentally alert and a great talker, was very silent. Leaning forward in her chair, her hands folded on her knees, her brows contracted, her eyes fixed on the ground, she seemed lost in thought.

Madame P…. asked her, "What are you thinking of, Daria? You look like a sybil on her stool. Are you going to utter oracles?"

"No, I'm not thinking of the future," she replied. "I'm thinking of the past, or rather of what there might have been. You're going to give me your opinion, Monsieur l'Ambassadeur. Yesterday I called on Madame Taneiev, you know, Anna Vyrubova's mother. There were five or six people present, the flower of the Rasputin set. They were arguing very seriously and looked very excited. My arrival was a cold douche as I'm not one of their crowd. Not I! After a somewhat awkward silence, Anna Vyrubova reopened the conversation, and n a peremptory tone, as if she wanted to teach me something, she declared that there would certainly have been no war if Rasputin had been at St. Petersburg instead of half dead at Pokrovskoe when things began to go wrong between us and Germany.

More than once she said, "If the *staretz* had been there, we should have had no war. I don't know what he would have done or advised, but God would have inspired him, whereas the ministers have proved incapable of seeing or preventing anything. It's an absolute disaster that he hasn't been here to open the Emperor's eyes. Just look what determines the fate of empires. A harlot revenges herself on a dirty *moujik* and the Tsar of all the Russias at once loses his head. And here's the whole world on fire!"

Madame P.... interrupted in a shocked tone. "Daria, you shouldn't say things like that in front of the Ambassador, even in fun. It's dreadful to think that such talk goes on among the intimate friends of Their Majesties."

Serious again, Countess R.... resumed. "All right, I'll be serious. Do you think the war was inevitable, Monsieur l'Ambassadeur? Could any personal influence have averted it?"

I replied, "In the way the problem was set by the will of Germany, the war was inevitable. In Petersburg, as in Paris and London, everything was done to save the cause of peace. It was impossible to go further in the path of concession. There was no alternative but to bow the knee to the Germanic powers and capitulate. Would Rasputin have advised the Tsar to do that?"

"You can't doubt it!" cried Madame P.... with indignation flaming in her eyes.

Thursday, August 13, 1914

Grand Duke Nicholas Nicholaievitch has informed me that the Vilna and Warsaw armies will take the offensive at dawn tomorrow. The armies earmarked for operations against Austria will do the same a little later. The Grand Duke leaves Petersburg this evening, taking with him my first Military Attaché, General de Laguiche, and the English Military Attaché, General Williams. General Headquarters is at Baranovici, between Minsk and Brest-Litovsk. I am keeping my second Military Attaché, Major Wehrlin, and my Naval Attaché, Commander Galland.

The Rumanian Government has declined the proposals of the Russian Government on the ground of the long and intimate friendship between King Carol and the Emperor Franz Joseph, but it has taken note of these proposals, the friendly nature of which it highly appreciates, and come to the conclusion that in the present phase of the conflict that divides Europe, its duty is to confine its efforts to the maintenance of the balance of power in the Balkans.

The warning Sazonov asked me to convey to our navy a week ago has been in vain. Two large German cruisers, The Goeben and The Breslau have succeeded in taking refuge in the Sea of Marmora. It is not even possible to doubt that the Turkish Government has been their accomplice.

There is great excitement at the Admiralty where the material damage to be expected from an attack on the Russian Black Sea coast, and still more its moral effect, is greatly feared.

Sazonov is looking still further ahead.

"By this surprise, the Germans have doubled their prestige in Constantinople," he said. "If we don't take immediate action, Turkey is lost to us, and not merely lost to us, but she'll come out against us. And then we shall have to distribute our forces over the Black Sea coast and the Armenian and Persian frontiers."

"What do you think should be done?"

"I've not yet come to any definite conclusion. At first sight, it seems to me we ought to offer Turkey a solemn guarantee of her territorial integrity as the price of her neutrality. We could add a promise of great financial advantages at the expense of Germany."

I encouraged him to explore that path for the solution that is so urgently required.

"Now I'm going to tell you a secret, a great secret," said Sazonov. "The Emperor has decided to re-establish Poland and grant her a large measure of autonomy. His intentions will be announced to the Poles in a manifesto that will shortly be published by Grand Duke Nicholas. His Majesty has ordered me to draw it up."

"Excellent! It's a magnificent move and it'll produce an enormous impression, not merely on the Poles but in France and England and throughout the world. When will the manifesto be issued?"

"In three or four days. I've submitted my draft to the Emperor and he has approved it. I'm sending it this evening to Grand Duke Nicholas, who may possibly require certain modifications of detail."

"But why does the Emperor entrust the publication of the manifesto to the Grand Duke. Why doesn't he issue it himself as a direct expression of his sovereign will? The moral effect would be all the more striking."

"That was my first idea too, but Goremykin and Maklakov, who are hostile to the reconstitution of Poland, observed, not without justice, that the Poles of Galicia and Posen are still under Austrian and Prussian domination and that the conquest of these two provinces is only an anticipation, a hope, so that the Emperor cannot consistently with his dignity address himself to future subjects. While Grand Duke Nicholas, on the other hand, would not exceed his functions of Russian Commander-in-Chief if he addressed himself to the Slav peoples he has come to deliver. The Emperor came round to this view."

Then we philosophized about the accession of strength Russia would gain from the reconciliation of the two nations under the scepter of the Romanovs. German expansion eastwards would thus be definitely arrested and all the problems of Eastern Europe would wear a new aspect, to the great advantage of Slavism. Lastly, and chiefly, a wider, more generous and liberal spirit would be introduced into the relations of Tsarism with the various racial groups of the Empire.

Friday, August 14, 1914

On the faith of God knows what rumors emanating from Constantinople, there is an idea in Paris and London that

Russia is meditating an attack upon Turkey and is keeping back part of her forces for this onslaught in the near future. Sazonov, who has been informed of this simultaneously by Isvolsky and Benckendorff, displayed some bitterness in telling me of his disappointment at finding himself the object of so unmerited a suspicion in the eyes of his allies.

"How could they attribute such an idea to us? It's not merely false but ridiculous! Grand Duke Nicholas told you himself that all our forces, without exception, are concentrated on the western frontier of the Empire, for one purpose and one purpose only – to crush Germany. Only this morning, when I made my report to the Tsar, His Majesty declared in his own words, 'I have told Grand Duke Nicholas to force his way to Berlin at the earliest possible moment and at any cost. I regard our operations against Austria as of secondary importance only. Our primary object is the destruction of the German army.' What more could anyone want?"

I soothed him as well as I could.

"Don't take things too much to heart. It's not in the least surprising that Germany is trying to make the Turks believe that you are preparing to attack them, hence a certain amount of agitation in Constantinople. The French and English ambassadors have reported the fact to their governments. That's all. The excellent news you have just given me will be all the more appreciated."

Saturday, August 15, 1914

The Belgians are offering a stout resistance at Hasselt. Will the French army arrive in time to save them?

Grand Duke Nicholas has sent to tell me from Baranovici that the concentration of his armies is proceeding appreciably ahead of schedule so that he proposes to extend his offensive.

Yesterday, a Russian advance guard entered Galicia at Sokal on the Bug and threw back the enemy in the direction of Lemberg.

This afternoon, I had a long talk with General Sukhomlinov, the War Minister, with a view to a speedy settlement of a great number of military questions with regard to transport, munitions, supplies etc. Then we spoke of the operations in progress.

The general plan is as follows:

> *(1) The north-western armies, three armies comprising a dozen corps, have taken the offensive. Two of these armies are operating north of the Vistula; the third is operating south of that river and has already struck west from Warsaw. A fourth army of three corps will advance on Posen and Breslau and connect up these three armies with the forces operating against Austria;*

(2) The south-western armies, three armies comprising twelve corps, have the task of overrunning Galicia.

There is something about General Sukhomlinov that makes one uneasy. Sixty-two years of age, the slave of a rather pretty wife thirty-two years younger than himself, intelligent, clever and cunning, obsequious towards the Tsar and a friend of Rasputin, surrounded by a rabble who serve as intermediaries in his intrigues and duplicities, he is a man who has lost the habit of work and keeps all his strength for conjugal joys. With his sly look, his eyes always gleaming watchfully under the heavy folds of his eyelids, I know few men who inspire more distrust at first sight.

Three days hence the Tsar is to go to Moscow to make a solemn proclamation to his people from the Kremlin. He has invited Buchanan and me to go with him.

Sunday, August 16, 1914

Grand Duke Nicholas's manifesto to the Polish nation is published this morning. The press is unanimous in its satisfaction, and most of the papers devote enthusiastic articles to celebrating the reconciliation of Poles and Russians in the bosom of the great Slav family.

The document is quite a work of art and has been drafted, on lines indicated by Sazonov, by one of the departmental heads of the Foreign Office, Prince Gregory Troubetzkoy. The translation into Polish has been done by Count Sigismund Wielopolsky, President of the Polish Group in the Council of Empire.

It was the day before yesterday that Sazonov asked Wielopolsky to come and see him, without giving him any reason. In a few words he told him what was afoot and then read him the manifesto. Wielopolsky listened, holding his breath, his hands clasped. After the moving peroration – "May the sign of the Cross, the symbol of the sufferings, and resurrection of the peoples glow in this new dawn!" – he burst into tears and murmured, "Blessed be God! Blessed be God!"

When Sazonov told me all this, I quoted to him what Father Gratry had said in 1863. "Since the partition of Poland, Europe has been in a state of mortal sin."

"Then I've done good work for the salvation of Europe," he cried.

From Poland we turned our conversation to Turkey. Sazonov is proposing to the French and British Governments to join with him in making the following declaration to the Ottoman Government:

(1) If Turkey will observe strict neutrality, Russia, France and England will guarantee the integrity of her territory;

(2) On the same condition, the three allied powers undertake, in case of victory, to secure the insertion in the peace treaty of a clause liberating

Turkey from the oppressive tutelage imposed on her by Germany in matters economic and financial. For example, this clause would provide for the cancellation of the contracts for the Bagdad railway and other German enterprises.

I congratulated Sazonov on this double proposal that seemed to me wisdom itself. In fact I referred specifically to the first paragraph in stating, "So even if we are victorious, Russia will make no claims, either territorial or political, on Turkey? I'm sure you realize the importance I attach to my question. No doubt you know that the absolute independence of Turkey is one of the guiding principles of French diplomacy."

Sazonov replied, "Even if we are victorious, we shall respect the independence and integrity of Turkey, provided she stays neutral. The utmost we shall ask is that there shall be a new regime for the Straits, a regime generally applicable to all the Black Sea states, Russia, Turkey, Bulgaria, and Rumania."

Monday, August 17, 1914

The French troops are making progress in the Upper Vosges and Upper Alsace. The Russian troops have embarked on a vigorous offensive on the frontier of East Prussia, on a line from Kovno to Königsberg.

The manifesto to the Poles is the subject of conversation everywhere. The general impression it has created remains excellent. The only criticism, more or less expressly stated, comes from partisans of the Extreme Right, where an understanding with Prussian reaction has always been considered a vital condition for the maintenance of Tsarism. The suppression of Polish nationalism is, of course, the very foundation of that understanding.

    At eight o'clock this evening I left for Moscow with Sir George and Lady Georgina Buchanan.

Chapter 4

Tuesday August 18, 1914

When I arrived in Moscow this morning, I went with Buchanan about half-past ten to the great Kremlin Palace. We were ushered into the St. George's Hall, where the high dignitaries of the empire, the ministers, delegates of the nobility, middle classes, merchant community, charitable organizations etc., were already assembled in a dense and silent throng.

On the stroke of eleven o'clock, the Tsar, the Tsaritsa, and the imperial family made their ceremonial entry. The grand dukes had all gone to the front and besides the sovereigns there were only the four young grand duchesses, the Tsar's daughters, the Tsarevitch Alexis, who hurt his leg yesterday and had to be carried in the arms of a Cossack, and Grand Duchess Elizabeth Feodorovna, the Tsaritsa's sister, Abbess of the Convent of Martha and Mary of Pity.

The imperial party stopped in the center of the hall, and in a full and firm voice the Tsar addressed the nobility and people of Moscow. He proclaimed that, as the traditions of his ancestors decreed, he had come to seek the moral support he needed in prayer at the relics in the Kremlin. He declared that a heroic national impulse was sweeping over all Russia, without distinction of race or nationality, and concluded, £From this place, the very heart of Russia, I send my soul's greeting to my valiant troops and my noble allies. God is with us!"

A continuous burst of cheering was his answer.

As the imperial group moved on, the Grand Master of Ceremonies invited Buchanan and myself to follow the royal family immediately after the grand duchesses.

Through the St. Vladimir Room and the Sacred Gallery, we reached the Red Staircase, the lower flight of which leads by a bridge with a purple awning to the Ouspensky Sobor, the Cathedral of the Assumption.

The moment the Tsar appeared, a storm of cheering broke out from the whole Kremlin where an enormous crowd, bare-headed and struggling, thronged the pavements. At the same time all the bells of the Ivan Veliky chimed in chorus, and the Great Bell of the Ascension, cast from the metal saved from the ruins in 1812, sent a thunderous boom above the din. Around us, Holy Moscow, with her sky-blue domes, copper spires and gilded bulbs, sparkled in the sun like a fantastic mirage.

The hurricane of popular enthusiasm almost dominated the din of the bells.

Count Benckendorff, Grand Marshal of the Court, came up to me and said, "Here's the revolution Berlin promised us!"

In so saying, he was probably interpreting everyone's thoughts. The Tsar's face was radiant. In the Tsaritsa's was joyous ecstasy.

Buchanan whispered, "This is a sublime moment to have lived to see. Think of all the history being made here and now!"

"Yes, and I'm thinking, too, of the historic past which is seeing its fulfilment here," I replied. "It was from this very spot on which we now stand that Napoleon surveyed Moscow in flames. It was by that very road down there that the Grand Army began its immortal retreat."

We were now at the steps of the cathedral. The Metropolitan of Moscow, surrounded by his clergy, presented to Their Majesties the cross of Tsar Michael Feodorovitch, the first of the Romanovs, and the holy water.

We entered the Ouspensky Sobor. This edifice is square, surmounted by a gigantic dome supported by four massive pillars, and all its walls are covered with frescoes on a gilded background. The iconostasis, a lofty screen, is one mass of precious stones. The dim light falling from the cupola and the flickering glow of the candles kept the nave in a ruddy semi-darkness.

The Tsar and Tsaritsa stood in front of the right ambo at the foot of the column against which the throne of the Patriarchs is set.

In the left ambo, the court choir, in 16th century silver and light blue costumes, chanted the beautiful anthems of the orthodox rite, perhaps the finest anthems in sacred music.

At the end of the nave, opposite the iconastasis, the three Metropolitans of Russia and twelve archbishops stood in line. In the aisles on their left was a group of one hundred and ten bishops, archimandrites and abbots. A fabulous, indescribable wealth of diamonds, sapphires, rubies and amethysts sparkled on the brocade of their miters and chasubles. At times the church glowed with a supernatural light.

Buchanan and I were on the Tsar's left, in front of the court.

Towards the end of the long service, the Metropolitan brought Their Majesties a crucifix containing a portion of the true cross, which they reverently kissed. Then, through a cloud of incense, the imperial family walked around the cathedral to kneel at the world-famed relics and the tombs of the patriarchs.

During this procession I was admiring the bearing and expressions of Grand Duchess Elizabeth, particularly when she bowed or knelt. Although she is approaching fifty, she has kept her slim figure and all her old grace. Under her loose white woolen hood, she was as elegant and attractive as in the old days before her widowhood, when she still inspired profane passions. To kiss the figure of the Virgin of Vladimir, which is set in the iconostasis, she had to place her knee on a rather high marble scat. The Tsaritsa and the young grand duchesses who preceded her had had to make two attempts, and clumsy attempts, before reaching the celebrated icon. She managed it in one supple, easy and queenly movement.

The service was now over. The procession was reformed, and the clergy took their place at its head. One last chant, soaring in triumph, filled the nave. The door opened.

All the glories of Moscow suddenly came into view in a blaze of sunshine. As the procession passed out, I reflected that the court of Byzantium, at the time of Constantine Porphyrogenetes, Nicephorus Phocas or Andronicus

Paleologue, can alone have seen so amazing a display of sacerdotal pomp.

At the end of the covered passage, the imperial carriages were waiting. Before entering them the royal family stood for a time facing the frantic cheers of the crowd.

The Tsar said to Buchanan and myself, "Come nearer to me, Messieurs les Ambassadeurs. These cheers are as much for you as for me."

Amid the torrent of acclamations, we three discussed the war that had just begun. The Tsar congratulated me on the wonderful ardor of the French troops and reiterated the assurance of his absolute faith in final victory. The Tsaritsa tried to give me a few kind words.

I helped her out. "What a comforting sight for your Majesty! How splendid it is to see all these people swept up in patriotic exaltation and fervor for their rulers."

Her answer was almost inaudible, but her strained smile and the strange spell of her rapt gaze, magnetic and inspired, revealed her inward intoxication.

Grand Duchess Elizabeth joined in our conversation. Her face in the frame of her long white woolen veil was alive with spirituality. Her delicate features and white skin, the deep, faraway look in her eyes, the low, soft tone of her voice, and the luminous glow around her brows all betrayed a being in close and constant contact with the ineffable and the divine.

As Their Majesties returned to the palace, Buchanan and I left the Kremlin amidst an ovation that accompanied us to our hotel.

I spent the afternoon seeing Moscow, lingering particularly over the places hallowed by memories of 1812. They stood out in sharp relief by contrast with the present moment.

At the Kremlin, the ghost of Napoleon seems to rise up at every step. From the Red Staircase, the Emperor watched the progress of the fire during the baneful night of September 16. It was there that he took counsel of Murat, Eugène, Berthier and Ney in the midst of the leaping flames and under a blinding shower of cinders. It was there that he had that clear and pitiless vision of his impending ruin. "All this," he said repeatedly, "is the herald of great disasters!"

It was by this road that he hastily went down to the Moskowa, accompanied by a few officers and men of his guard. It was there that he entered the winding streets of the burning city.

"We walked," says Ségur, "upon an earth of fire, under a sky of fire, between two walls of fire."

Alas, does not the present war promise us a second edition of this Dantesque scene? And how many chapters will be added to the edition?

North of the Kremlin, and between the Church of St. Basil and the Iberian Gate, lies Red Square, of glorious and tragic memory. If I had to give a list of those spots in which the visions and sentiments of the past have most vividly passed before my eyes, I should include the Roman Campagna, the Acropolis in Athens, the Eyub cemetery in Istambul, the Alhambra in Granada, the Tartar city of Pekin, the Hradschin in Prague, and the Kremlin of Moscow. This curious conglomeration of palaces, towers, churches, monasteries, chapels, barracks, arsenals and bastions, this incoherent jumble of sacred and secular buildings, this complex of functions as fortress, sanctuary, seraglio, harem, necropolis and prison, this blend of advanced civilization and archaic barbarism, this violent contrast of the crudest materialism and the most lofty spirituality, are they not the whole history of Russia, the whole epic of the Russian nation, the whole inward drama of the Russian soul?

Towering above the banks of the Moskowa to the south of Red Square, the Church of St. Basil rears its prodigious and paradoxical architecture, the architecture of dreams. The most conflicting styles, Byzantine, Gothic, Lombard, Persian, and Russian seem to have been incorporated. Yet an imposing harmony emerges from all these slender, aspiring, twisting, many-hued forms, and all this riot of imagination.

It pleases me to think that the Italian Renaissance was introduced into the Kremlin by Sophy Paleologue, niece of the last Emperor of Constantinople, who fled to Rome. In 1472, she married the Tsar of Moscow, Ivan III, known to history as 'Ivan the Great.' It was through her that he henceforth regarded himself as heir to the Byzantine Empire. He took the two-headed eagle as Russia's new arms. She surrounded herself with Italian artists and engineers. In her reign, a gentle breeze of Hellenism and classical culture tempered the rigors of Muscovite barbarism for a time.

Towards evening, I ended my walk on Sparrow Hill, the view from which embraces Moscow and the whole vale of the Moskowa. It used to be called the 'Hill of Salvation' because Russian travelers, when they had their first glimpse of the holy city from this spot, used to stop for a moment to cross themselves and offer up a prayer. Thus, for the Slav Rome, Sparrow Hill awakes the same memories as Monte Mario for the Latin Rome. The same feeling of wondering and pious admiration made the pilgrims of the Middle Ages fall on their knees when they beheld the City of Martyrs from the heights that crown the banks of the Tiber.

At half-past two in the afternoon of September 14, 1812, in brilliant sunshine, the advance guard of the French army ascended Sparrow Hill in open order. They stopped as if smitten dumb with the majesty of the sight. Clapping their hands, they cried out gleefully, "Moscow! Moscow!"

Napoleon came up and in a transport of delight he called out, "So this is the famous city!" But he immediately added, "It was high time!"

Chateaubriand has summed up the scene in a metaphor rich in picturesque romanticism. "Moscow, a European princess on the frontier of her empire, arrayed in all the glories of Asia, seemed to have been brought there to wed Napoleon."

Did any vision of that kind flit through the mind of the Emperor? I doubt it. Thoughts far more serious, uneasy forebodings, already claimed him.

At ten in the evening I left for St. Petersburg.

From the political point of view, today's happenings have left me with two strong impressions.

The first came to me in the Ouspensky Sobor as I watched the Emperor standing before the iconostasis. His person, his entourage, and the whole setting of the ceremony, seemed an eloquent interpretation of the very principle of Tsarism as it was defined in the imperial manifesto of June 16, 1914, ordering the dissolution of the first Duma.

> *As it is God himself who has given Us our supreme power, it is before His altar alone that We are responsible for the destinies of Russia.*

My second impression is the frantic enthusiasm of the Muscovite people for their Tsar. I never thought that the monarchical illusion and imperial fetishism were still so deeply rooted in the heart of the *moujik*. There are very many Russian proverbs that express this unshakeable faith of the poor and lowly in their master. "The Tsar is good; it is his servants who are bad. The Tsar is not guilty of the sufferings of his people; the *tchinovniks* hide the truth from him." But there is also another proverb it is wise to remember because it explains, on the other side of the coin, all the desperation and protest of the popular mind: "It's very high up to God. It's a very long way to the Tsar."

And to set a true value on the ovations that the Tsar received this morning on Red Square, one must not forget that on this same spot, on December 22, 1905, it was found necessary to fire on the crowd that was singing the 'Marseillaise.'

Wednesday, August 19, 1914

I returned to St. Petersburg this morning.

The French troops are making progress in the valleys of the Vosges on the Alsace side. The forts of Liège are still resisting, but the German army is not allowing itself to be held up by these forts and is marching straight on Brussels.

The Russian troops are rapidly concentrating on the frontier of East Prussia.

Thursday, August 20, 1914

Sazonov came for a tête-à-tête luncheon with me today. We discussed in an academic sort of way the objects it will be our business to attain when peace comes, objects we shall only obtain by force of arms. Indeed, we have no doubt that Germany will accept none of our demands until we have put her out of the field. The present war is not the kind of war that ends with a political treaty after a battle of Solferino or Sadowa. It is a war to the death in which each group of belligerents stakes its very existence.

"My formula's a simple one," said Sazonov. "We must destroy German imperialism. We can only do that by a series of military victories, so we have a long and very stubborn war before us. The Emperor has no illusions on that score. But great political changes are essential if *Kaisertum* is not to rise at once from its ashes and the Hohenzollerns are never again to be in a position to aspire to universal dominion. In addition to the restitution of Alsace-Lorraine to France,

Poland must be restored, Belgium enlarged, Hanover reconstituted, Slesvig returned to Denmark, Bohemia freed, and all the German colonies given to France, England and Belgium etc."

"It's a gigantic program, but I agree with you that we ought to do our utmost to realize it if we want our work to be lasting."

Then we worked out the forces of the respective belligerents, their reserves of man-power, and financial, industrial, agricultural etc. resources. We looked into our chances of deriving advantage from the internal dissensions of Austria and Hungary, a subject which inspired me to remark, "There's another factor we must not neglect, public opinion among the German masses. It is very important that we should be well informed as to what is going on there. You ought to organize an intelligence service in the great socialist centers that are nearest to your territory: Berlin, Dresden, Leipzig, Chemnitz, Breslau."

"It's very difficult to organize."

"Yes, but indispensable. Don't forget that after a military defeat it will undoubtedly be the German Socialists who will force the jackboot caste to make peace. If we could only help them."

Sazonov started and in a sharp, dry voice exclaimed, "Not that! No, no! Revolution will never be one of our weapons!"

"You may be quite certain that it's a weapon our enemies will use against you! Germany hasn't waited for a possible defeat of your armies, nor even for the outbreak of war, to establish an intelligence service in your working class circles.

You won't deny that the strikes that broke out in Petersburg during the President of the Republic's visit were instigated by German agents."

"I know that only too well, but I tell you again, revolution will never be one of our weapons, even against Germany."

Our conversation rested there. Sazonov had ceased to be at all expansive. The evocation of the specter of revolution had suddenly frozen him.

To ease his mind, I took him to Krestovsky Island in my car. There we walked about under the splendid trees that stretch to the sparkling, checkered waters of the Neva estuary.

We spoke of the Tsar.

I said to Sazonov, "What a wonderful impression he made on me the other day in Moscow. He was the living embodiment of resolution, persistence and strength."

"He made the same impression on me and it seemed to me a very happy augury, but a much needed augury, for after all ..."

He stopped abruptly as if he dare not pursue his thought.

I pressed him to continue.

He took my arm and said in a tone of affectionate confidence, "Don't forget that the Emperor's salient characteristic is a mystic resignation."

Then he told me the following significant anecdote he had heard from his brother-in-law, Stolypin, ex-President of the Council, who was assassinated on September 18, 1911.

It was in 1909, when Russia was beginning to forget the nightmare of the Japanese War and the troubles that followed it. One day, Stolypin asked the Tsar's approval for a serious piece of domestic legislation. Nicholas II listened to him absent-mindedly and then shrugged his shoulders in a skeptical, indifferent sort of way, as much as to say, 'That or something else, what does it matter?'

At last he remarked in a melancholy tone, "Peter Arkadievitch, I succeed in nothing I undertake. I've no luck at all. And anyhow, the human will is so impotent."

Stolypin, a courageous and resolute character, protested vigorously.

The Tsar then asked him, "Have you ever read 'The Lives of the Saints'?"

"Yes ... some of it at any rate. If I remember rightly, there are quite twenty volumes of it."

"And do you know on what day my birthday falls?"

"How could I forget it? It is May 6."

"What Saint's Day is it?"

"Forgive me, Sire, I'm afraid I've forgotten."

"The Patriarch Job."

"Then God be praised! Your Majesty's reign will end gloriously, for Job, after piously enduring the most cruel tests of his faith, found blessings and rewards showered upon his head."

"No, no, Peter Arkadievitch, believe me! I have a presentiment – more than a presentiment, a secret conviction – that I am destined for terrible trials. But I shall not receive my reward on this earth. How often have I not applied to myself the words of Job, 'Hardly have I entertained a fear than it comes to pass and all the evils I foresee descend upon my head.' "

It is certain that this war is going to compel all the belligerents to put forth their last ounce of moral strength and organizing power. The story Sazonov has just told me brings me to an observation I have often made since I came to live among the Russians, an observation which in a way sums up their national physiognomy.

If the word 'mysticism' is used in its broad sense, the Russian is preeminently a mystic. He is a mystic not merely in his religious life but also in his social, political and emotional life. Behind all the reasoning that dictates his actions, a certain belief is always apparent. He reasons and acts as if he believes that human events are produced by secret, superhuman forces, by occult, arbitrary and autocratic powers. This disposition, more or less avowed and conscious, is directly connected with his imagination which is naturally uncontrolled and dispersive. It is also the product of his atavism, geographical position, climate and history.

Left to himself, he feels no need to enquire how things happen, or what are their practical and necessary determining factors, or by what rational and successive agencies they can be produced or averted. Indifferent to logical certainty, he has no taste for considered and accurate observation or analytical and deductive enquiry. He relies less on his intelligence than on his imagination and emotional faculties. He cares less about understanding than about "sensing" and divination. Usually he acts only on intuition or by routine and natural helplessness.

From the religious point of view, his faith is contemplative, visionary, filled with vague hopes, superstitious fears and Messianic expectations; always in search of direct communication with the invisible and the divine. From the political point of view, the conception of effective cause is utterly foreign to him. Tsarism seems to him a metaphysical entity. He attributes to the Tsar and his ministers intrinsic virtue, self-contained dynamic force and a kind of magic power to govern the empire, redress abuses, effect reforms, establish the reign of justice etc. By what legislative measures, through what administrative machinery can they effectually do so? That is their business, their secret.

In his emotional life also, the Russian constantly feels himself the submissive instrument of strange forces that lead him where they will. By way of apology for his sins and shortcomings, extravagances and surrenders, he usually pleads ill luck, fate, the mysterious influence of the Beyond and frequently even sorcery and the enchantments of the devil.

Such views do not exactly promote personal, responsible effort and manly, sustained action, and that is why the Russian so often surprises us with his indifference, his 'wait and see' attitude and his passive and resigned inaction.

Conversely – and though it is almost impossible to appeal to his soul – he is capable of the most splendid impulses and the most heroic sacrifices. And his whole history proves that he is always true to himself when he feels himself really called upon.

Pope Pius X died last night. Will any conclave ever open in graver circumstances or in the midst of a greater upheaval of human affairs? Will the College of Cardinals find in its ranks a pontiff with sufficient humanity, depth of piety, strength of character and astuteness of intellect to play the capital and unprecedented role which the war offers to the Holy See?

Friday, August 21, 1914

On the Belgian and French fronts, our operations are taking a bad turn. I have received an order to make representations to the Imperial Government to accelerate the projected offensive of the Russian armies as much as possible.

I went to the War Minister and put the French Government's request to him with considerable vigor. He sent for an officer and immediately dictated to him, from my dictation, a telegram to Grand Duke Nicholas.

Then I questioned General Sukhomlinov about the operations in progress on the Russian front. I took note of what he told me in the following terms:

> *(1) Grand Duke Nicholas is determined to advance full-speed on Berlin and Vienna, more especially Berlin, passing between the fortresses of Thorn, Posen and Breslau;*

(2) The Russian armies have taken the offensive along the entire front;

(3) The forces attacking East Prussia have already advanced 20 to 45 kilometers on hostile territory; their line is approximately Soldau-Neidenburg-Lyck-Angerburg-Insterburg;

(4) In Galicia, the Russian troops advancing on Lemberg have reached the Bug and the Sereth;

(5) The forces operating on the left bank of the Vistula will advance straight on Berlin the moment the northwestern armies have succeeded in "fixing" the enemy;

(6) The twenty-eight corps now at grips with Germany and Austria represent approximately 1,120,000 men.

Yesterday the Germans entered Brussels. The Belgian army is withdrawing to Antwerp. Between Metz and the Vosges, the French army has been compelled to retire after suffering heavy losses.

Saturday, August 22, 1914

The Germans are outside Namur. While one of their corps is bombarding the town, their main body is continuing its progress towards the sources of the Sambre and the Oise. The plan of the German offensive through Belgium is now being revealed in all its grandeur.

Sunday, August 23, 1914

Our allies from across the Channel are now beginning to appear on the Belgian front. As a matter of fact, an English cavalry division has already scattered a German column – at Waterloo! Wellington and Blücher ought to have turned in their graves. A great battle is opening between Mons and Charleroi.

The Russians are advancing in East Prussia. They have just occupied Insterburg.

Monday, August 24, 1914

The Ministry wires me from Paris:

> *Information from an unimpeachable source has brought to our knowledge the fact that two active corps which were originally opposed to the Russian army have now been transferred to the French front and replaced on Germany's eastern frontier by landwehr formations. The German General Staff's plan of campaign is too clear for there to be any need for us to insist on the necessity of the Russian armies prosecuting their offensive à outrance in the direction of*

Berlin. Inform the Russian Government at once and insist.

I made immediate representations to Grand Duke Nicholas and General Sukhomlinov and simultaneously informed the Emperor.

This evening I am in a position to assure the French Government that the Russian army is continuing its march on Königsberg and Thorn with all possible energy and speed. An important action is about to open between the Narev and the Vkra.

This very afternoon, Prince Catacuzene, an aide-de-camp of Grand Duke Nicholas, has been brought to the French Hospital in St. Petersburg. He was shot through the chest near Gumbinnen. Doctor Cresson, the Senior Medical Officer, had a few minutes' talk with him. The wounded officer is still quivering with the ardor, the spirit of the offensive, that animates the Russian troops. He has enthusiastically affirmed that Grand Duke Nicholas is bent on forcing his way to Berlin at any cost.

Tuesday, August 25, 1914

The Germans have won at Charleroi. They have also inflicted a serious check upon us near Neufchâteau, south of the Belgian Ardennes. All the French and English armies are retreating on the Oise and the Semoy.

These tidings, though censored, have started a current of vague alarm in St. Petersburg against which I struggle to the best of my ability, availing myself of a subterfuge that Tolstoy attributes to Prince Bagration in 'War and Peace.' It is a subterfuge that ought to find a place in the moral breviary of all Commanders-in-Chief. On the battlefield of Austerlitz, the Prince was receiving one alarming message after another. He received them with the most perfect composure and even an air of approval, as if what he was being told was exactly what he had expected.

In the north of East Prussia, the Russians have cut the crossings of the Alle and the Angerapp. The Germans are withdrawing towards Königsberg.

Japan declared war on Germany the day before yesterday. A Japanese squadron is bombarding Kiaochau.

Wednesday, August 26, 1914

The French and English armies are continuing their retreat. The entrenched camp at Maubeuge is holding. An advance guard of German cavalry is passing through the suburbs of Roubaix.

I have seen to it that these events should be presented by the Russian press in the most suitable (and perhaps truest) light, i.e. as a temporary and methodical retirement, a prelude to a *volte face* in the near future for the purpose of a more formidable and vigorous offensive. All the papers support this theory.

Grand Duke Nicholas has sent me a message through Sazonov:

The withdrawal ordered by General Joffre is in conformity with all the rules of strategy. We must hope that henceforth the French army will expose itself as little as possible, refuse to let itself be broken through or demoralized, and reserve all its offensive capacity and liberty to maneuver until the time when the Russian army is in a position to deal decisive blows.

I asked Sazonov, "Won't that time be soon? Don't forget that our losses are enormous and that the Germans are 250 kilometers from Paris! "

He replied, "I believe that Grand Duke Nicholas has decided to start an important operation to hold down the largest possible number of Germans on our front."

"Somewhere round Soldau and Mlava, no doubt."

"Yes."

In that short answer I thought I detected a certain reticence, so I begged Sazonov to be a little more explicit.

"Think what a serious moment this is for France," I said.

"I know. I'm not forgetting what we owe France. The Tsar and the Grand Duke don't forget it either. You can count on our doing everything in our power to help the French army. But, from the practical point of view, the difficulties are great. General Jilinsky, who is commanding the north-western front, considers that an offensive in East Prussia is doomed to certain defeat because our troops are still too scattered and their concentration is meeting with many obstacles. You know how Masuria is intersected by forests, rivers and lakes. Janushkevitch, Chief of the General Staff, shares Jilinsky's views and is protesting strongly against the offensive. But Danilov, the Quartermaster-General, is insisting, no less forcibly, that we have no right to leave our ally in danger and ought to attack at once, notwithstanding the indubitable risks of the plan. Grand Duke Nicholas has just ordered an immediate attack. I shouldn't be surprised if the operation had already begun."

Thursday, August 27, 1914

The Germans are at Péronne and Longwy.

A Ministry of National Defense has been established in Paris. Viviani remains President of the Council, without portfolio; Briand becomes Minister of Justice; Delcassé, Minister for Foreign Affairs; Millerand, War Minister; Ribot, Finance Minister. Two Unified Socialists, Jules Guesde and Marcel Sembat, enter the Cabinet.

This combination has produced an excellent effect here. It is interpreted as both a striking demonstration of our national solidarity and a guarantee of the inflexible resolution with which France will prosecute the war.

Friday, August 28, 1914

Grand Duke Nicholas has kept his word. On his imperative and repeated orders, General Samsonov's five corps attacked the enemy yesterday in the Mlava-Soldau region. The point of attack has been chosen well to compel the Germans to bring up a large force, for a Russian victory in the direction of Allenstein would have the double result of clearing their path to Allenstein and cutting the line of retreat of the German army which has just been beaten at Gumbinnen.

Saturday, August 29, 1914

The battle at Soldau is still raging furiously. Whatever may be its ultimate result, it is very satisfactory that the action should be drawn out so that the French and English armies may have time to reform and advance once more.

The Russian southern armies are forty kilometers from Lemberg.

Sunday, August 30, 1914

As I entered Sazonov's room this morning I was struck with the gloomy and strained look in his face

"Anything new?" I said.

"Nothing good."

"Aren't things going well in France?"

"The Germans are approaching Paris."

"Yes, but our armies are intact and their moral is excellent. I am confidently awaiting their *volte face*. And what about the Battle of Soldau? "

He was silent, biting his lips, and with gloom written all over his face.

I went on, "A check?"

"A great disaster, but I've no business talking to you about it. Grand Duke Nicholas doesn't want the news known for several days. It will get about only too soon and too fast as our losses have been ghastly."

I asked him for details but he told me he had had no precise information.

"Samsonov's army has been destroyed. That's all I know." After a short silence he continued in a simple, natural tone. "We owed this sacrifice to France as she has shown herself to be a perfect ally."

I thanked him for this thought. Then, in spite of the heavy weight we both had on our minds, we turned to a discussion of current affairs.

In the city, no one as yet knows anything about the Soldau disaster, but the continued retreat of the French army and the rapid march of the Germans on Paris are giving rise to the most pessimistic expectations among the public. The leaders of the Rasputin clique are even announcing that France will soon be compelled to make peace. To the highly-placed individual who came to tell me of this I replied that the character of the statesmen who have just come into power makes such a suggestion utterly unthinkable, and that in any case the game is anything but lost and perhaps the day of victory is nigh at hand.

Monday, August 31, 1914

At Soldau the Russians have lost 110,000 men – 20,000 killed or wounded and 90,000 prisoners. Two of the five corps engaged, the 13th and 16th have been surrounded. All the artillery has been lost.

The judgment of the High Command was only too accurate: the offensive was premature. The initial cause of the disaster was the inadequate concentration of the troops and the extreme difficulty in which the transport found itself in a region intersected by rivers and dotted with lakes and forests. It appears, too, that the disaster was aggravated by a great strategic mistake. It is said that General Artamanov, who was in command of the left wing, fell back twenty versts without informing General Samsonov.

One point where the battle raged most fiercely was the village of Tannenberg, thirty-five kilometers north of Soldau. It was here that in 1410 King Vladislas V of Poland overthrew the Teutonic Knights, the first victory of Slavism over Germanism. The Teutons have waited five hundred and four years for their revenge, but it has been all the more terrible.

Tuesday, September 1, 1914

Sazonov told me this morning that, according to a telegram from Isvolsky, the Government of the French Republic has decided to remove to Bordeaux if the Commander-in-Chief considers that the higher interests of national defense compels him not to bar the German road to Paris.

"It is a grievous but splendid decision," he said to me," and one I should have expected from French patriots."

Then he read out to me the telegrams sent on August 30 and 31 by Colonel Ignatiev, Attaché at French G.H.Q. Every word went to my heart like a knife.

> *The German army, turning the left flank of the French army, is advancing irresistibly on Paris by stages averaging thirty kilometers. In my opinion, the entry of the Germans into Paris is now only a question of days, unless the French have sufficient forces at their disposal to carry out a counter-attack against the turning group without running a risk of being separated from the other armies.*

Fortunately he recognizes that the spirit of the troops remains excellent.

Sazonov asked me, "Is there really no means of defending Paris? I thought that Paris was so well fortified. I cannot hide from you that the capture of Paris would have a deplorable effect here, especially after our Soldau disaster. People are ultimately bound to find out that we have lost 110,000 men at Soldau."

Taking up Colonel Ignatiev's telegrams, I countered his conclusions to the best of my ability by asserting that the entrenched camp of Paris was strongly armed and insisting that General Galliéni's character guaranteed a stubborn resistance.

A decree, signed yesterday evening, declares that the City of St. Petersburg will henceforth be called 'Petrograd.' As a political demonstration and a protest of Slav nationalism against German intrusion, the step is as emphatic as opportune, but from a historical point of view it is a mistake. The present capital of the Empire is not a Slav city; it represents only the recent past of Russian life. It is situated in a Finnish region, at the gates of Finland, where Swedish culture predominated so long, and on the borders of the Baltic provinces where German influence still holds sway. Its architecture is wholly western, its physiognomy quite modern. That is exactly what Peter the Great desired to make of St. Petersburg – a modern, western city. The name 'Petrograd' is thus not merely a mistake but a historic contradiction in terms.

Wednesday, September 2, 1914

The Russian General Staff's communiqué announces the Soldau disaster in the following terms:

> *In the south of East Prussia, the Germans, with much superior forces, have attacked two of our army corps which have sustained considerable losses. General Samsonov has been killed.*

The public is not deceived by this economy of language. Everywhere all sorts of versions of the battle are being hawked round in undertones. The losses are put still higher. General Rennenkampf is accused of treason. It is said that the Germans have spies even among the men around General Sukhomlinov himself. It is also said that General Samsonov has not been killed but killed himself, refusing to survive the destruction of his army.

General Bielaiev, Chief of Staff of the Army at the Ministry of War, assures me that the vigorous offensive of the Russians in East Prussia, and the rapidity of their advance on Lemberg, are compelling the Germans to bring back east the troops that were on their way to France:

"I can assure you," he said, "that the German General Staff never expected to see us in the field straightaway. They thought our mobilization and concentration would be a far slower business. They had calculated that we could not take the offensive anywhere before the 15th or 20th September, and they thought that between now and then they would have time to finish with the French army. So I consider that henceforth the Germans have failed in the execution of their original design."

Thursday, September 3, 1914

From the Oise to the Vosges, the seven German armies, a terrible steel monster, are proceeding with their outflankinging movement at a speed, and with a skill in maneuver, and a concentration of force, such as no other war has ever known. At the present moment, the line of the

French and English armies runs thus from east to west: Belfort-Verdun-Vitry-le François-Sézanne-Meaux-Pontoise.

Fortunately, in Galicia, the Russians have been brilliantly successful. They entered Lemberg yesterday. The retreat of the Austro-Hungarians has assumed the character of a rout.

Since August 27, the Russians, starting from the Kovel-Rovno-Proskurov line, have advanced 200 kilometers. In this operation they have captured 70,000 men and 300 guns. On the Lublin-Kholm front, the Austro-Hungarians are still offering resistance.

Friday, September 4, 1914

The threat hanging over Paris has started a wave of pessimism in Russian society, and the victory of Lemberg is almost forgotten. No one doubts that the Germans will storm the entrenched camp of Paris, and then France will be obliged to capitulate, so it is said. Germany will then bring her whole mass against Russia.

Where do these rumors come from? By whom are they spread?

Only too much light has been thrown on this subject by a conversation I have just had with one of my secret informers, N….. I have my doubts about him, like all men of his trade, but he is well informed about what is said and done in the immediate entourage of the sovereigns. Besides, at the moment he has a special and tangible reason for telling me the truth.

After praising the wonderful patriotism with which France is inspired he continued, "I have come to Your Excellency to be cheered up a little, as I shall not hide from you that I am hearing the most sinister prophecies on all sides."

"Surely they could wait for the result of the battle that is beginning on the Marne! And even if this battle turns out unfavorably for us, the issue will be in no way desperate."

I supported my statement with a number of facts and reasonable prognoses that left me in no doubt, or so I said, of our ultimate victory so long as our *sang froid* and tenacity did not fail us.

"That's true," continued N....., "quite true. It does me good to hear you talk like this. But there's one factor you have not allowed for and which plays a large part in the pessimism I have observed in every quarter, and particularly in high places."

"How do you mean, 'particularly in high places'?"

"Yes, it's among the upper ranks of the court and society that the greatest nervousness is shown, among those who are in daily touch with the sovereigns."

"Why?"

"Well, because it is in that quarter that people have long been convinced that the Emperor is dogged by ill-luck. They know that he fails in everything he undertakes, that fate is always against him, and in short that he is manifestly doomed to misfortune. Besides it's said that the lines of his hand are terrifying."

"Do you mean to say that people let themselves be swayed by that sort of tomfoolery?"

"What do you expect, Monsieur l'Ambassadeur? We are Russians and therefore superstitious. Anyhow, isn't it obvious that the Tsar is predestined to disasters?"

Lowering his voice as if he were telling me some terrible secret, and fixing me with his sharp, yellow eyes in which dull flames glowed from time to time, he gave me a list of the incredible series of accidents, miscalculations, reverses and disasters that has marked the reign of Nicholas II over the last nineteen years.

The series opens with the coronation when two thousand *moujiks* were crushed to death in a stampede in Khodynsky meadows, near Moscow. A few weeks later, the Tsar went to Kiev and saw a steamer with three hundred spectators founder in the Dnieper under his eyes. After a further few weeks he saw his favorite minister, Lobanov, die in his train quite suddenly. Living as he did in constant peril of the bombs of anarchists, his whole soul was longing for a son, a Tsarevitch. Four girls were successively born to him, and when God at last gave him an heir, the child bore the germ of an incurable disease. As he has no taste for either pomp or company, all he desires is to forget the responsibilities of power in the tranquil delights of family life. His wife is an unhappy neurotic who carries an atmosphere of unrest and worry about with her.

But that's not all: The Tsar had dreamed of the ultimate reign of peace on earth, but was dragged by a few schemers at his court into the war in the Far East. His armies were beaten, one after another, in Manchuria. His fleets were sunk, one after another, in the Chinese seas.

Then a fierce tempest of revolution swept across Russia. Risings and massacres followed each other in uninterrupted succession in Warsaw, the Caucasus, Odessa, Kiev, Vologda, Moscow, the Baltic provinces, Kharkov, St. Petersburg and Kronstadt. The murder of Grand Duke Sergius Alexandrovitch opened the era of political assassinations. And just when the hurricane had begun to die down, Stolypin, the President of the Council who was hailed as the savior of Russia, fell one evening under the revolver of a member of the Secret Police right in front of the imperial box in Kiev theater.

Having reached the end of this lugubrious list, N…. concluded, "Your Excellency will admit that the Tsar is doomed to misfortune and that we have a right to quake when we contemplate the prospects before us in this war."

"But it's not by quaking that one controls fate," I protested, "for I'm one of those who believe that fate is obliged to reckon with us. But as you are so sensitive to evil influences, have you failed to observe that today the Tsar has among his adversaries a man who takes second place to no one so far as ill-luck is concerned – Emperor Franz Joseph? There's no risk at all in a bout with him. You simply can't help winning!"

"Yes, but there's Germany too. We're not equal to beating her."

"No, not by yourselves, but you have France and England at your side. So for goodness' sake don't start with the assumption that you're not equal to beating Germany. Fight with all your might, all the heroism you are capable of, and you will see that victory will seem more certain every day."

Cardinal della Chiesa has been elected Pope. He is taking the name of Benedict XV. Since the faraway days of Gregory VII, no role so magnificent and pre-eminent has been offered to the Vicar of Christ.

Saturday, September 5, 1914

Agreement has been reached in London as to the wording of the declaration whereby France, England and Russia engage not to make peace separately. This clause appeared in the Franco-Russian military convention of 1892. The accession of England to our alliance has made this new agreement necessary, and its solemn announcement will probably have a very great effect.

The Russians have occupied Strij, eighty kilometers beyond Lemberg. Their cavalry advance-guard has approached the Carpathian passes. Vienna is in a panic.

Sunday, September 6, 1914

At the moment, the whole interest of the war is focused on the western front. The German First Army, under the command of General von Kluck, which is operating on the extreme right of the outflanking wing, has just turned suddenly southwards, leaving Paris on its right, as if it were trying to outflank our left wing and throw it back over the Seine in the direction of Fontainebleau. Thus the decisive hour has struck. Is the French army going to stand fast at last? In the events now upon us, the stake is nothing less than the future of France, the future of Europe, the future of the world.

Monday, September 7, 1914

In Galicia, the operations of the Russian army are developing splendidly. The Austro-Hungarians have just suffered two severe reverses, one in front of Lublin and the other in the neighborhood of Rava Russka. On the other hand, the Russians are giving way before the German thrust in East Prussia.

In France, the battle continues stubbornly. For the moment, the Germans seem to have given up the idea of a direct attack on Paris.

Tuesday, September 8, 1914

Maubeuge surrendered yesterday after a frightful bombardment lasting eleven days. On the rest of the front, and particularly north-east of Paris, there is violent and uninterrupted fighting. But nothing decisive has happened yet.

General Bielaiev has confided to me that Hindenburg's army, which is operating in East Prussia, has received considerable reinforcements and the Russians are compelled to evacuate the region of the Masurian Lakes.

"From the point of view of sound strategy, our retreat ought to have begun several days ago, but Grand Duke

Nicholas wanted to do everything to take the weight off the French army."

Wednesday, September 9, 1914

East of Paris, from the Ourcq to the environs of Montmirail, the French and English troops are slowly advancing. A general decision cannot be far away now.

Russian public opinion, with a very true instinct, has taken far more interest in the battle of the Marne than in the victories in Galicia. It is plain that the issue of the war is being fought out on the western front. If France goes down, Russia will be compelled to abandon the struggle. The fighting in East Prussia proves that afresh every day. It shows that the Russians are not in the same category as the Germans, who overwhelm them in their superior tactical training, generalship and the wealth of transport facilities at their disposal. On the other hand, the Russians seem to be quite equal to the Austro-Hungarians, and even their superior in the matter of poise and tenacity under fire.

Thursday, September 10, 1914

East of the Vistula, on the frontiers of western Galicia and Poland, the Russians have broken the enemy's line between Krasnik and Tomassov, but in East Prussia General Rennenkampf's army is in confusion.

From France the news is satisfactory. Our troops have crossed the Marne between Meaux and Chateau-Thierry.

Outside Sézanne, the Prussian Guard has been thrown back north of the marshes of St. Gond. If our right wing, the 'hinge' between Bar-le-Duc and Verdun, holds firm, the whole German line will be dislocated.

Friday, September 11, 1914

Victory! We have won the Battle of the Marne! Along the whole front the German armies are retreating northwards. Paris is now out of reach. France is saved! The Russians, too, have won a great victory between Krasnik and Tomassov. The Austro-Hungarian forces, supported by German reinforcements, amounted to more than a million men. Their artillery comprised more than 2,500 guns. On the other side of the coin, General Rennenkampf's army has had to evacuate East Prussia. The Germans are in occupation of Suvalki.

Chapter 5

Saturday, September 12, 1914

The Marne victory is hailed as a deliverance in all Russian social circles. Congratulations are pouring in to the Embassy. But the recent disaster at Soldau, and disquieting rumors over the last two days as to the course of the great battle in progress in East Prussia are casting a general gloom over men's minds and rendering them almost indifferent to the brilliant successes in Galicia. And even if the public pays a generous tribute to the heroism of the French army and General Joffre's skill in maneuver, it does not fail to add that if it were not for the terrible massacre of Soldau, the Germans would now be in Paris.

Rasputin has recovered from his wound and has returned to Petrograd. It has been easy for him to prove that his recovery is striking proof of divine protection.

When he speaks of the war, it is only in veiled, ambiguous, and apocalyptic terms, and the conclusion is drawn that he does not approve of it and anticipates great misfortunes.

Someone else has just come back to Petrograd on whose return I have equally little cause to congratulate myself, as he has done nothing but give vent to lugubrious prophecies since his arrival. I mean Count Witte, who was in Biarritz when war broke out. He called on me the day before yesterday.

My personal acquaintance with him is confined to a single meeting in Paris in the autumn of 1905. He was returning from America after signing the Peace of Portsmouth, and he spoke very bitterly of France, which he accused of giving insufficient support to her ally, Russia, against Japan. At the time I was much struck by his acute mind, broad views, and the somewhat contemptuous authority of his language and of his whole personality.

Let me give a few biographical details. Sergius Yulievitch Witte was born on June 29, 1849, in the Caucasus, where his father was Rector of the university department. His mother, a Fadeiev, belonged to an old Russian family. He took the mathematics course at Odessa University, but lack of means soon compelled him to break off his studies. He then obtained a post in the South-Western railways. He was still only a stationmaster at Popielna, a little hamlet near Kiev, when Vishnegradsky, the President of the Company, 'discovered' him and promoted him at one step to the post of Manager.

In 1889, Vishnegradsky was made Finance Minister, and he immediately sent for Witte to come to St. Petersburg and made him his right-hand man. Their close cooperation promptly raised Russian credit to a level it had never reached before.

In 1892, however, Vishnegradsky had to retire, worn out by work. Witte succeeded him. His strength of character, experience, and talents soon secured him an outstanding place among the political leaders of the Empire. He became President of the Committee of Ministers at the end of 1903, but he did not succeed in foiling the insane combination of intrigue and speculation that led to the outbreak of the Manchurian War on February 8, 1904. After the disasters of Mukden and Tsushima it was universally recognized that he alone was of a stature to conduct the peace negotiations, and on September 5, 1905, he had the melancholy honor of signing the Treaty of Portsmouth.

As a reward for his services, Nicholas II gave him the title of Count, but at the bottom of his heart he hated this proud and ironic nature, and cold, penetrating and acid intellect, in contact with which he always felt himself gauche and disarmed.

Revolutionary troubles rapidly grew worse, however, and the dynasty was threatened.

Hitherto, Witte had always been a sincere advocate of autocracy. In his view, the Western states had no particular reason to boast of their constitutional dogmas, and Tsarism, though part of its machinery could perhaps do with renovation, was perfectly adapted to the instincts, manners, and powers of the Russian people. But, faced with this urgent peril, he did not hesitate.

On October 30, after interminable discussions with the terrified Tsar, he induced him to sign the famous Manifesto which seemed destined to be Russia's Magna Charta and, conceding the principle of various fundamental liberties, established an immediate imperial Duma. A week later he was appointed President of the Council of Ministers.

During the following months the situation did anything but improve. Emboldened by their first success, the parties of the Left put forward new claims and the arrogance and audacity of the revolutionaries greatly increased. Simultaneously, in a violent reaction to these events, the handiwork of the 'Black Bands' mobilized the rural masses in the cause of orthodox absolutism, and massacres of liberals, intelligentsia and Jews occurred in every part of the Empire.

Witte soon realized that he could never come to terms either with the Duma, because it was pursuing a program of sedition, or with the Conservatives, because they would never forgive him for the Manifesto of October 30. Therefore, preferring to keep himself for the future, he offered his resignation to the Tsar who was only too glad to see him go. But before surrendering his portfolio, he gave himself the pleasure of a last success in the service of which he is a past master, in finance.

On April 16, 1906, he negotiated in Paris a loan of two thousand million francs on terms very favorable to the Russian Treasury. On May 5, Nicholas II finally accepted his resignation and appointed as his successor Ivan Loguinovitch Goremykin, the present President of the Council.

Count Witte arrived here from Biarritz a week ago, and, as I have said, called on me the day before yesterday. As an excuse for his visit, he reminded me of our meeting in Paris in the autumn of 1905, and at once, without any preliminaries, opened a discussion, head erect, eyes fixed on me, and his speech firm, precise, and slow.

"This war's madness," he said. "It has been forced on the Tsar's by stupid and short-sighted politicians. It can only have disastrous results for Russia. France and England alone can hope to derive any benefit from victory. And anyhow, a victory for us seems to me highly questionable."

"Of course the benefits to be derived from this war, as from any other war," I replied, "depend upon victory. But I presume that if we are victorious, Russia will get her share, and a large share, of the advantages and rewards. After all, forgive me for reminding you that if the world is now on fire, it is in a cause that first and foremost was in Russia's interest, a cause that is eminently the Slav cause and did not affect either France or England."

"No doubt you're referring to our standing in the Balkans, our pious duty to protect our blood brothers, our historic and sacred mission in the East? Why, that's a romantic, old-fashioned chimera. No one here, no thinking man at least, now cares a fig for these turbulent and vain Balkan folk who have nothing Slav about them and are only Turks christened by the wrong name. We ought to have let the Serbs suffer the punishment they deserved. What did they care about their Slav brotherhood when their King Milan made Serbia an Austrian fief? So much for the origin of this war ... Now let's talk about the profits and rewards it will bring us. What can we hope to gain – an increase in territory? Great Heavens! Isn't His Majesty's empire big enough already? Haven't we, in Siberia, in Turkistan, in the Caucasus, and in Russia itself, enormous areas that have not yet been opened up? What are these conquests they are dangling before our eyes? East Prussia? Hasn't the Emperor too many Germans among his subjects already? Galicia? It's full of Jews! Besides, the moment we annex Austria and Prussia's Polish territories, we shall lose the whole of Russian Poland. Don't you make any mistake: when Poland has recovered her territorial integrity, she won't be content with the autonomy she's been so stupidly promised. She'll claim, and get, her absolute independence. What else have we to hope for? Constantinople, the Cross on Santa Sophia, the Bosphorus, the Dardanelles? It's too mad a notion to be worth a moment's consideration! And even if we assume a complete victory for our coalition, with the Hohenzollerns and Hapsburgs reduced to begging for peace and submitting to our terms, it means not only the end of German domination but the proclamation of republics throughout Central Europe. That means the simultaneous end of Tsarism. I prefer to remain silent as to what we may expect if we are defeated."

"What practical conclusions do you come to?"

"My practical conclusion is that we must extract ourselves from this stupid adventure as soon as possible."

"You'll appreciate that I can't follow you in your criticisms of your Government for its support of Serbia. But you argue as if it was responsible for the war. It was not your Government that wanted the war, nor indeed the French or British Governments. I can guarantee that the three governments did all that was honorably possible to save peace. In any case, our business at the moment is not to ascertain whether the war could or could not have been avoided, but to win victory. Why, the conclusions to which you yourself come on the assumption of our defeat are so terrifying that you daren't mention them. As for promptly extracting yourselves from this stupid adventure, it's an idea that astonishes me in a statesman of your intelligence. Can't you see that the gigantic struggle in which we are involved is a duel to the death, and that a compromise peace would mean the triumph of Germany?"

Looking incredulous, he replied, "So we've got to go on fighting?"

"Yes, until victory."

He half-shrugged his shoulders. Then, after a moment's hesitation, he resumed. "I'm afraid you credit certain idle rumors and believe me inspired by ill-feeling towards France. That's how you account for everything you don't like in what I have said."

"If I had credited you with ill-feeling towards France, particularly at the present moment, I shouldn't have received you, Monsieur le Comte. At any rate, I should have broken off our conversation long ago. All I know is that you are hostile to the policy of the Triple Entente."

"Yes, but I've always been an advocate of the French alliance."

"On condition that it was completed by an alliance with Germany."

"I admit it."

"What about Alsace-Lorraine? How would you deal with that in your inclusion of Germany?"

"The difficulty did not seem to me insurmountable. In any case, I should never have sacrificed the French alliance to the German alliance. I have given convincing proof of that."

"Are you referring to what happened at Bjorkö between Emperor Nicholas and Emperor Wilhelm in July 1905?"

"Yes, but it's a subject on which I'm bound to silence. Do you mind my asking what you know about it?"

"Our information about the incident is very imperfect, and in the interests of the alliance itself we have not tried to clear up the semi-confidences my predecessor, Monsieur Bompard, received from you. If I had to sum up the various pieces of information, I should say that at the Bjorkö meeting Emperor Wilhelm proposed to the Tsar an agreement incompatible with the French alliance and that, owing to your personal intervention, the scheme came to nothing."

"That's quite accurate."

"Forgive me for asking you a question in return. Did the agreement proposed by Emperor Wilhelm bind France to make common cause with Germany in future?"

"I'm sworn to secrecy on this matter. All I can tell you is that Emperor Wilhelm has never forgiven me for having brought his scheme to nought. And yet they accuse me of being a Germanophile! As a matter of fact, Emperor Nicholas hates me far more, not only because I frustrated the German intrigue, but, and this is my worst offence, because shortly afterwards I submitted for his signature the famous Manifesto of October 30, 1905, which gave legislative power to the Duma. Since then, the Emperor has regarded me as his enemy and goes about telling his intimates that I dream of succeeding him as President of the Russian Republic. How absurd! What a pity! From the Emperor's feelings towards me you can imagine what the Empress thinks. But enough of all these trifles ... I'm afraid I've kept you too long, Monsieur l'Ambassadeur, and perhaps forced too many of my opinions on you. Only please remember that in one important affair I proved myself a true friend to France."

"I shall never forget it, and I'm grateful for your confidences."

He rose from his chair, and, straightening himself awkwardly after the manner of tall men, he took his leave in the most friendly terms.

When he had gone, I went for a walk on the Islands. As I strolled in the solitary avenue which is my favorite haunt, I turned this long conversation over in my mind. I could still see the tall figure of the old statesman, an enigmatic, unnerving individual, a great intellect, despotic, disdainful, conscious of his powers, a prey to ambition, jealousy, and pride. I feel that if the war goes badly for us, his strength of character will bring him to the fore again. But I also think how evil an influence the spread of his ideas on the war may have in a country in which public opinion is so emotional and unstable, and how dangerous it is to tell a Russian that Russia must extricate itself from this stupid adventure as soon as possible."

Sunday, September 13, 1914

In France, the Germans are still retreating, abandoning prisoners, wounded and unwounded, guns and transport. The left wing of the French army has crossed the Aisne, the center is making progress between the Argonne and the Meuse, and the right wing is forcing the enemy back in the direction of Metz.

In the east of East Prussia, General Rennenkampf's army looks as if it ought to escape the catastrophe with which it was threatened. It has practically succeeded in forcing a passage through the Masurian Lakes and is falling back on Kovno and Grodno.

In Galicia, the Russians have crossed the lower San, and in the Bukovina they have occupied Czernowitz.

Today is the birthday of Saint Alexander Nevsky, the Tsar of Novgorod, who defeated the Swedes and the Teutonic Knights on the banks of the Neva in 1241. On the spot where the national hero won his victory, Peter the Great built a monastery as vast and sumptuous as the famous Lauras at Kiev and Serghievo.

Surrounded by walls and moats like a monastic citadel, the Laura of Petrograd comprises a cathedral, eleven churches, numerous chapels, the Metropolitan's residence, the monks' cells, a seminary, an ecclesiastical academy and three cemeteries. I often take my walks there to enjoy the charm of peace and silence it gives, the atmosphere of religious resignation, and the sweet humanity it breathes.

Today, a huge crowd filled the courts and sanctuaries. In the Cathedral of the Trinity, engulfed in one great cloud of incense, the pious were swarming round the shrine of Saint Alexander. The throng was quite as great in the Church of the Annunciation around the bronze slab on which this modest and eloquent epitaph may be read: *Here lies Suvorov.* Women were in a large majority. They were praying for their husbands, brothers, and sons fighting away at the front.

Several groups of peasants, men and women, made a touching picture with their grave and rapt gaze.

I was particularly struck by one *moujik*, an old man with snow-white hair and beard, swarthy complexion, broad and deeply wrinkled forehead, melancholy, luminous and distant eyes – a typical patriarch. Standing before an icon of Saint Alexander, he was turning his cap in his bony fingers. Nor did he stop for a moment except to cross himself fervently while bowing low. He muttered an interminable prayer, a prayer very different no doubt from those that are being offered up at the present time in the churches of France, for the way of prayer varies with different races. When a Russian soul beseeches God's help, what it expects is not so much the strength to will and act as the strength to suffer and endure. This old man's face and pose were so expressive that he seemed to me to personify the patriotism of the Russian peasant.

In the evening I went to the Marie Theater for a performance of Glinka's 'Life for the Tsar.' The Director of the imperial Theaters had invited my English and Japanese colleagues, the Belgian and Serbian Ministers, and myself, to be present this evening as a demonstration in honor of the Allies had been prepared.

Before the curtain rose, the orchestra played the Russian national anthem, the 'Boje Tsaria Kranie,' which Prince Lvov composed about 1825, a hymn with a broad sweep that produces a noble, religious effect. How many times had I heard it before? But I had never realized so forcibly how foreign the melody of the national anthem is to Russian music and how German it is in the direct tradition of Bach and Handel. But that did not prevent the public from listening to it in a patriotic silence which ended in an outburst of prolonged cheering.

Next came the 'Marseillaise,' received with transports of delight. Then 'Rule Britannia,' which was likewise hailed with loud cheers.

Buchanan was in the box next to mine and I asked him why the orchestra played 'Rule Britannia' and not' God Save the King.' He replied that, as the latter was the same as the Prussian national anthem, the authorities feared a mistake which would have shocked the public.

Next came the Japanese national anthem, which was suitably welcomed. I calculated that it was only nine years since Mukden and Tsushima!

At the opening notes of the 'Brabançonne,' a storm of grateful and admiring cheers burst. Everyone seemed to be saying, 'Where should we be now if Belgium had not resisted?'

The ovation to the Serbian national anthem was more restrained – in fact, very restrained. Many people seemed to be reflecting, 'If it had not been for the Serbs, we should still be at peace!'

Then we had to sit through 'The Life for the Tsar,' a stale and turgid work, with its too obvious calls to loyalty and its too old-fashioned borrowings from Italian opera, although the public enjoyed it all the same because Glinka's drama reaches the very fibers of the Russian conscience.

Monday, September 14, 1914

In France, the Germans are slowly retiring northwards and seem to have prepared strong positions on the Aisne. If they manage to hold us up in these lines, the victory of the Marne will not have been as decisive as we could have hoped it would be. It is only by the results of the aftermath that the importance of a victory can be measured.

Anyhow, I was not surprised by a telegram I receive this morning in which Delcassé instructs me to impress on the Russian Government that it is essential for the Russian armies to press home their offensive directly against Germany. The fact is that Bordeaux is afraid that our Allies may have had their heads turned by their relatively easy successes in Galicia and may neglect the German front in order to concentrate on forcing their way to Vienna.

This very morning I went to the War Office and told General Sukhomlinov of the French Government's concern.

He replied, "But our direct offensive against Germany began on August 16, and we're continuing it vigorously and on the largest possible scale. You know as much as I do about our operations in East Prussia. What more can we do, I ask you."

"How soon will the Niemen and Narev armies be able to resume their advance?"

"Oh, not for a long time yet. They've suffered too many casualties. I'm afraid they may even have to retreat a little further yet. But I don't mind telling you, in strict secrecy, that

Grand Duke Nicholas is preparing an operation on a wide front in the direction of Posen and Breslau."

"Excellent!"

"I mustn't hide from you that it will take a long time to organize this operation. We can't take any more risks. Don't forget, Monsieur l'Ambassadeur, that we've already sacrificed 110,000 men at Soldau to help the French army."

"We should have made the same sacrifice to help the Russian army, but without diminishing the practical importance and moral effect of the service you rendered us then, forgive me for remarking that it was not our fault if General Artamanov retreated 20 versts on the left wing without notifying his Army Commander."

We returned to the matter that was the reason for my visit. I reiterated my desire to obtain an assurance that the Russian armies would not allow themselves to be deflected towards Vienna and neglect their principal objective – Germany.

"I am not forgetting," I said, "that the final decision as regards operations is the province of the Commander-in-Chief, but I know also that Grand Duke Nicholas always attaches great importance to your views and suggestions. So I'm relying on you to back up my request to the Grand Duke."

He fixed his eyes on me, eyes that were sharp and cunning under their heavy lids.

"But we can't stop our advance in Galicia where we are gaining brilliant successes every day. Remember that since the campaign started, the Austrians have already lost

200,000 men killed or wounded, in addition to 60,000 prisoners and 600 guns."

"Your Excellency too must remember that the Germans are only 70 kilometers from Paris. What would you say if they were 70 versts from Petrograd, halfway between Luga and Gatchina? Besides, I'm not asking you to suspend your operations in Galicia, but merely not to get too involved there and forget that our main objective is the destruction of the German armies."

A smile, a hypocritically pleasant smile, spread over his face.

"We're both absolutely agreed on that, Monsieur l'Ambassadeur. I'm quite sure we shall always understand one another."

"So I can rely on you to telegraph Grand Duke Nicholas?"

"I'll do more than that. I'll send him one of my officers this very evening."

Before withdrawing, I asked the Minister about the result of the recent fighting in East Prussia. He replied that it had been extremely severe at Tilsit, Gumbinnen and Lyck, but that the Russian army had succeeded in making its way out of the Mazurian Lakes region and at the moment was falling back on Kovno.

"So all East Prussia has been lost?"

"Yes."

"What are your losses?"

"I don't exactly know."

"A hundred thousand men?"

"Perhaps."

Tuesday, September 15, 1914

As I distrust General Sukhomlinov and all the doubtful intrigues in which he is an agent, I again took up the question of the direct offensive against Germany with Sazonov this morning and asked him to put our representations before the Emperor on my behalf.

"For greater accuracy," he said, "draft the answer yourself that you want His Majesty to give."

I then drafted the following:

> *As soon as the Austro-Hungarian armies in Galicia have been put out of action, the direct offensive of the Russian armies against Germany will be pressed with the greatest energy.*

"That's all right," Sazonov said. "I'll write to His Majesty at once."

At eleven this evening, the Tsar had me informed that he accepted my draft and had wired Grand Duke Nicholas accordingly.

Wednesday, September 16, 1914

The Battle of the Marne is being continued on the Aisne, with the difference that the Germans have dug themselves in on strong defensive positions, so that the struggle is assuming the character of siege warfare.

The Russians are on the heels of the Austrians between Sandomir and Jaroslav.

Since mobilization, the Government has prohibited the sale of spirits – vodka – in the whole territory of the Empire. This great reform was introduced by the order of February 13, 1914, and the whole credit for it is the Emperor's. It is being carried out so methodically and strictly as to leave one astonished at the effectiveness of Russian bureaucracy. The effects of the reform are seen in a decrease in crimes of violence and an appreciable increase in the output of labor.

Thursday, September 17, 1914

Grand Duke Nicholas has just issued a proclamation to the nations of Austria-Hungary, inviting them to throw off the Hapsburg yoke and realize their national aspirations at last.

Simultaneously, Sazonov is pressing the Rumanian Government to occupy Transylvania and join in the occupation of the Bukovina by the Russian troops.

Saturday, September 19, 1914

The bombardment of Rheims and the destruction of the cathedral are affecting Petrograd very deeply. No event of the war has made such a striking impression on the Russian imagination, an imagination that is excessively emotional, hungering after melodrama, indifferent, and all but blind to reality, except when it appears in the form of picturesque and theatrical events, or moving and dramatic scenes.

Sunday, September 20, 1914

The Emperor is on a tour of inspection the armies at the front.

As a rule, the meetings of the Empress and Rasputin take place in Madame Vyrubova's little house on the Sredniaya, but yesterday the *staretz* was received at the palace itself and his visit lasted nearly two hours.

Tuesday, September 22, 1914

This morning I was called on by a Frenchman, Robert Gauthiot, Professor at the École des Hautes-Études in Paris. He has come straight from Pamir where he was engaged on an ethnological and linguistic expedition.

In the second week of August he was in the neighborhood of Chorog, a valley 4,000 meters high on the slopes of the Hindu Kush. He had continued on for twelve days beyond the last Russian post guarding the frontier of Ferghana, the ancient Sogdiana. On August 16, a native, who had gone to get him supplies from this post, told him that Germany had declared war on Russia and France. He started back immediately and has reached Petrograd in one stage, via Marghelan, Samarkand, Tiflis, and Moscow.

I told him the extraordinary series of events that has marked the last two months. He told me how very impatient he was to get back to France and rejoin his territorial regiment. Then we explored the future. We calculated what a colossal effort will be required of us to destroy the power of Germany, and so on. I am particularly interested in his views because he has paid frequent and long visits to Germany.

Among the most noteworthy of his remarks were these. "I have spent a good deal of time among the German Socialists. I know their doctrines well and their habits of mind even better. You may be quite certain, Monsieur l'Ambassadeur, that they will do all they can to help in the war and fight as hard as the most inveterate *junker*. Why, I'm a Socialist myself. I'm actually anti-militarist, but you can see it doesn't prevent me from going to defend my country."

I congratulated him on his eagerness to perform his military duty and have asked him to lunch with me tomorrow.

When he had gone, I reflected that I had had before me eloquent proof of the patriotism with which the French intellectuals are inspired, notwithstanding all appearances to the contrary. Here is one of them who hears of the war when he is in the depths of the Pamir, 4,000 meters up on the Roof of the World. He is alone, left to his own resources, away from the contagious fever of the sublime national impulse that is sweeping over France, yet he does not hesitate a moment. All his socialist and pacifist theories, the interest of his scientific expedition, and his own personal interests vanish before the vision of the Motherland being in danger. He rushes to the rescue.

Count Kokovtsov, ex-President of the Council, whose clear-eyed patriotism and high intelligence I so much admire, has been to see me at the Embassy. He has just returned from an estate of his near Novgorod.

"You know," he said, "that temperamentally I'm not prone to optimism, but all the same I think the war is going well for us. As a matter of fact, I never thought our war with Germany could have any other beginning. We've suffered some reverses, but our armies are intact and our moral is excellent. In a few months from now, we shall be strong enough to crush our terrible opponent."

Then he talked about the terms of peace we shall have to impose on Germany, and expressed himself with a violence that astonished me in a man who usually weighs his words so carefully.

"When the hour of peace strikes, we must be ruthless, ruthless! Public opinion will drive us to ruthlessness anyhow. You've no idea how furious the *moujiks* are with Germany."

"That's really most interesting. You noticed it yourself?"

"Only the day before yesterday, I was leaving that morning and taking a walk in my grounds when I saw a very old peasant who lost his only son a long time ago and has his two grandsons in the army. On his own initiative, and without my asking him, he told me how much he feared that the war would not be fought out to the bitter end, the hateful German brood destroyed and the evil weed of the Niemetz rooted out of the soil of Russia. I congratulated him on his patriotism in accepting the risks to which the two grandsons, his sole means of support, were exposed. He replied, 'Look, barin. If we're unlucky enough not to destroy the Niemetz, they'll come here, they'll reign over the whole of Russia, and then they'll harness you and me – yes, you as well – to their ploughs.' That's what our peasants are thinking."

"Their reasoning is very sound, at any rate in a symbolic sense."

Thursday, September 24, 1914

I have had a talk with the Minister for Agriculture, Krivoshein, whose personal authority, lucid intellect and political talents seem to have won him a high degree of confidence and favor with Nicholas II.

Yesterday he had a long conference with the Emperor whom he found in excellent spirits. During the conversation His Majesty casually remarked, "I shall fight this war to the bitter end. To wear down Germany I shall exhaust all my resources. I'll retreat to the Volga, if necessary." The Tsar also said, "In starting this war, Emperor Wilhelm has dealt a terrible blow to the principle of monarchy."

Saturday, September 26, 1914

In accordance with the promise I received from the Emperor on September 15, the Russian army is about to resume the offensive in the direction of Berlin, via Breslau. All the preparations are complete and a cavalry corps, consisting of

120 squadrons, has already been sent forward with infantry support.

On this subject, General de Laguiche writes to me as follows from Baranovici. "I have received a formal promise that they will not allow themselves to be deflected towards Vienna. I can assure you that there is no dissentient voice on this subject, not one that asks for anything other than an advance on Berlin. The Austrian is not the enemy now. We are attacking Germany with our whole soul invested in our task and a burning desire to close with her at the first possible moment. I am touched to see how anxious the military leaders are about French intentions and aspirations. Everything is being done with the single purpose of coming up to the expectations of our Ally. This has struck me very forcibly."

Sunday, September 27, 1914

I have lunched at Tsarskoe Selo with Countess B....., whose sister is very friendly with Rasputin. I asked her about the *staretz*.

"Has he seen much of the Emperor and Empress since his return?"

"Not much. I've an idea that Their Majesties are keeping him at a distance to a certain extent at the moment. For example, yesterday he was at my sister's house, quite near here. He telephoned, in our presence, to the palace to ask Madame Vyrubova if he could see the Empress in the evening. She replied he had better wait a few days. He seemed very annoyed at this answer and left us at once, without even saying goodbye. Until recently, he wouldn't even have asked if he could go to the palace. He'd have gone straight there."

"How can you account for this sudden decline in his fortunes?"

2Simply the fact that the Empress has been torn from her old fits of melancholia. From morning to night she's busy with her hospitals, sewing committees and hospital train. She has never looked so well."

"Is it true that Rasputin has told the Emperor that this war will be disastrous to Russia and must be stopped at once?"

"I doubt it. Last June, just before Khinia Gusseva's attempt on his life, Rasputin was frequently telling the Emperor to beware of France and make friends with Germany. Of course, he was only repeating the words old Prince Mestchersky had had such difficulty in teaching him. But since his return from Pokrovskoe, he has been talking very differently. Only the day before yesterday he said to me, 'I'm very pleased this war has come. It has delivered us from two great evils: drink and German friendship. Woe to the Tsar if he stops the conflict before Germany has been crushed!' "

"Good, but does he talk in the same way to the sovereigns? Only a fortnight ago I had a very different report about what he was saying."

"He may have said something different. Rasputin is not a politician with a system or program from which he draws his inspiration no matter what. He's a *moujik*, illiterate, impulsive, visionary, capricious and a bundle of contradictions. But as he's very cunning and feels that his position at the palace is shaken, I should be surprised if he spoke openly against the war."

"Are you under his spell?"

"I? Not in the least! Physically I find him disgusting. He has dirty hands, black nails and an unkempt beard. It is horrific, but I'll admit he amuses me all the same. He has extraordinary verve and imagination. At times he is actually eloquent. He has a gift for metaphor and a deep sense of mystery."

"Is he really so eloquent?"

"Yes. I assure you that some days he has a very original and arresting way of speaking. He is familiar, mocking, violent, merry, ridiculous and poetic by turns. And with all this, not a trace of affectation. On the contrary, he has the most extraordinary effrontery and the most staggering cynicism."

"You describe him to the life."

"Tell me honestly. Wouldn't you like to know him?"

"No, indeed! He's too compromising. But please keep me *au fait* with all he is sayings and doings, as I'm uneasy about him."

Monday, September 28, 1914

I told Sazonov what Countess B..... told me yesterday about Rasputin and he went purple in the face at once.

"For Heaven's sake, don't mention that man's name to me! I loathe him. He's not merely an adventurer and a charlatan: he's the incarnation of the Devil himself. He's the Antichrist!"

So many legends have already gathered around the *staretz* that it seems to me useful to give some authentic facts.

Grigory Rasputin was born in 1871 at Pokrovskoe, a wretched hamlet on the borders of Western Siberia, between Tiumen and Tobolsk. His father was a simple *moujik*, a drunken, thieving horse-dealer. His name was Eflin Novy. The nickname of Rasputin, which young Grigory soon received from his comrades, is eloquent of this period of his life and prophetic of the future. It is a term of peasant slang, derived from the word *'rasputnik,'* which means "debauchee," "rake," and "womanizer."

Grigory was often thrashed by enraged fathers, and even publicly whipped by order of the *ispravnik*, but one day he found his road to Damascus. The exhortations of a priest whom he was driving to Verkhoturie monastery suddenly awakened his mystic instincts. But his robust temperament, strong passions and unbridled imagination immediately drove him into the licentious sect known as the *Khlisty*, or 'Flagellants.'

Among the innumerable sects that are more or less detached from the established Church — and reveal so strangely the lack of moral discipline among the Russian people, their hunger for mystery and their taste for the indefinite, the extreme and the absolute — the *Khlisty* are distinguished by the gross excesses and sensuality that mark their practices. They inhabit principally the regions of Kazan,

Simbirsk, Saratov, Ufa, Orenburg and Tobolsk. Their number is put at about 120,000.

The most lofty spirituality seems to inspire their doctrine, as they aim at nothing less than communicating directly with God, steeping themselves in the Word and incarnating Christ. But to attain this celestial communion, they resort to all the indulgences of the flesh. The faithful, men and women assemble at night, sometimes in an *isba*, sometimes in a forest clearing, and there, calling upon God, singing hymns and yelling chants, they dance in a ring, faster and faster. Soon they are overcome with giddiness and fall down in ecstasy or convulsions. The leader of the dance whips those whose energies flag. Then, filled and intoxicated with the 'divine influx,' they couple like brute beasts. The service ends with monstrous scenes of sensuality, lust and incest.

Rasputin's richly-endowed temperament marked him out as ripe for the 'divine influx.' His exploits during the nocturnal activities soon won him popularity. His gifts for mysticism developed simultaneously. Traveling through the villages, he delivered evangelical addresses and told parables. Gradually he ventured into prophecy, exorcism and incantations. He even boasted of having performed miracles. For a hundred versts around Tobolsk no one doubted that he was a holy man. Yet, even in this period, he had some tiresome brushes with justice over too glaring misdemeanors, and would have come out of them rather badly if the ecclesiastical authorities had not already taken him under their wing.

In 1904, his reputation for piety and the scent of his virtues reached Petersburg. The famous visionary Father

John of Kronstadt, who had consoled and sanctified the dying moments of Alexander III, desired to know the young Siberian prophet. He received him at the Monastery of Saint Alexander Nevsky and congratulated himself on observing, from clear signs, that he was marked out by God. After this appearance in the capital, Rasputin returned to Pokrovskoe, but from that day on the horizon of his life was extended.

He entered into relations with a whole gang of more or less illuminist, charlatan and dissolute priests, hundreds of whom may be met with among the dregs of the Russian clergy. It was then that he took as his acolyte a vulgar, blustering, erotic and 'miracle-working' monk, worshipped by the mob, but a fierce enemy of liberals and Jews. He was Father Heliodorus, who was later to raise the standard of revolt in his monastery at Tsarytsin and keep the Holy Synod in check through the violence of his reactionary fanaticism.

Before long, Grigory was not satisfied with the company of *moujiks* and priests. He was seen gravely walking with archpriests and abbots, bishops and archimandrites, who all agreed with John of Kronstadt in seeing in him a spark of God.

Yet he had to withstand the continuous assaults of the Devil, and often enough he yielded. At Tsarytsin, he deflowered a nun whom he had undertaken to exorcise. At Kazan, he was drunk one fine June evening and came out of a drinking den driving before him a naked prostitute whom he thrashed with his belt, a proceeding that caused a great scandal in the town. At Tobolsk, he seduced Madame L……, the wife of an engineer and a woman of a great piety, and he drove her to such a pitch that she went everywhere proclaiming her passion for him and glorying in her shame. It was she who initiated him into the refined joys of women of society.

Through such exploits, that accumulated as time went on, his reputation for holiness increased from day to day. People knelt in the streets as he passed. They kissed his hands, touched the hem of his robe, called out, "Our Christ, our Savior, pray for us, poor sinners! God will hear thee ...' and he would reply, "In the name of the Father, the Son and the Holy Spirit, I bless you, little brothers. Trust and obey. Christ will soon return. Be patient and remember his death. Mortify your flesh for the love of Him."

In 1905, the Archimandrite Theophanes, Rector of the Theological College at Petersburg, a prelate of the greatest piety and the Empress's confessor, was unhappily inspired to summon Rasputin to see for himself the marvelous effects of grace upon this simple soul that the powers of evil tormented so pitilessly. Then, touched by his frank fervor, he took him under his wing and introduced him into his own particular circle, a very considerable one. At its head was a very influential group comprising: Grand Duke Nicholas Nicolaievitch, then Commander of the Imperial Guard and now Commander-in-Chief of the Russian armies; his brother Grand Duke Peter; their wives; Grand Duchesses Anastasia and Militza, daughters of the King of Montenegro. Grigory had only to make his appearance to amaze and fascinate this idle and credulous company that was given to the most absurd practices of spiritualism, occultism, and necromancy.

Soon among all the mystic coteries, there was quite a scramble for the Siberian prophet, the *Bojy tchelloviek,* the 'Man of God,' and the Montenegrin Grand Duchesses distinguished themselves by their excessive devotion to him. As early as 1900, they had brought the magician, Philip of Lyons, to the Russian Court, and itt was they who presented Rasputin to the Tsar and Tsaritsa in the summer of 1907.

Yet, when on the point of granting him an audience, the sovereigns had one last hesitation. They consulted with the Archimandrite Theophanes, who fully reassured them about him.

"Grigory Efimovitch," he said, "is a peasant, a man of the people. Your Majesties will do well to hear him, for it is the voice of the Russian soil which speaks through him. I know all the charges against him, I know his sins which are numberless and most of them heinous, but there dwells in him so deep a passion of repentance and so implicit a trust in divine pity that I would all but guarantee his eternal salvation. Every time he repents, he is as pure as the child washed in the waters of baptism. Manifestly God has called him to be one of His chosen."

From the moment of his entrance into the palace, Rasputin obtained an extraordinary ascendancy over the Tsar and Tsaritsa. He wheedled them, dazzled them and dominated them. It was almost like sorcery.

Not that he flattered them; quite the contrary. From the first day, his manner towards them was rough and he treated them with a bold and disingenuous familiarity in which the two sovereigns, nauseated with adulation and sycophancy, thought they recognized the voice of the Russian soil.

He soon became the friend of Madame Vyrubova, the Empress's inseparable companion, and by her was initiated into all the secrets of the imperial couple and the Empire. All the intriguers at court, all the place-hunters and aspirants for titles and livings, naturally tried to enlist his support. His humble residence on the Kirotchnaïa, and later the Anglisky Prospekt, was besieged day and night by applicants, generals and officials, bishops and archimandrites, Councilors of the Empire and Senators, aides-de-camp and chamberlains, maids-of-honor and society women. There was an unending procession of them.

When he was not with the sovereigns or the Montenegrin Grand Duchesses, he was usually to be found at the house of old Countess Ignatiev, whose salon on the French Quay comprised the official champions of autocracy and theocracy. The highest dignitaries of the Church liked to congregate around her. Promotions in the ecclesiastical hierarchy, nominations to the Holy Synod, and the gravest questions of dogma, discipline and Church liturgy were discussed before her. Her moral authority, which was universally recognized, was a valuable help to Rasputin.

Sometimes she had celestial visions. One evening, during a spiritualistic séance, Saint Seraphin of Sarov, who was canonized in 1903, had appeared to her with a flaming halo around his head. He had declared, "A great prophet is among you. It is his mission to reveal the will of Providence to the Tsar and to lead him into glorious paths." She realized at once that he was referring to Rasputin. The Emperor was immensely impressed with this oracle for, as supreme guardian of the Church, he had taken a decisive part in the canonization of the blessed Seraphin and had a very special reverence for him.

Among Rasputin's patrons in his early days was another curious individual, the therapeutist Badmaiev. He is a trans-Baikal Siberian, a Buriat Mongol. Although he has not a single university degree, he carries on the profession of medicine, not clandestinely but openly in the public eye. It is a very curious sort of medicine, a kind of alchemy with a flavor of sorcery. When he first knew Rasputin, in 1906, a very unfortunate thing had just happened to him, a tribulation such as occasionally overtakes even the most honest of men. Towards the close of the Japanese War, a highly-placed client of his had shown his gratitude by sending him on a political mission to the hereditary chiefs of Chinese Mongolia. He was commissioned to distribute two hundred thousand rubles among them to secure their support. When he came back from Urga, he presented a report enumerating the brilliant results of his journey, and on the strength of this document was appropriately congratulated. But a little later it was discovered that he had kept the two hundred thousand rubles for himself.

The incident was beginning to have a somewhat ugly look when the intervention of the highly-placed client settled everything. The therapeutist then returned to his cabalistic operations with an easy mind. Never before had the sick and ailing flocked in such numbers to his consulting room on the

Liteïny, for it was rumored that he had brought back from Mongolia all sorts of medicinal herbs and magic remedies, obtained with immense difficulty from Thibetan sorcerers.

Secure in his ignorance and illuminism, Badmaiev does not hesitate to treat the most difficult and obscure cases in the whole realm of medicine. Yet he has a preference for nervous diseases, mental affections, and the baffling disorders of feminine physiology. He has established a secret pharmacopoeia. Under grotesque names, and in equally grotesque forms, he himself prepares the medicaments he orders. Thus he carries on a dangerous trade in narcotics, stupefactives, anesthetics, emmenagogues, and aphrodisiacs. He christens them with names such as 'Elixir du Thibet,' 'Poudre de Nirvritti,' 'Fleurs d'asokas,' 'Baume de Nyen-Tchen,' 'Essence de lotus noir,' and so on. And all he does is to get the substances for his drugs from a chemist who is in league with him.

On several occasions the Emperor and Empress have called him in to the Tsarevitch when ordinary doctors seemed powerless to stop the child's hemorrhage. It was thus that he met Rasputin, and their respective charlatanisms at once recognized each other and coalesced.

But ultimately sane elements in the capital were aroused by all the scandals that gathered around the name of the *staretz* of Pokrovskoe, and at long last his perpetual presence in the imperial palace, the part he had admittedly played in certain arbitrary or unfortunate actions on the part of the supreme authority, the insolent carelessness of his speech, and the cynical effrontery of his morals roused a storm of indignation in all quarters, so that, in spite of strict censorship, the press began to denounce the ignominy of the Siberian "magician," although, of course, it was careful not to implicate Their Majesties.

However, the public soon read between the lines of what was being published, and the 'Man of God' felt that it would be advisable for him to disappear for a time, so, in March 1911, he took up the pilgrim's staff and departed for Jerusalem. This unexpected decision filled his devotees with grief and admiration. None but a sainted soul could give such a reply to the calumnies of the wicked! Then he spent the summer at Tsarytsin with his excellent friend and colleague, the monk Heliodorus.

The Empress, however, kept in constant touch with him by letter and telephone, and in the autumn she told him she could endure his absence no longer. Besides, since the *staretz* had been allowed to go, the Tsarevitch's attacks of hemorrhaging had become more frequent. Suppose the child died!

The mother had not a single day's peace; she was a prey to an unending series of nervous crises, muscular spasms and fainting fits. The Tsar loves his wife and is absolutely devoted to his son, and he had a most trying time.

At the beginning of November, Rasputin returned to Petersburg. The insanities and orgies immediately began again, but already certain dissensions began to be observable among his disciples. Some thought him compromising and unduly licentious; others were concerned at his growing influence over Church and State affairs.

As it happened, the ecclesiastical world was still quivering with indignation over a shameful appointment forced on the weak-willed Emperor. Grigory had obtained the bishopric of Tobolsk for one of the friends of his youth, an illiterate, obscene and debauched peasant, Father Varnava. About the same time it was learned that the Procurator of the Holy Synod had received orders to ordain Rasputin a priest. This time there was an explosion.

On December 29, Monsignor Hermogenes, Bishop of Saratov, the monk Heliodorus and certain priests had an altercation with the *staretz*. They abused and buffeted him, shouting out, "Accursed!" "Sacrilegious priest!" "Fornicator!" "Filthy beast!" "Devil's viper!"

Taken aback at first, and crouching against the wall, Grigory tried to reply with a volley of counter-abuse. Then Monsignor Hermogenes, who is a giant, struck him hard on the head several times with his pectoral cross and cried out, "Down on your knees, you wretch! On your knees to the sacred icons! Ask God's pardon for all your filthy knaveries! Swear that you'll never pollute the palace of our beloved Tsar with your dirty presence again!"

Rasputin, quivering with fear and bleeding at the nose, beat his breast, stammered out prayers and swore never to appear in the Emperor's presence again, leaving the room under a fresh shower of curses and abuse.

Yet, the moment he was out of this trap, he went straight to Tsarskoe Selo and he had not long to wait for the joys of revenge. A few days later, on the express orders of the Procurator, the Holy Synod deprived Monsignor Hermogenes of his see and exiled him to the monastery of Khirovitsy in Lithuania. The monk Heliodorus was arrested by the police and shut up in the penitentiary monastery of Floristchevo, near Vladimir.

At first the police were powerless to prevent this scandal from leaking out. Speaking in the Duma, the leader of the Octobrist Party, Gutchkov, attacked Rasputin's relations with the Court in veiled terms. In Moscow, the religious and moral metropolis of the Empire, the best and most respected interpreters of orthodox Slavism, Count Cheremetiev, Samarin, Novosilov, Drujinin, and Vasnetsov, protested publicly against the servility of the Holy Synod. They even demanded the convocation of a national ecclesiastical council to reform the Church. The Archimandrite Theophanes himself raised a dignified voice against Grigory. His eyes had at length been opened to the true character of 'the Man of God,' and he could not forgive himself for having introduced him to the Court. Although he was the Empress's confessor, by an immediate decree of the Holy Synod he was sent to Taurida.

The President of the Council at this time was Kokovtsov, who was also in charge of the Ministry of Finance. An upright, honest, and courageous character, he did what was possible to enlighten his master as to the unworthiness of the *staretz*. On March 1, 1912, he begged the Emperor to let him send Grigory back to his home.

"This man has obtained Your Majesty's confidence by false pretenses," he said. "He is a charlatan and libertine of the worst description. Public opinion is roused against him. The papers —"

The Emperor interrupted his minister with a scornful smile. "You mean to say you take notice of what the papers say?"

"Yes, Sire, when they attack my sovereign and the prestige of the dynasty. At the present time it is the most loyal papers that are most severe in their criticism."

The Emperor, irritated, interrupted him again. "These criticisms are ridiculous. I hardly know Rasputin."

Kokovtsov hesitated to continue, but proceeded. "Sire, in the name of the dynasty and of your heir, I beg you to let me take the steps necessary to secure the return of Rasputin to his village and prevent him from coming back again."

In cold tones, the Emperor replied, "I shall tell him myself to go and never return."

"May I conclude that this is Your Majesty's decision?" asked Kokovtsov.

"Yes, it is my decision." Then, with a glance at the clock, that showed the time as half-past twelve, the Emperor held out his hand to Kokovtsov: "Goodbye, Vladimir Nicolaievitch, I need not detain you anymore."

At four o'clock the same day, Rasputin rang up Senator D….., a close friend of Kokovtsov, and said to him in a contemptuous tone, "Your friend the President tried to frighten Papka this morning. He said all sorts of nasty things about me, but he had no luck at all. Papka and Mamka still love me. You can ring up Vladimir Nicolaievitch and tell him so from me."

On May 6, all the ministers were present in full uniform in the imperial palace to congratulate the Empress whose birthday it was. When Alexandra Feodorovna passed Kokovtsov, she turned her back on him.

A few days before this ceremony, the *staretz* had left for Tobolsk. He did not go because he was told to, but of his own free will, to see how things were getting on in his little place at Pokrovskoe. As he bade farewell to the sovereigns, he had uttered this formidable prophecy with a fierce scowl. "I know that the wicked are watching me. Don't listen to them. If you abandon me, you will lose your son and your crown within six months."

The Empress exclaimed, "How could you think of our abandoning you! Are you not our only protector, our best friend?"

Then she had knelt down and asked his blessing.

In October, the imperial family stayed for a time at Spala in Poland, where the Tsar often went to enjoy the hunting in the wonderful forest of Krolova. One day, the young Tsarevitch was coming back from sailing on the lake, and miscalculating his jump on to the landing stage, caught his hip against the deck. At first the contusion seemed superficial and harmless, but a fortnight later, on October 16, a swelling appeared in his groin, the thigh began to inflame, and then his temperature suddenly rose.

Doctors Feodorov, Derevenko and Rauchfuss were hastily summoned, and diagnosed a sanguinous tumor that was becoming septic. An operation was necessary, but the hemophiliac tendency of the child made any incision out of the question. Yet his temperature rose every hour. On October 21, it reached 39.8C.

The parents never left the sick boy's bedroom as the doctors did not conceal their extreme anxiety. In Spala Church, the priests prayed day and night in relays. By order of the Emperor, a solemn service was simultaneously held in Moscow before the miraculous icon of the Iverskaia Virgin, and from morning to night the people of Saint Petersburg thronged to Our Lady of Kazan.

On the morning of the 22nd, the Empress came down for the first time to the drawing-room where she was met by Colonel Narishkin, the duty aide-de-camp; Princes Elizabeth Obolensky, her lady-in-waiting; Sazonov, who had come to make his report to the Emperor; and Count Ladislas Wielopolsky, Director of the imperial hunting establishments in Poland. Alexandra Feodorovna was pale and emaciated, but she wore a smile.

To the anxious questions that were put to her, she replied in a calm voice, "The doctors notice no improvement yet, but I am not a bit anxious myself now. During the night I have received a telegram from Father Grigory and it has reassured me completely." When she was pressed for details, she simply read out this wire. "God has seen your tears and heard your prayers. Grieve no more. Your son will live."

On the next day, the 23rd, the invalid's temperature fell to 38.9C. Two days later, the tumor in the groin began to dry out. The Tsarevitch was saved.

During the year 1913, several persons made further attempts to open the eyes of the Tsar and Tsaritsa to the behavior and moral degeneracy of the *staretz*. The first was Dowager Empress Marie Feodorovna, and she was followed by the Empress's sister, the pure and noble Grand Duchess Elizabeth Feodorovna. And how many more there were! But to all these warnings and pleadings, the sovereigns returned the same imperturbable reply. "These are all calumnies. The saints are always exposed to calumny."

In the religious jargon with which Rasputin habitually clothes his erotic tastes, one idea is perpetually recurring. "It is by repentance alone that we can win our salvation. We must therefore sin in order to have an opportunity for repentance. So when God places temptation in our way, it is our duty to yield to it so that we may secure the necessary condition precedent to a salutary penitence. Besides, was not the first word of life and truth that Christ uttered to mankind 'repent'? But how can we repent if we have not sinned?"

His homely sermons abound with ingenious disquisitions on the pardoning power of tears and the redemptive virtue of contrition. One of his favorite arguments, an argument that has the greatest effect on his feminine clientele, is the following: "It is not the horror at the sin that usually prevents us from yielding to temptation, for if sin was really a horror to us, we should not be tempted to commit it. Does a man ever want to eat anything he thoroughly dislikes? No, what really stops us and frightens us is the hurt to our pride that repentance involves. Absolute contrition implies absolute humility. No one likes humbling himself, even before God. That is the whole secret of our resistance to temptation. But the Sovereign Judge is not deceived, not for a moment! And

173

when we are in the valley of Jehoshaphat he will know how to remind us of all the chances for salvation he has offered us that we have rejected."

These sophisms were employed by a Phrygian sect even as early as the second century of our era. The heretic Montanus calmly put the same proposition to his fair Laodicean friends and secured the same practical results as Rasputin.

If the activities of the *staretz* were confined to the spheres of lust and mysticism, so far as I am concerned he would remain nothing but a more-or-less curious psychological, or physiological, study, but by force of circumstances this ignorant peasant has become a political instrument. Around him has gathered a regular clientele of influential people who have linked their fortunes with his.

Of these, the most eminent is the Minister of justice, Stcheglovitov, who is also leader of the Extreme Right in the Council of the Empire. He is a man of intellect, fluent and acid of speech, and he brings a good deal of calculation and elasticity to the realization of his designs. But he is only a recent acquisition to Rasputinism. Almost as important is the Minister of the Interior, Nicholas Maklakov, whose amiable docility is highly agreeable to the sovereigns. Then comes the Procurator of the Holy Synod, Sabler, a contemptible and servile character. Through him the *staretz* as it were controls the whole episcopate and all the high ecclesiastical offices. Next in order I should place the First Procurator of the Senate, Dobrovolsky, then Sturmer, Member of the Council of the Empire, then the Governor of the imperial palaces,

General Voyeikov who is a son-in-law of the Minister of the Court. At the end I should place Bieletzky, Director of the Police Bureau, a very bold and cunning individual. It is easy to imagine the enormous powers represented by a coalition of such influences in an autocratic and centralized state like Russia.

To counterbalance the evil influence of this cabal, I can find only one man in the personal entourage of the sovereigns, Prince Vladimir Orlov, son of the former ambassador to Paris and Director of His Majesty's Military Chancellery. A man of upright judgment, proud and wholeheartedly devoted to the Emperor, he has always denounced Rasputin and never ceased to fight against him, a fact that has naturally attracted to him the enmity of the Empress and Madame Vyrubova.

Wednesday, September 30, 1914

In the Galician Carpathians, the Austro-Hungarians are putting up a fierce defense of the Uszok Pass that leads into Transylvania.

In the east of East Prussia, the Germans are making great efforts to cross the Niemen between Kovno and Grodno at the very points where the Grand Army crossed on June 25, 1812.

Thursday, October 1, 1914

The Turkish Government has closed the Straits on the pretext of the presence of an Anglo-French squadron off the entrance to the Dardanelles. This action does incalculable harm to Russia, which is left without maritime communications except by Vladivostok and Archangel. Now it must be remembered that Vladivostok is 10,500 kilometers from Petrograd and that the port of Archangel may be closed by ice at any time now until the end of May.

The closing of the Straits is all the more serious because, for some time, I have been receiving reports from Moscow, Kiev and Kharkov that the old Byzantine dream is reviving.

"This war will have no meaning for us unless it brings us Constantinople and the Straits. Tsarigrad must be ours, and ours alone. Our historic mission and our holy duty is to set the cross of Pravoslavie, the cross of the Orthodox Faith, on the dome of Saint Sophia once more. Russia would not be the chosen nation if at long last she did not avenge the age-old wrongs of Christianity."

That is what is being said and spread in political, religious, and university circles, and even more in the obscure depths of the Russian conscience.

Friday, October 2, 1914

Grand Duchess Elizabeth Feodorovna, sister of the Empress and widow of Grand Duke Sergius, is a strange creature whose whole life is a series of enigmas.

Born at Darmstadt on November 1, 1864, she was a flower of exquisite loveliness when at the age of twenty she married the fourth son of the Emperor Alexander II.

I remember dining with her in Paris a few years later, somewhere about 1891. I can still see her, tall and slender, with limpid, frank and penetrating eyes, sweet, soft lips, delicate features and a straight, aristocratic nose. All her lines were pure and graceful, and there was a delightful rhythm to her movements and gestures. Her conversation revealed a charming woman's mind – unaffected, contemplative and gentle.

Since that time a good deal of mystery had gathered around her and certain details of her married life remained inexplicable.

Physically, Sergius Alexandrovitch was very tall. He had a good figure but a disagreeable face, distinguished by grayish-white eyebrows and a hard look. Morally, he was quarrelsome and despotic by nature, and both his intellect and education were poor. On the other hand, his artistic perceptions were very well developed. He was a very different man from his brothers Vladimir, Alexis and Paul. He lived within himself, preferred solitude and had a reputation for oddity.

After his marriage he was even less understood. He certainly showed himself the most suspicious and inquisitorial of husbands. He would not allow his wife to remain alone with anyone or to go out by herself. He spied on her correspondence and her books, even forbidding her to read 'Anna Karenina' for fear of its arousing unhealthy curiosity or too violent emotions. He was always finding fault with her in harsh and cutting terms. Even in public he sometimes spoke rudely to her. Of a calm and docile nature, she merely bowed under the lash of his bitter tongue. Alexander III, the kind and considerate giant, was sorry for her and showed his affection, but observing that he was arousing his brother's jealousy, he had to give this up before long.

One day, after a violent outburst on the part of the Grand Duke, old Prince B...., who had witnessed the scene, offered the young woman his sympathy.

She seemed surprised and answered in a frank tone, "I'm not to be pitied. People may say what they like, but I'm happy because I'm very dearly loved."

He certainly did love her, but in his own way, a way that was esthetic and irritable, wayward and ambiguous, covetous and incomplete.

In 1891, Grand Duke Sergius was appointed Governor-General of Moscow. It was the period when the famous Procurator of the Holy Synod, Constantine Pobiedonostsev, 'the Russian Torquemada,' enjoyed unbounded influence over Alexander III and was trying to restore the doctrines of theocratic absolutism and bring Russia back into the traditions of Byzantine Muscovy.

Grand Duchess Elizabeth had been baptized into the Lutheran Confession. The new Governor-General could not, however, decently appear in the Kremlin with a heretical wife, and so he ordered her to abjure Protestantism and accept the national faith. It is said that she had already been inclined that way for some considerable time. Whatever the reason, she adopted the creed of the Russian Church with her whole soul.

No conversion was ever more sincere, thorough and complete. Hitherto the cold, dry observances of Lutheranism had been but poor sustenance to the imaginative faculties of the young woman. The experience of marriage had not been any better. All her instincts for dreams and emotion, fervor and tenderness, suddenly found its outlet in the mysterious rites and pomp and pageantry of orthodoxy. Her piety soared to amazing levels. She knew heights and depths whose existence she had never even suspected.

In the glory of his position as Governor-General, that equaled that of a viceroy, Sergius Alexandrovitch soon blossomed out as a protagonist of the reactionary crusade that was the sum total of the domestic policy of the "Most Pious Tsar" Alexander III. One of his first acts was the expulsion *en masse* of the Jews who had gradually made their way into Moscow and who were now roughly driven back into their ghettoes in the western provinces. Then he issued a whole series of vexatious edicts imposing all sorts of restrictions on the professors and students of the University. Finally he adopted a haughty attitude towards the bourgeois, just to remind them that their liberalism, mild though it was, was not to his taste.

As always happens in such cases, the officers and officials around him were only too glad to improve on his dictatorial ways. The general hatred he thus aroused filled him with pride.

In May 1896, the coronation of Nicholas II marked a glorious date in the history of orthodox autocracy. The ideal of the Muscovite Tsars, the intimate association of Church and State, was seen to be the *leitmotiv* of the new reign. Only the catastrophe in Khodinsky meadows, where two thousand *moujiks* perished through the carelessness of the police, cast a sinister, though passing, shadow over the brilliant gaiety of the Holy City.

Two years later, the monument of the "Martyr Tsar," Alexander II, was unveiled in the Kremlin in front of the Cathedral of the Archangel. During the ceremonies on this occasion, the Procurator of the Holy Synod, Constantine Pobiedonostsev, received the highest honor the Empire could give, the Order of Saint Andrew, founded in 1698 by Peter the Great. The "orthodox and most Christian" army was drawn into in the festivities by a magnificent review.

In 1900, Nicholas II took it upon himself to revive an ancient custom of his ancestors that had fallen into disuse for more than fifty years: He came to perform his Easter duties in Moscow, to confirm once more, as he put it, the religious and national sentiments that joined the hearts of the sovereign and his people. Nothing was left undone to make these solemnities as impressive as possible. Throughout Holy Week, services and processions succeeded one another with unprecedented pomp, both in the Kremlin and the principal sanctuaries of the city.

Before leaving Moscow the Emperor addressed the following rescript to Grand Duke Sergius:

Your Imperial Highness,

By the grace of God I have realized my great desire, and the desire of the Empress Alexandra Feodorovna, to be with our children and spend the days of Holy Week, receive Holy Communion and stay in Moscow for the most solemn of all ceremonies among the greatest of our national sanctuaries under the protecting shadow of our age-old Kremlin.

Here, where lie the mortal remains of the saints beloved of the Lord, among the tombs of the sovereigns who brought Russia unity and organization, the very cradle of autocracy, fervent prayers have been offered up to the King of Kings, and a sweet joy has possessed Our soul as it has filled those of the faithful children of Our dear Church who have thronged the temples.

May God hear those prayers! May He strengthen the believers, succor those whose faith is shaken, bring back those who have strayed from the true path and bless the Empire of Russia which rests firmly on the unshakable foundation of orthodoxy, the holy guardian of the eternal Verities, love and peace.

Associating myself with the prayers of my people, I draw fresh strength to serve Russia for her good and her glory, and I rejoice to be able at this moment to convey to Your Imperial Highness – and through you to the City of Moscow, Moscow so dear to my heart – the sentiments by which I am inspired.

Christ is risen,

Nicholas.

Moscow, April 9, 1900

Thus from time to time some great religious, political, or military ceremony draws the eyes of the Russian people and the Slav world to the sacred mount on which the Kremlin stands. In this active and brilliant life, Elizabeth Feodorovna played her part. She made a graceful hostess at the magnificent receptions in the Alexander and Illinskoe palaces. She threw herself enthusiastically into much religious, charitable, educational and artistic work. The picturesque setting and moral atmosphere of Moscow had a profound effect on her esthetic sensibilities. She had once been told that the mission assigned by Providence to the Tsars was to realize the Kingdom of God on the soil of Russia. The thought that she was helping, however modestly, in such a task fired her imagination.

Satisfied with the part assigned to her, a miracle of purity and charm, reserve and guilelessness, with her graceful lines and exquisite attire, she exhaled a perfume of idealism, mystery and voluptuous charm that made her all that life could wish.

Yet the ultra-reactionary policy, of which Grand Duke Sergius boasted of being one of the principal authors, aroused a spirit of opposition in intellectual circles and among the working masses throughout Russia that became more violent every day. A group of fearless anarchists, Guerchouny, Bourtzev, Savinkov and Azev, founded a 'Fighting Organization,' the exploits of which were soon to equal the Nihilist feats of 1877-1881. Plots and assassinations followed one another at short intervals with alarming regularity. A Minister of Education, two Ministers for the Interior, Commissioners of Police, and provincial governors and magistrates, were struck down one after the other. Towards the end of 1904, the situation, particularly in Moscow, suddenly became much worse owing to the disasters in the Far East.

Grand Duke Sergius immediately took the most radical measures. With his fierce scowl and cruel sneer, he let everyone know that he would not show the slightest mercy.

On February 17, 1905, as he was driving across the Kremlin and about to reach the Senate Square at three o'clock in the afternoon, the terrorist Kalaiev threw a bomb at him. It caught him on the breast and blew him to pieces.

At that moment Grand Duchess Elizabeth was in the Kremlin where she was organizing a Red Cross sewing guild for the armies in Manchuria. When she heard the dreadful sound of the explosion, she ran out, just as she was, without a hat, and was seen to throw herself on the corpse of her husband whose head and arms, torn from his body, lay among the debris of the carriage. Then she returned to the grand-ducal palace and passed the whole of her time in prayer.

She remained in prayer continuously for the five days preceding the funeral, and this long communion with the Deity inspired her to a curious step. On the night before the obsequies, she sent for the Prefect of Police and ordered him to take her at once to Tanganka prison where Kalaiev was waiting his summons to appear before a court martial.

When she was shown into the assassin's cell she asked him, "Why did you kill my husband? Why have you burdened your conscience with such a horrible crime?"

The prisoner had at first received her with a look of angry suspicion, but he observed that she spoke in gentle tones to him and said "my husband," and not "the Grand Duke."

"I killed Sergius Alexandrovitch," he replied, "because he made himself the instrument of tyranny and of the exploitation of the working class. I have done justice in the name of the socialist and revolutionary people."

"You are wrong," she replied. "My husband loved the people and thought of nothing but their welfare. So there is no excuse for your crime. Close your ears to your pride and repent. If you tread the path of re repentance, I will plead with the Emperor to give you your life and I will pray to God to forgive you, as I have already forgiven you myself."

Touched and amazed at this language, he was yet brave enough to reply, "No, I'm not sorry. I must die for my cause. I shall die."

"Then, as you have deprived me of any means of saving your life, and will certainly soon appear before God, at any rate let me do what I can to save your soul. Here's the Gospel. Promise me to read it carefully until the hour of your death."

He shook his head and replied, "I'll read the Gospel if you, in turn, will promise me to read this story of my life that I've just finished writing. It will help you to understand why I killed Sergius Alexandrovitch."

"No, I won't read your diary. All I can do is to go on praying for you."

She went out, leaving the Gospel on the table.

In spite of her rebuff, she wrote to the Emperor to ask for a pardon for the assassin, but meanwhile the public had heard of her visit to Tanganka prison. The most extraordinary and romantic versions got abroad, but they all agreed that Kalaiev had agreed to plead for a pardon.

A few days later she received from the prisoner a letter that ran more or less like this:

> *You have taken advantage of my position. I did not say I was sorry, because I am not. If I agreed to hear what you had to say, it was only because I regarded you as the unfortunate widow of a man whom I had executed. I was sorry for your grief, nothing more. The account*

you have given of our interview is an insult to me. I don't want the mercy you have asked for me.

The trial proceeded. The preliminary enquiries were very prolonged owing to a useless search for accomplices, the chief of which was Boris Savinkov. On April 4, Kalaiev was condemned to death.

The next day, the Minister of Justice, Sergius Manushkin, was making his report to the Emperor and asked him if he intended to commute Kalaiev's sentence in view of Grand Duchess Elizabeth's plea.

Nicholas II remained silent and then casually remarked, "Is there anything else you want to talk about, Sergius Serguievitch?" and he dismissed him.

The Tsar immediately sent for Kovalensky, the Director of the Police Department, and gave him secret orders. Kalaiev was then transferred to the Fortress of Schlusselburg, the famous State prison.

At eleven o'clock in the evening of May 23, the Attorney-General's deputy, Feodorov, entered the cell of the condemned man, whom he had known when they were students together, and said to him: "I am authorized to tell you that if you will ask for pardon, His Majesty the Emperor will deign to grant it you."

Kalaiev replied, calmly and firmly, "No, I wish to die for my cause."

Feodorov persisted to the best of his ability, in noble and humane terms.

Kalaiev broke down but was not to be moved, concluding with the remark, "As you're so good to me, let me write to my mother."

"Certainly you may write to her, and I'll see she gets your letter at once."

When the prisoner had finished his letter, Feodorov made a last despairing effort to make him change his mind.

Summoning up all his courage, but losing none of his unruffled calm, Kalaiev declared solemnly, "I want to die. I must die. My death will be even more useful to my cause than the death of Grand Duke Sergius."

The deputy realized that he would never succeed in overcoming such heroic resolution. He left the cell and went to the Governor of the fortress to order the execution.

The scaffold had already been erected in the courtyard of the prison. The executioner, a convict in a red cap, was waiting on the steps. He was a parricide named Philippiev, and had been borrowed from the penal settlement at Orel on account of his herculean strength and professional skill.

The Governor's residence was at the far end of the court. It wore a festive look that evening. Merry shouts and loud laughter were heard at every moment. When Feodorov entered there, he found a lively company, the principal officials of the fortress and all the officers stationed at Schlusselburg, who were frolicking and feasting. By way of whiling away the time preceding the execution, they were swilling champagne and toasting Baron von Medem, Deputy Chief of Staff to the Imperial Corps of Police, who had been sent by the Minister of the Interior to be present for the condemned man's last moments.

Now Kalaiev was extremely anxious to see his counsel, whose presence at the execution was legally permissible. This gentleman, Jdanov, had come to Schlusselburg especially the previous evening and had asked several times to be taken to his client. But he was known as an advanced socialist and the imperial police feared that Kalaiev would give him some last message for the revolutionary party. So, in spite of the express provisions of the law, Jdanov was refused admittance to the fortress.

When Feodorov left the cell, he was succeeded by a priest. The prisoner received him kindly but declined all religious assistance.

"I have settled accounts with life," he said. "I need neither your prayers nor your sacraments. All the same, I am a Christian and I believe in the Holy Spirit. I feel it still within me and I am sure it will not abandon me. That's enough for me." As the priest persisted kindly in his desire to fulfil his mission, Kalaiev continued, "It's very good of you to pity me. Let me embrace you."

They fell into each other's arms.

At two o'clock in the morning, the prisoner was taken from his cell, his hands were bound and he was led into the courtyard of the fortress. He ascended the scaffold with a firm step. Not a shade of emotion passed over his face as he listened while the verdict was read out to him, an interminable proceeding.

When the clerk of the court had finished, Kalaiev said, in a very simple tone, "I'm glad I've kept my composure to the end.2

Then two jailers dressed him in a long white shroud that covered his head, and the executioner called out, "Get on the stool!"

Kalaiev demurred. "How can I get on the stool? You've covered my head. I can't see a thing."

Phillipiev took him in his strong arms, lifted him on to the stool, and quickly fastened a rope round his neck. Then he swiftly knocked away the support. But the rope was too long – kKalaiev's feet still touched the floor. The victim gave a terrible start and cries of horror arose from the spectators assembled round the scaffold.

The executioner had to shorten the rope and begin all over again.

After this sinister tragedy, Elizabeth Feodorovna considered that she had finished with the world. Henceforward she devoted herself exclusively to the consolations of religion. She spent all her time in works of asceticism, piety, penitence and charity.

On April 15, 1910, she realized an ambition she had held in mind for a considerable period. She established a religious community for women and had herself appointed Abbess. Taking the name of "Martha and Mary," the convent was established in Moscow in a part of the city on the right bank. The nuns devoted themselves particularly to the succor of the sick and poor. But at the moment when she was thus saying farewell to the world, Elizabeth Feodorovna made a last concession to feminine taste; she had the dress of her order designed by a Moscow artist, the painter Nesterov. The costume comprises a long robe of fine, pearl-gray baize, a cambric wimple drawn close around the face and neck, and a long white woolen veil that falls over the breast in broad folds. The general effect is simple, austere and attractive.

There is a lack of warmth in the relations between Grand Duchess Elizabeth and Empress Alexandra. The original cause, or at any rate the principal reason, for their estrangement is Rasputin. In Elizabeth Feodorovna's eyes, Grigory is nothing but a lascivious and sacrilegious impostor, an emissary of Satan.

The two sisters have often had disputes about him that have several times led to an open quarrel. They never mention him now. Another reason for the coolness between them is their rivalry in piety and good works. Each of them claims superiority in knowledge of theology, observance of scriptural injunctions, meditations on the eternal life, and adoration of the crucifix. The result is that Grand Duchess Elizabeth's appearances at Tsarskoe Selo are rare and short.

What is the origin of this extraordinary domination of the mystic sensibilities in the case of Grand Duchess Elizabeth and her sister, the Empress Alexandra? It seems to me it is a legacy from their mother, Princess Alice, daughter of Queen Victoria, who was married in 1862 to the hereditary Prince of Hesse-Darmstadt and died in 1878 at the age of thirty-five.

Brought up in the strictest tenets of Anglicanism, Princess Alice, shortly after her marriage, conceived a strange passion, a passion wholly ethical and intellectual, for the great rationalist theologian of Tübingen, David Strauss, the celebrated author of 'The Life of Jesus,' who died four years before herself.

Under the manners of a Swabian philistine and unfrocked minister, David Strauss concealed the soul of a romantic. In the early days of his fame, he had felt the temptation of love and the bulwark of his books was not enough to save him from the spell of the 'eternal feminine.' A young girl, a stranger (who was dazzled by his growing fame) offered herself to him, as Bettina von Arnim offered herself to Goethe. He had respected this naive flower, but in breathing its fragrance he had tasted mortal poison. When he recovered his self-possession, he was able to compare himself to "the fakirs of India who boast of gaining a superhuman glory by heroic mortifications while the jealous gods send them female visions to seduce them from their faith.

A few years later, another witch once more deranged his studious life. This time it was not a fair and frank German lily, but a perverse creature, Agnes Schebest, an opera singer of great gifts and amazing beauty. He loved her passionately, so much so that, unable to do without her, and fearing to lose her, he married her.

Of course, she lost no time in betraying him with a fervor of sensuality and a callous audacity that seemed to heighten her beauty.

At first, he refused to open his eyes. "The world," he wrote, "calls me credulous. Perhaps I am only a slave." Ultimately he was forced to admit he had been deceived, and after a terrible scene, he turned away the sinner.

Then he went back to his work. But after the frenzy of passion, he found the interpretation of Holy Writ somewhat insipid. He could not remain in one place, for an inward unrest made him change his residence time and again. He carried his sorrows from Ludwigsburg to Stuttgart, from Heidelberg to Cologne, from Weimar to Munich, from Heilbronn to Darmstadt. The historic evolution of doctrine gave him pleasure no longer. Even Hegelian dreams revolted him. Amid this general bankruptcy of his character, he became daily more soured, his irony more acid, his dialectics more destructive. Weary of a life from which he had nothing to expect, he longed for dissolution.

It was then that he first knew Princess Alice. He at once obtained a great influence over her, but the romance of their minds and hearts was still wrapped in a deep mystery, although it is impossible to doubt that he shook her faith to the depths and that she passed through a terrible crisis.

Thus it may be that her daughters have inherited from her their tendency towards religious exaltation. Perhaps, too, they betray the influence of an atavism far more ancient. Have I not found the names of Saint Elizabeth of Hungary and Mary Stuart among their female ancestry?

Saturday, October 3, 1914

Grand Duke Nicholas is making preparations for a general offensive in Poland and Galicia. The operations will develop in the region of Warsaw and extend to the San and the Carpathians. If they succeed the Russian army will immediately make a beeline for Cracow and Breslau.

Monday, October 5, 1914

At the moment, the Emperor is making a round of the battle fronts to encourage his troops and receive their salute: *Ave, Cæsar, morituri te salutant!* [Hail, Caesar. Those who are about to die salute you!]

According to General Bielaiev, Chief of Staff of the Army, Grand Duke Nicholas means to carry through the next offensive with the greatest possible vigor and intensity "in the hope of deciding the war with one great blow."

Thursday, October 8, 1914

The Russian offensive runs all along the line, and there is violent fighting from the confluence of the Bzura, which joins the Vistula 60 kilometers above Warsaw, to the source of the San, i.e. the western chain of the Carpathians. The frontline thus extends for more than four hundred kilometers.

The transport movements that have preceded this vast operation have been carried out with the most perfect skill and organization.

Simultaneously, the Russian troops have gained a brilliant success between Augustov and Suvalki on the frontier of East Prussia.

Sunday, October 11, 1914

Count Joseph Potocki, who arrived yesterday from his Antoniny property in Volhynia, has been to lunch at the Embassy.

He has confided to me the disappointment of his Polish compatriots.

"The manifesto of August 16 filled us with a great hope. We thought that Poland was to be reborn. When the manifesto was issued, I had it read out in church by the priest. We all dissolved in tears. I wept like a child. But we are already feeling that the Russians are trying to get out of their promises. They are giving us to understand, and later on it will be their excuse, that the manifesto was signed by Grand Duke Nicholas and not by the Emperor; that it is an initiative of the military authorities, not an act of the supreme power. They will resort to other subterfuges, no doubt. And in any case, these magnificent promises are conditional on the conquest of Prussian Poland. Do you really think the Russian army will ever enter Posen? Here we are, seventy-two days after mobilization, and it has only reached the Vistula. Anyhow, the Russians can't hold their own with the Germans. I simply daren't tell you all I think, all I anticipate ... No, no, the day of Poland's resurrection is a long way off yet."

I did my best to revive his faith.

"The promise to restore Poland has been sworn in the face of Europe. I can assure you that it is the Emperor's personal intention. No doubt the reactionaries are secretly working to secure that the manifesto of August 16 shall remain a dead letter. I often hear of their intrigues. But their calculations are much too obvious. In opposing the restoration of Poland, they are merely trying to pave the way for a reconciliation between Russia and Germany. Thus the whole policy of the alliance is involved, and on that point the Emperor will never give way. The Allies will see to that, if necessary. As to your military expectations, forgive me if I regard them as an impression, not an opinion. This war will be very long and very stern, but our victory is not in doubt so long as we display tenacity and loyalty."

He shrugged his shoulders skeptically and then talked about the evil situation in which most Polish families find themselves at the present moment.

"To begin with," he said, "most of the fighting is on Polish soil. It is our towns, fields and estates that are being ravaged, burnt and looted by both sides. But that isn't all. Owing to the partition of Poland, this war is having the most dreadful effects. Look at my family. I'm a Russian subject; my brother's an Austrian subject. One of my brothers-in-law is a German subject, another a Russian. All my cousins and nephews are similarly distributed by the necessities of inheritance among the three countries. Although we are all of the same race, we are condemned to civil war."

At the Marie Theater this evening, we had Tchaikovsky's ballet, 'Le Lac des Cygnes,' a picturesque and poetic work of high symphonic quality. The theater was filled with as brilliant an audience as was to be seen on a subscription night in the days before the war.

Is the inference that Russian society is indifferent to the war? No, indeed. On the battlefields, the Russian officers show a wonderful spirit of dash and heroism. In the front line dressing-stations, the finest of society ladies are rivaling each other in courage, endurance and devotion. In every quarter, public generosity is at work on an unparalleled scale. Gifts are flowing in from every side, particularly anonymous gifts that are almost always the largest. In every part of the Empire, relief work for the wounded, sick, necessitous and refugees is going on under most ingenious forms. Taking the Russian people as a whole, their social and patriotic solidarity is all that could be desired. There is no ground whatever for charging them with not taking seriously the terrible trial in which the future of the nation is at stake.

But it would be vain to ask them to go without their theaters, music and ballets. One might as well ask the Spanish to give up their bull fights. Nor are the observations to which I have been inspired today by contemplation of the brilliant audience at the Marie Theater confined to the upper and propertied classes, for the cheaper seats were crammed to the roof. The numberless theaters of Petrograd are full every night, and it is the same in Moscow, Kiev, Kazan, Kkarkov, Odessa, Tiflis, &c.

In one of the intervals I called on Teliakovsky, the Director of the Imperial Theaters. I found him with General M….. and two officers who have just come back from the front. Of course we talked about the great battle that is developing west of the Vistula, the opening moves of which have been terribly bloody.

"In short," said Teliakovsky, "we're letting thousands and thousands of men be massacred for the sake of restoring Poland. I hope to goodness we shan't persevere in this mad course."

General M….. broke in.

"But we've made a promise, a solemn promise. It's an obligation of honor to restore Poland."

"That's all right," replied Teliakovsky; "let's take Posen, if we can, but we should go on and take everywhere else that really wants us. Let's have Armenia and Constantinople."

As I went back to my box, I passed Potocki, looking as gloomy as ever.

"Oh Ambassador," he sighed, "I've been thinking over what you said this morning. I'm sorry to say you haven't convinced me at all."

Monday, October 12, 1914

The King of Rumania, Carol I, died yesterday in his seventy-sixth year.

A submissive vassal of the German powers, he was always an admirer – I might almost say under the spell – of their military, political and moral superiority, and never harbored the slightest doubt about their victory in the immediate future. As long as he was alive, we had no chance whatever of rallying Rumania to our cause.

The new king, Ferdinand I, will have an open mind and his hands free. Besides, his wife, Queen Marie, is the granddaughter of Queen Victoria through her father, the Duke of Edinburgh, who succeeded the Duke of Saxe-Coburg and Gotha in 1893. Her mother is Grand Duchess Marie, daughter of Tsar Alexander II, and her sister is Grand Duchess Victoria, wife of Grand Duke Cyril Vladimorovitch. She thus has family ties, ties that are very close and affectionate, with the English and Russian courts.

Tuesday, October 13, 1914

Warsaw is in danger from a violent counter-attack by the Germans north of the Pilica. The Russian resistance is magnificent.

Wednesday, October 14, 1914

A Jew from Odessa, employed to buy corn by a large exporting house, came to see me this morning on a business matter.

Struck by his intelligence and sagacity, I questioned him about the state of public feeling among the lower classes, especially the *moujiks*. I could not have found a better authority on this subject, as his work obliges him to travel continuously in every part of the Empire and brings him into daily contact with the masses.

This is more or less what he says. "The patriotic impulse has not died down among the masses. On the contrary, hatred of Germany seems even more marked than in the first days of the war. Everyone is determined to carry the struggle through to victory. No one doubts that victory. In Moscow, however, there is some uneasiness owing to the rumors coming from Petrograd. The Empress and those about her are suspected of carrying on a secret correspondence with Germany. This suspicion extends to Grand Duchess Elizabeth, the Empress's sister, Abbess of the Convent of Martha and Mary in Moscow, who spends her life in good works. The Emperor's weakness with the Empress, Vyrubova and Rasputin comes in for severe criticism. On the other hand, the popularity of Grand Duke Nicholas increases every day. People are beginning to talk a good deal about Constantinople, particularly in the southern provinces."

Thursday, October 15, 1914

The German thrust at Warsaw has been stayed. The Russians are extending their offensive, but the operations are greatly hampered by the state of the roads that have been turned into quagmires by the autumn rains. In places, the mud is more than a meter deep. In 1807, in the same region and at the same time of the year, Napoleon had to admit the impossibility of maneuvering troops on such a spongy soil.

The remarks made to me by the Jewish broker from Odessa yesterday have been confirmed somewhat curiously this morning. A French manufacturer, Goujon, who has been established in Moscow for forty years, came to see me this morning, and said, "Several of my Russian friends, commercial and industrial leaders, have asked me on their behalf to put a question to you that will no doubt appear somewhat strange. Is it true that the court clique have succeeded in shaking the Emperor's determination to continue the war until Germany is completely defeated? My friends are extremely anxious. They say they are quite positive about it, so much so that they've come to Petrograd with me this morning and intend to ask an audience of the Emperor. But before doing so, they want to consult you, and will be extremely grateful if you'll receive them."

I told Goujon all that I know about the intrigues in progress among the Empress's entourage, intrigues that need very careful watching. As to the Emperor's determination, I told him of the accumulation of evidence I am continually receiving.

"You can assure your friends from me that I have unlimited confidence in the Emperor's word, his loyalty to the alliance, and his determination to carry the war through to final and complete victory. They will understand, of course, that I cannot receive them. It would look as if I were coming between the Tsar and his subjects. If you hear anything definite about the intrigues at the palace, don't neglect to let me know."

I have just told Sazonov of this conversation and he has entirely approved what I said.

He added, "I'm very glad indeed about this. It's enabled you to feel the pulse of Russia. You can see for yourself it beats strongly."

Monday, October 19, 1914

At two o'clock this afternoon, there was a memorial service for King Carol in the chapel of the Winter Palace.

While the interminable funeral service was in progress, I had a talk with the Procurator of the Holy Synod, Vladimir Sabler, the successor and rival of the formidable Pobiedonostsev, fierce guardian of orthodox traditions and discipline; otherwise a nice, kind man.

"Ambassador," he said, "why weren't you present yesterday evening at the sacred concert got up by the clergy of Petrograd in aid of the wounded? There was nothing but religious music in the program. We began with the Russian national anthem and then the 'Marseillaise.' It's a fact, the 'Marseillaise' was sung by Russian clergy! They put their hearts into it too. And I of all people, the Procurator of the Holy Synod, actually encored the 'Marseillaise.'

"You were absolutely right, Your Excellency," I said. "The 'Marseillaise' was in no way out of place in your sacred concert. At the present moment, it is an epitome of every Frenchman's national faith."

Then he smilingly told me of the terrible scandal at court and in Russian high society when the Tsar Alexander III allowed the 'Marseillaise' to be played in his presence in July 1891, during the visit of the French fleet to Kronstadt.

Tuesday, October 20, 1914

The Russian offensive is in full flow on a front of 450 kilometers from Vloslavsk to Jaroslav.

In the Constantinople quarter, the sky is even darker and the storm is approaching. Sazonov tells me that Grand Duke Nicholas will not allow himself to be deflected from his plan by the threat from Turkey. He will spare as little as possible for the defense of the Caucasus, and will keep all his troops for the principal theater of operations. It is in Berlin where all the accounts will be taken. General de Laguiche writes to me in the same vein.

Wednesday, October 21, 1914

West of the Vistula, the Germans are retreating all along the line.

A terrible battle is in progress in France and Belgium, in the region of Arras and on the line of the Yser.

Thursday, October 22, 1914

The victory of the Russian armies is becoming more pronounced and extensive.

It is a case of now or never for Rumania to take the field against Austria-Hungary, especially as she is no longer held back by the objections of King Carol. But Bratiano, the President of the Council, who is now the sole master of Rumanian policy, is showing himself increasingly undecided and timid.

Friday, October 23, 1914

Up to the present, the students of Russian universities have been exempted from military service so that they can finish their courses. A decree has now been issued authorizing the Minister for War to call them to the colors. The reason for this measure is the enormous losses suffered by the Russian armies in Poland and Galicia. After a six months' course in certain special schools, students possessing certain degrees will be granted commissions as secondlieutenants.

This decree has come in for severe criticism in conservative circles. One of the leaders of the Right in the Council of the Empire said to me, "It's ridiculous! Our corps of officers is to be contaminated. All these students are nothing but revolutionary viruses that will infect the army."

In the university towns such as Petrograd, Moscow, Kazan and Kiev, the students have been organizing patriotic demonstrations. The Moscow students have even thought that the best way to prove their nationalist fervor is to loot the shops of Germans.

Saturday, October 24, 1914

Following up their campaign against everything German, the Government has decided that the 'Petrograder Zeitung,' the influential 'Petersburg Gazette,' which has been published in German since 1726, is to be suppressed on December 31 next. The German party in Russia, the party of the 'Baltic Barons,' will thus lose its official organ.

In many ways the animosity against the Germans throughout the Empire – even Germans who are Russian subjects – recalls the nationalist outburst of 1740 that put an end to the regime of the Birens, Ostermanns, Munnichs, Lowenwoldes and all the other German favorites of which Herzen wrote so picturesquely. "They wrangled over Russia as if it were a jug of beer."

Sunday, October 25, 1914

Sazonov has shown me a letter he has just received from a student at Kazan. It runs as follows:

> *Your Excellency,*
>
> *I have not the honor of knowing you. I am about to join the army. If this war is to bring us Constantinople, I will die twenty times and gladly. But if we are not to have Constantinople, I shall die but once, with death in my heart. I beg Your Excellency to reply with*

a simple 'yes' or 'no' on the enclosed postcard on which I have given my name and address.

Monday, October 26, 1914

I have dined quite privately at Tsarskoe Selo with Grand Duchess Marie Pavlovna.

The Grand Duchess is absolutely delighted at the great successes the Russian army has just gained in Poland.

"I attach the greatest importance to these successes," she said. "We may legitimately call them a victory. In the first place, the German army has lost its prestige in the eyes of our men. They thought it invincible. In the second place, it has removed any possibility of a premature peace with Germany." I made cautious enquiries about Rasputin. She replied, "Alas, some believe in him more than ever. He is more than ever the 'Man of God'! Some do not doubt that our successes are due to his prayers. Some have even asked him more than once to give his blessing to the plan of campaign. What a pity!"

"Does he ever talk about peace?"

"I don't know, but I should be greatly surprised if he had. He's too cunning not to feel that he would not be listened to at a time like this."

Wednesday, October 28, 1914

For the Jews of Poland and Lithuania, the war is one of the greatest disasters they have ever known. Hundreds of thousands of them have had to leave their homes in Lodz, Kielce, Petrokov, Ivangorod, Skiernewice, Suvalki, Grodno, Bielostock etc. Almost everywhere the prelude to their lamentable exodus has been the looting of their shops, synagogues, and houses. Thousands of families have taken refuge in Warsaw and Vilna. The majority are wandering aimlessly like a flock of sheep. It's a miracle that there have been no pogroms (organized massacres). But not a day passes where the armies are without a number of Jews being hanged on a trumped-up charge of spying.

Incidentally, Sazonov and I have been talking of the Jewish question and all the religious, political, social and economic problems it raises. He informed me that the Government was considering what modifications could be made in the far-too-arbitrary and vexatious regulations to which the Russian Jews are subjected. A new law is about to be issued in favor of the Jews of Galicia who will become subjects of the Tsar. I have encouraged him to be as tolerant and liberal as possible.

"I'm speaking to you as an ally. In the United States, there is a very large, influential and wealthy Jewish community who are very indignant at your treatment of their co-religionists. Germany is very skilfully exploiting this quarrel with you, which means a quarrel with us. It 's matter of importance for us to win the sympathy of Americans."

Chapter 6

Thursday, October 29, 1914

At three o'clock this morning, two Turkish destroyers entered the port of Odessa, sank a Russian gunboat, and fired on the French mail boat 'Portugal,' doing considerable damage. Then they fled at top speed, pursued by a Russian destroyer.

Sazonov has received the news very calmly. He immediately applied to the Emperor for orders, and then said to me, "His Majesty has decided that not a man shall be withdrawn from the German front. Our first concern is to beat Germany. The defeat of Germany will necessarily involve the ruin of Turkey. We shall keep down to a minimum the forces required for defense against the Turkish fleet and army."

Among the general public there is great excitement.

Friday, October 30, 1914

The Russian Ambassador in Constantinople, Michael de Giers, has received orders demanding that he return his passports.

At Sazonov's request, the three allied Governments are still trying to keep Turkey neutral and pressing her immediately to dismiss the German officers serving in the Ottoman fleet and army.

The attempt has no chance of success, however, as Turkish cruisers have just bombarded Novorossisk and Theodosia as well.

These attacks, which have not been preceded by a declaration of war or any sort of notice, this series of provocations and outrages, have made the whole Russian nation almost beside itself with fury.

Sunday, November 1, 1914

As Turkey has refused to sever her ties with the German powers, the Russian, French and English Ambassadors have left Constantinople.

West of the Vistula, the Russian armies are still advancing victoriously across the whole front.

Monday, November 2, 1914

The Tsar Nicholas has issued a proclamation to his people.

> *Under German command the Turkish feet has had the treacherous effrontery to attack our Black Sea coasts. We share with all the peoples of Russia the unshakable conviction that the rash intervention of Turkey will only hasten that country's downfall and open Russia's path towards the solution of the historic problem which our ancestors have bequeathed to us on the shores of the Black Sea.*

I questioned Sazonov about the meaning of this last phrase which seems to have been drawn from the Sibylline Books.

"We shall have to make Turkey pay dearly for her mistake of today," he replied. "We must have tangible guarantees on the Bosphorus. As regards Constantinople, personally I don't want the Turks to be cleared out. I'd gladly leave them the old Byzantine city with a good-sized kitchen-garden all round – but no more!"

Tuesday, November 3, 1914

Two days ago, Countess I….. sent me the following letter:

My Dear Friend,

Don't be afraid I'm going to ramble, but a strange and mysterious being has asked me to translate his thought for France and send it on to you. I warn you it's just a mass of incoherencies.

I also send the Russian original, if the enclosed scrawl can be called an "original." Perhaps you will find someone better qualified than I to seize the mystic, and perhaps prophetical meaning of this letter. It is Madame Vyrubova who has sent

> it to me with a request to translate it, for I imagine the idea has emanated from higher up.
>
> Your Friend,
>
> O.I.

Enclosed in this letter was a sheet of paper gashed with a large, uneven, heavy and uneducated handwriting, a jumble of jerks, stabs and contortions. The letters were so clumsy and misshapen that it was exceedingly difficult to make them out. But, taken as a whole, the sheet was as expressive as an etching. One could feel the trembling of the hand as it traced each word, and before one's eyes rose the vision of a being endowed with imagination and audacity, a thing of impulses and sensuality. The signature was almost easy to read: Rasputin.

Madame L.....'s translation from the Russian runs as follows:

> God grant that you may live after the manner of Russia, and not of the critics of the country, the cipher, for example. From that moment God will give you the miracle of strength. Your armies will see the strength of Heaven. Victory is with you and on you!
>
> Rasputin.

The piece of paper on which this unintelligible scrawl was written has had the top left corner torn off, the corner on which the imperial arms are stamped. Rasputin must have written this note in Tsarskoe Selo palace itself.

After somewhat anxious reflection, I dictated to Countess L….. a nebulous reply that enshrines the following notion: "The French nation, whose intuition is very quick, well knows that the Russian people embody their love of their country in the person of the Tsar." My letter ended thus: "Your Prophet may be easy in his mind. France and Russia are at one in the loftiness of their common ideal."

Wednesday, November 4, 1914

The strength of the Russian troops assigned to operations in Asia against the Turks is 160,000 men. The plan of the Russian General Staff is immediately to secure all the strategic positions that command the gateways into Azerbaidjan, and then remain on the defensive.

Countess L….. writes to me:

> *Your answer to my letter was perfect and your letter has reached august hands. I have ascertained that I had good reason to think that the order to translate came from high up.*
>
> *All good wishes.*
>
> *O.I.*

Thursday, November 5, 1914

An Anglo-French squadron has bombarded the advance forts of the Dardanelles.

In Armenia, the Russians have carried by storm the fortress of Bayazid that commands the road to Van. They began their campaigns of 1828 and 1877 in the same way.

England is annexing the Island of Cyprus, which she has occupied since 1878 in accordance with the terms of her alliance with Turkey.

In northern France and Belgium, the Germans are exhausting themselves in frantic and furious efforts to force their way through to Calais.

Friday, November 6, 1914

In the region of Warsaw, the Germans are threatened with the outflanking of their left wing and are hastening their retreat in a westerly direction.

In Galicia, the obstinate fighting that has been in progress for three weeks on the San resulted yesterday in a general and precipitate retreat by the Austrians.

Grand Duke Nicholas has asked me to forward to General Joffre the following telegram:

> *Following on our successes on the Vistula, a complete victory has just been gained by our troops. The Austrians are in disorderly flight on the whole of the Galician front. The strategic*

maneuver of which I informed you when it began has thus come to a happy conclusion, being crowned with the most important success gained by us since the beginning of the war.

Saturday, November 7, 1914

I have had a talk with the Chief of the General Staff. I asked him what would probably be the immediate effect of the rout of the Austrians on the course of the operations.

I give a summary of what I took down from General Bielaiev's dictation:

(1) In the Austrian theatre:

The Austrian army may be considered as crushed. Its debris are being mercilessly pursued into the defiles of the Carpathians. The intention of the Grand Duke is to send twelve cavalry divisions with infantry support into the upper valley of the Theiss with a view to threatening Buda-Pesth; but for the time being these troops will not proceed more than a hundred kilometers. These twelve divisions comprise 48,000 men, of which 30,000 are Cossacks. The latter include the special brigade known as the 'savage brigade' because it is recruited from the fiercest and most warlike tribes of the Caucasus. The Grand Duke anticipates that this mass of cavalry will produce a panic in Hungary;

(2) In the German theater:

The German armies are retreating all along the line, but it looks as if they will stop on the Thorn-Posen-Breslau-Neisse line where a series of fortified positions is being prepared in feverish haste. The German forces consist of seven corps, to which should perhaps be added five corps of recent formation (the five corps operating in East Prussia are not included in this number). The Russian forces comprise thirty-seven corps (not including the five corps in East Prussia). Grand Duke Nicholas's intention is to press forward on Berlin on a front of approximately 250 kilometers, resting his left on the Carpathians.

Sunday, November 8, 1914

Yesterday the Japanese captured Tsing-Tau and have taken 2,300 prisoners.

In Poland, a Russian cavalry division has advanced 250 kilometers west of Warsaw and penetrated German territory as far as Pleschen, which is 30 kilometers northwest of Kalisz.

Monday, November 9, 1914

The attack by the Turks has shaken the Russian national conscience to its depths.

Naturally, the shock and indignation have been nowhere greater than in Moscow, the sacred metropolis of orthodox nationalism. In the heady atmosphere of the Kremlin, all the romantic utopias of Slavism have suddenly been roused to life. As in the days of Aksakov, Kireievsky and Katkov, Muscovite brains have been intoxicated the last few days with the thought of Russia's divine mission on earth.

It has inspired me to re-read the poems of Tiutchev, the poet of *slavianophilstvo*, and particularly his verses called 'Russian Geography,' which had such a success in days gone by:

> *Moscow, the City of Peter and the City of Constantine, these are the three sacred capitals of the Russian Empire. But where are its frontiers on the north and the east, on the south and the west? Destiny will show us in the future. Seven inland seas and seven great rivers; from the Nile to the Neva, the Elbe to China, the Volga to the Euphrates, the Ganges to the Danube — there is the Russian Empire, and it will last throughout the centuries! The spirit has predicted this, and Daniel has prophesied it.*

It was Tiutchev, too, who wrote this famous apocalypse:

> *Soon the days will be fulfilled, the hour will sound! And in Byzantium, born again, the ancient vault of Saint Sophia will once more shelter the altar of Christ. Kneel before that altar, O Tsar of 'Russia, and rise, Tsar of all the Slavs!*

Tuesday, November 10, 1914

With his usual calm and haughty audacity, Count Witte is carrying on his campaign in favor of peace.

He is going about saying, "Lose no time in extracting us from this sorry venture. Russia will never have so favorable an opportunity again. We have just beaten the Austrians and driven back the Germans. It is the utmost we can ever do. Henceforward, our military power can only wane. We shall require months and months to bring our effectives up to strength and complete our artillery and supplies, but within three weeks the Germans, with the help of their railways, will return to attack us with new armies, superior in numbers and provided with all the munitions they require. And this time they'll finish us off. That's what the Emperor and his ministers have to realize, if they, are capable of realizing anything."

This specious talk, uttered in his slow, deliberate and contemptuous voice, is having a great effect.

I complained to Sazonov, "What makes Count Witte's intrigues particularly ill-timed and indecent," I said, "is the fact that in France and England politicians of all parties have voluntarily submitted to strict discipline in the interests of national solidarity. Look at our socialists. Not a fault to find with them. The only false note is here. And he who utters it, nay shouts it on the house-tops, is not a private individual but a former President of the Council and still one of His Majesty's Secretaries of State, a member of the Council of Empire and President of the Higher Committee of Finance! "

"You're perfectly right, I'm sorry to say. Count Witte's intrigues are not merely indecent, they're positively criminal. I've denounced them several times to the Emperor and His Majesty has been very indignant."

"But why doesn't the Emperor punish him? Why doesn't he take away his title of Secretary of State and deprive him of his seat in the Council of Empire, or at any rate of the presidency of the Finance Committee?"

"Because ... because ..." His words ended in a despairing sigh.

I continued. "But you should take action against this pacifist propaganda. It might easily become dangerous."

"I'll be seeing the Emperor over the next few days and advise him to see you so that he can tell you himself that Count Witte's babble doesn't matter a bit."

Wednesday, November 11, 1914

During the ten months of my acquaintance with Russian society, one of the phenomena that have amazed me most is the freedom, or rather the license, with which the Emperor, Empress and imperial family are discussed. In this home of autocracy, where the police, the Okhrana, the Fortress of Peter and Paul, and Siberia, are such terrible and ever-present realities, the crime of *lèse-majesté* is the habitual sin of conversation in society.

I had further proof of it to-day when I was at tea with Madame B...... She told me of several new features in Witte's peace campaign and then flamed up against the Emperor who tolerates this outrage.

"He is mortally afraid of Witte. He'll never have the courage to deal with him. He's always been the same since the beginning of his reign. He has neither courage nor will."

"Is it fair to say he has no will? I should have thought that he'd held the reins pretty tight on a good many occasions."

But Madame B..... was not to be appeased. Her eyes sparkling with intelligence and irritation, she continued her indictment with a frown.

"No, he hasn't an ounce of will. How could he expect to have, seeing that he hasn't the slightest personality? He's obstinate, but that's a very different thing. When an idea has been put in his head – he never has ideas of his own – he takes it up and clings to it simply because he hasn't the strength of mind to want any other. But what annoys me most about him is that he hasn't any courage. He's always doing underhand things. He won't enter into a frank and free discussion on a subject that is of importance to him. To avoid opposition, he invariably acquiesces in everything that is said to him, and always complies with one's requests. The moment his back is turned, he orders the opposite. Look at the way he dismisses his ministers. It is just when he's determined to get rid of them that he gives them the friendliest reception and shows them special confidence and kindness. They open their newspaper some fine morning and learn that their health obliges them to take a long rest. Have you ever heard anything more disgraceful than the dismissal of Kokovtsov at the beginning of this year? Why, I shouldn't send one of my servants away in such a humiliating fashion and without a word of explanation!"

Thursday, November 12, 1914

At the club today I had a talk with old Prince T..... and B..... (the Director of the Imperial Hunting Establishments) who were personal friends of Alexander III. In veiled terms they conveyed to me how deplorable the discredit into which the imperial family has fallen seemed to them, and how dangerous the perpetual web of intrigues around the Empress was for Russia and the dynasty. I did not conceal from them that I, too, was very uneasy about these intrigues:

"How can the Emperor tolerate a real hotbed of treason within the four walls of his own palace? How can he let his own authority be flouted in this way? Why doesn't he take strong action? He could put everything right in a moment with a word or a stroke of his pen. After all, he's the master. Of course, I know Russia has passed beyond the feudal stage, the times of Ivan the Terrible or Peter the Great, but the Tsar is still the Tsar, the autocrat that is to say, and his power is enormous."

Prince T..... broke in.

"His power is far less than you think. From a practical point of view, he is dependent upon his officials for information, or advice, or the carrying out of his orders. And he lets things slide because he has little initiative or will, and at heart is pretty much of a fatalist. It is the bureaucracy that really governs the Empire."

B..... joined in.

"With very few exceptions, it has always been the same. The Tsars have always been more or less in the hands of their *tchinovniks*. You remember Madame Svetchin's remarks: 'It's marvelous how much those who can do everything cannot do!' And she was speaking of none other than Nicholas I!"

Saturday, November 14, 1914

This morning, Buchanan told Sazonov in my presence that the British ministers had discussed at great length the new problems that had arisen in the east owing to the deeds and misdeeds of the Turkish Government. He added that Sir Edward Grey had not failed to inform them of the views of the Russian Government and the aspirations of the Russian people.

He wound up with a solemn declaration:

The Government of His Britannic Majesty have been led to recognize that the question of the Straits and Constantinople must be solved in the manner Russia desires. I am happy to inform you accordingly.

After a moment's surprise, Sazonov's face lit up with delight, but, overcoming his emotions, he replied with calm dignity.

"Monsieur l'Ambassadeur, I accept your intimation with heartfelt gratitude. Russia will never forget the proof of friendship that England has given her today. Never!"

Then they shook hands and warmly congratulated one another.

Sunday, November 15, 1914

In Poland, the operations of the Russian army are developing successfully (1) between the Vistula and the Warta, in and around Leczyca; (2) in South-western Poland, between Czestochova and Cracow.

In Galicia, the Russians are still making progress across the Carpathians.

In East Prussia, they are approaching the Gumbinnen-Angerburg front, where the German line is strongly fortified.

General de Laguiche, who has just been round the Russian army fronts in Poland, has been telling me of the enormous difficulties of their advance in the region from which the enemy has just retired. All the railways and roads have been systematically destroyed. Not a station, not a bridge is left. In many places a series of trenches has been cut across the roads for several versts. The troops are displaying amazing energy in the repair of the roads, such is their impatience to get on. The men are in fine fettle. There are few sick, but thousands of horses have had to be replaced. The units that have suffered the most are those that were engaged in operations in Galicia and have had to be sent north. Five army corps, forming a single column, spent four days in passing through forests so marshy that the trees on either side of the one available road had to be cut down to fill up the holes.

After describing the retreat of the Germans in a westerly direction, General de Laguiche concluded with his usual wisdom. "The enemy's retreat is voluntary, without letting himself be held and without being touched in his vitals. This enemy may therefore appear again. What is the motive behind this retreat? It is a question we should put to ourselves if we are to be prepared against surprise and not to be embarrassed in the execution of our own plans. We are witnessing successes that are well calculated to give us every satisfaction, but the task before us is one and indivisible, for there will be no victory until the enemy's armies have ceased to exist."

Wednesday, November 18, 1914

Buchanan told Sazonov this morning that the British Government finds itself compelled to annex Egypt. It hopes that the Russian Government will offer no objection. Sazonov hastened to express his approval.

Four days ago England abandoned Constantinople to Russia. Today Russia has abandoned Egypt to England. Thus is fulfilled, after an interval of sixty-one years, the program that Tsar Nicholas I laid before Sir Hamilton Seymour, the British Ambassador, in January 1853, a program that was the origin of the Crimean War.

Thursday, November 19, 1914

Between the Vistula and the Warta, about 100 kilometers from Warsaw, the Germans are engaged in a violent offensive to hold up the Russian advance on Silesia. Near Kutno, the Russians seem to have suffered a reverse that is said to have cost them 30,000 men.

A great battle is about to begin further south, in the region of Lodz.

The Grand Master of the Ceremonies has informed me that the Emperor desires to see me and will receive me the day after tomorrow, Saturday, at Tsarskoe Selo.

Friday, November 20, 1914

The new Bulgarian Minister, Madjarov, presented his credentials to His Majesty this afternoon.

After declaring his friendly feelings for the Bulgarian nation, the Emperor spoke to him in a warning tone.

"I must not hide from you that the attitude of your Government towards Serbia is making a very painful impression upon me and that all my people feel it as much as I myself. If your Government takes advantage of the present situation to attack Serbia as sovereign of the greatest of the Slav States, I shall solemnly proclaim that Bulgaria has forfeited her place in the Slav family."

Saturday, November 21, 1914

This morning Sazonov said to me, "The Emperor will receive you at four o'clock. Officially he has nothing to say, but he wants to talk to you frankly and without restraint. I warn you your audience will be a long one."

At three o'clock, I left in a special train for Tsarskoe Selo. Snow was falling heavily. Under the wan light from the sky, the great plain in which Petrograd is set lay pale, misty and drab. It made me feel gloomy, with its reminder of the plains of Poland, where, at this very moment, thousands of men are dying and thousands others suffer the tortures of wounds.

Although my audience was a private one, I had to put on my full dress uniform, as is fitting for a meeting with the Tsar, Autocrat of all the Russias. The Director of Ceremonies, Evreinov, went with me. He also was a symphony of gold braid.

From Tsarskoe Selo station to the Alexander Palace is a short distance, less than a verst. In the open space before one reaches the park, a little church, medieval in style, raises its pretty cupola above the snow. It is the Feodorovsky Sobor, one of the Empress's favorite resorts for private devotion.

The Alexander Palace showed me its most intimate side, for ceremonial was reduced to a minimum. My escort consisted only of Evreinov, a household officer in informal uniform, and a footman in his picturesque (Tsaritsa Elizabeth) dress with the hat adorned with long red, black and yellow plumes.

I was taken through the audience rooms, then the Empress's private drawing-room, down a long corridor leading to the private apartments of the sovereigns in which I passed a servant in very plain livery who was carrying a tea tray. Further on was the foot of a little private staircase leading to the rooms of the imperial children. A lady's maid flitted away from the landing above. The last room at the end of the corridor is occupied by Prince Mestschersky, personal aide-de-camp. I waited there barely a minute. The gaily and weirdly bedecked Ethiopian who mounted guard outside His Majesty's study opened the door almost at once.

The Emperor received me with that gracious and somewhat shy kindness that is all his own.

The room in which he received me is small and has only one window. The furniture is plain and comfortable. There are plain leather chairs, a sofa covered with a Persian rug, a bureau and shelves arranged with meticulous care, a table spread with maps, and a low book case with photographs, busts and family souvenirs on the top shelf.

As usual the Emperor hesitated over his preliminary remarks, which are kind personal enquiries and attentions, but soon he became more at his ease:

"Let's make ourselves at home and be comfortable first, as I shall keep you some time. Have this chair. We'll put this little table between us. That's better. Here are the cigarettes – Turkish. I've no business to smoke them as they were given to me by a fresh enemy, the Sultan, but they're extremely nice, and, anyhow, I haven't any others. Let me have my maps. And now we can talk."

He lit his cigarette, offered me a light, and went straight to the heart of the subject:

"Great things have happened in the three months since I saw you last. The splendid French army and my dear army have already given such proof of valor that victory can't fail us now. Don't think I'm under any illusion as to the trials and sacrifices the war still has in store for us, but so far we have a right – and even a duty – to consider together what we should have to do if Austria or Germany sued for peace. You must observe that it would unquestionably be in Germany's interest to treat for peace while her military power is still formidable. But isn't Austria very exhausted already? Well, what should we do if Germany or Austria asked for peace?"

"The first question," I said, "is to consider whether peace can be negotiated if we are not forced to dictate it to our enemies. However moderate we may b,e we shall obviously have to insist on guarantees and reparations from the Central Powers, demands they will not accept before they are at our mercy."

"That's my own view. We must dictate the peace, and I am determined to continue the war until the Central Powers are destroyed. But I regard it as essential that the terms of the peace should be discussed by us three – France, England and Russia – and by us three alone. No Congress or mediation for me! So when the time comes, we shall impose our will upon Germany and Austria."

"What is your general idea of the terms of peace, Sire?"

After a moment's consideration the Emperor resumed.

"What we must keep before us as our first object is the destruction of German militarism, the end of the nightmare from which Germany has made us suffer for more than forty years. We must make it impossible for the German people even to think of revenge. If we let ourselves be swayed by sentiment, there will be a fresh war within a very short time. As for the precise terms of peace, I must tell you at once that I accept here and now any conditions France and England think it their duty to put forward in their own interests."

"I thank Your Majesty for that intimation. I am certain that the Government of the Republic in turn will meet the wishes of the imperial Government in the most sympathetic spirit."

"What you say encourages me to tell you all I think, but I'm only giving you my own view as I don't like to open questions of this kind without consulting my ministers and generals." He drew his chair close to mine, spread a map of Europe on the table between us, lit another cigarette, and continued in an even more intimate and familiar tone. "This is more or less my view of the results Russia is entitled to expect from the war, results failing which my people will not understand the sacrifices I have require of them. In East Prussia, Germany must accept a rectification of the frontier. My General Staff would like this rectification to be extended to the mouths of the Vistula. That seems to me excessive. I'll look into the question. Posen and possibly a portion of Silesia will be indispensable to the reconstitution of Poland. Galicia and the western half of the Bukovina will enable Russia to obtain her natural frontier, the Carpathians. In Asia Minor, I shall have to consider the question of the Armenians of course. I certainly could not let them return to the Turkish yoke. Ought I to annex Armenia? I shall only do so if the Armenians expressly ask me to, otherwise I shall establish an autonomous regime for them. Lastly, I shall be compelled to secure my Empire a free passage through the Straits."

As he stopped at these words I pressed him to enlighten me further.

He continued. "I am far from having made up my mind. The matter is of such grave importance. But there are two conclusions to which I am always being brought back. First, that the Turks must be expelled from Europe. Secondly, that Constantinople must in future be neutral, with an international regime. I need hardly say that the Mohammedans should receive all necessary guarantees that sanctuaries and tombs will be respected. Western Thrace to the Enos-Midia line should be given to Bulgaria. The rest, from that line to the shores of the Straits, but excluding the environs of Constantinople, would be assigned to Russia."

"So, if I have understood you correctly, the Turks will be confined to Asia, as in the days of the first Osmanlis, and have Angora or Koniah for their capital. The Bosphorus, the Sea of Marmora, and the Dardanelles will thus form the western frontier of Turkey."

"Exactly."

"Your Majesty will forgive me for interrupting again to remind you that in Syria and Palestine France has a precious heritage of historical memories, and moral and material interests. May I assume that Your Majesty would acquiesce in any measures the Government of the Republic might think fit to take to safeguard that inheritance?"

"Certainly."

Then he spread out a map of the Balkans and indicated broadly his view of the territorial changes we should desire.

"Serbia should annex Bosnia, Herzegovina, Dalmatia and Northern Albania. Greece should have southern Albania with the exception of Valona, which must be assigned to Italy. If Bulgaria behaves properly, she should receive compensation in Macedonia from Serbia." He carefully folded up the map of the Balkans and as carefully returned it to its exact place on his table. Then, crossing his arms and leaning back in his chair, he fixed his eyes on the ceiling and asked in a dreamy voice, "What about Austria-Hungary? What's to become of her? "

"If the victories of your armies develop beyond the Carpathians, and Italy and Rumania enter the field, Austria-Hungary will hardly survive the territorial sacrifices Emperor Franz Joseph will be obliged to accept. When the Austro-Hungarian partnership has gone bankrupt, I imagine the partners won't wish to go on working together, at any rate on the same terms."

"I think so too. When Hungary loses Transylvania, she'll have some difficulty in keeping the Croats under her sway. Bohemia will demand its autonomy at the least, and Austria will thus find herself reduced to her ancient hereditary states – the German Tyrol and the district of Salzburg." Hereupon he lapsed into silence for a moment, his brows contracted and his eyes half-closed as if he were repeating to himself what he was about to tell me. Then he cast a glance at the portrait of his father on the wall behind me and continued. "But it is primarily in Germany that the great changes will take place. As I have said, Russia will annex the former Polish territories and part of East Prussia. France will certainly recover Alsace-Lorraine and possibly obtain the Rhine Provinces as well. Belgium should receive a substantial addition of territory in the region of Aix-la-Chapelle. She thoroughly deserves it! As for the German Colonies, France and England will divide them as they think fit. Further, I should like Schleswig, including the Kiel Canal zone, to be restored to Denmark. And Hanover? Wouldn't it be wise to revive Hanover? By setting up a small independent state between Prussia and Holland, we should do much towards putting the future peace on a solid basis. After all, it is that which must guide our deliberations and actions. Our work cannot be justified before God and History unless it is inspired by a great moral idea and the determination to secure the peace of the world for a very long time to come."

As he uttered these last words, he sat up in his chair and his voice quivered a little under the influence of a solemn religious emotion. In his eyes shone a strange light. His conscience and his faith were visibly at work. But neither in his attitude nor his expression was there a suggestion of pose. Nothing but perfect simplicity.

"Doesn't it mean the end of the German Empire?" I said.

He replied in firm tones. "Germany can adopt any organization she likes, but the imperial power cannot be allowed to remain with the House of Hohenzollern. Prussia must return to the status of a kingdom only. Isn't that your opinion also, Ambassador?"

"The German Empire, as conceived, founded and governed by the Hohenzollerns, is so obviously directed against the French nation that I shall certainly not attempt its defense. France would have a great guarantee if all the powers of the German world ceased to be in the hands of Prussia."

Our talk had already lasted more than an hour. After a few moments of reflection the Emperor remarked, as if he had suddenly remembered something, "We mustn't think merely of the immediate results of the war. We must consider the remoter future, too. I attach the very greatest importance to the maintenance of our alliance. The work we have set out to do, and which has already cost us such efforts and sacrifices, will be permanent only if we remain united. As we know, we are striving for the peace of the world, and it is essential that our work should be permanent."

As he delivered himself of this finale, an obvious and necessary finale, to our conversation, I could see in his eyes the same strange, mystic light I had observed a few minutes earlier. His ancestor, Alexander I, must have worn this fervent and inspired expression when he preached to Metternich and Hardenberg about the Holy Alliance of kings against peoples. Yet, in Madame von Krüdener's friend, there was a certain theatrical affectation, a kind of romantic exaltation. Nicholas II, on the other hand, is sincerity itself. He endeavors to contain rather than give rein to his feelings, to conceal rather than to deploy his emotions.

The Emperor rose, offered me another cigarette, and remarked in the most casual and friendly way, "What glorious memories we shall share, my dear Ambassador! Do you remember ...?" He proceeded to remind me of the days immediately preceding the war, that harassing week from July 25 to August 2. He recounted even the most trivial details and laid particular emphasis on the personal telegrams that had passed between the Emperor William and himself. "He was never sincere, not for a moment. In the end he was hopelessly entangled in the net of his own perfidy and lies. Have you ever been able to account for the telegram he sent me six hours after giving me his declaration of war? It's utterly impossible to explain what happened. I don't remember if I've ever told you. It was half-past one in the morning of August 2. I had just received your English colleague who had brought me a telegram from King George begging me to do everything possible to save peace. I had drafted, with Sir George Buchanan's help, the telegram with which you are familiar, which ended with an appeal for England's help in arms as the war was forced on us by Germany. The moment Buchanan had left, I went to the Empress's room, as she was already in bed, to show her King George's telegram and to have a cup of tea with her before retiring myself. I stayed with her until two in the morning. Then I wanted to have a bath, as I was very tired. I was just getting in, when my servant knocked at the door, saying he had a telegram for me. 'A very important telegram, very important indeed. A telegram from His Majesty Emperor Wilhelm.' I read the telegram, read it again, and then repeated it aloud, but I couldn't understand a word of it. *What on earth does Wilhelm mean?* I thought, pretending that it still depended on me as to whether war was averted or not. *He implores me not to let my troops cross the frontier? Have I suddenly gone mad? Didn't the Minister of the Court, my trusted Fredericks, at least six hours ago bring me the declaration of war the German Ambassador had just handed to Sazonov?* I returned to the Empress's room and read her Wilhelm's telegram. She had to read it herself to bring herself to believe it. She said to me immediately, 'You're not going to answer it, are you?' 'Certainly not,' I replied. There's no doubt that the object of this strange and farcical telegram was to shake my resolution, to disconcert me, and to inspire me to some absurd and dishonorable step. It produced the opposite effect in me. As I left the Empress's room, I felt that all was over forever between me and Wilhelm. I slept extremely well. When I awoke at my usual hour, I felt as if a weight had fallen from mind. My responsibility to God and to my people was still enormous, but at least I knew what I had to do."

"I think, Sire, I could give a somewhat different explanation of Emperor Wilhelm's telegram."

"Really? Let me have it."

"Emperor Wilhelm is not a man of courage."

"He is not."

"He's a comedian and a braggart. He never dares to go right through with what he undertakes. He has often reminded me of an actor playing the murderer in melodrama who suddenly finds that his weapon is loaded and that he's really going to kill his victim. How often have we not seen him frightened by his own pantomime? When he ventured on his famous Tangier pronouncement in 1905, he stopped quite suddenly in the middle of his scenario. I am inclined to think that the moment he had issued his declaration of war, he got frightened. He realized the formidable results of his action and wanted to throw all the responsibility onto you. Perhaps, too, he clung to some fantastic hope of producing, by his telegram, some unexpected, inconceivable, miraculous event that would enable him to escape the consequences of his crime."

"Well, your explanation is quite in keeping with Wilhelm's character." The clock struck six. "My word, it's late!" the Emperor said. "I'm afraid I've wearied you, but I'm glad to have had an opportunity of talking freely to you."

As he led me to the door, I asked him about the fighting in Poland.

"It's a great battle," he said, "and raging with the greatest fury. The Germans are making frantic efforts to break our line. They won't succeed and they can't remain long in their present positions, so I hope that before long we shall resume our advance."

"General de Laguiche wrote to me recently that Grand Duke Nicholas still keeps a march on Berlin as his one and only objective."

"Yes, I don't yet know where we shall be able to break through – between the Carpathians and the Oder, perhaps, or between Breslau and Posen. Or north of Posen. It depends a good deal on the fighting now in progress around Lodz and in the neighborhood of Cracow. But Berlin is certainly our sole objective. The fighting is equally violent on your side. This furious Yser battle is going in your favor. Your marines have covered themselves with glory. It's a serious reverse for the Germans, nearly as serious as their defeat on the Marne. Well, goodbye, my dear Ambassador! Once more, I'm very glad to have been able to talk so freely with you! "

Tuesday, November 24, 1914

The Russians are keeping the upper hand in the furious struggle raging west of Warsaw, and particularly between Lodz and Lowicz, but the issue of the battle is not yet determined.

Grand Duchess Marie Pavlovna asked me to dinner this evening. Besides herself, only her ladies-in-waiting and particular cronies were present. She was very anxious to know what the Emperor said to me during my last audience. I told her only as much as is good for her to know and pass on. For instance, I told her that the Emperor had vigorously confirmed his determination to continue the war until German power was utterly overthrown.

"He has also given me to understand that he cannot allow the imperial power to remain with the House of Hohenzollern."

"Splendid! Splendid!" The Mecklenburger in her came out, and once more I could see all the ancient and jealous animosity of the little German courts towards arrogant Prussia. Her eyes sparkling with rage, she continued. "We've had quite enough of the Hohenzollerns. Quite enough! They've been the curse of Germany. Munich, Stuttgart, Dresden, Darmstadt, Schwerin, Weimar, Meiningen, Coburg – none of them wants them anymore. It's only perhaps in Baden that there is some slight attachment to them because they're really the same family."

We talked about Empress Alexandra Feodorovna.

"I noticed," I said, "that the Emperor mentioned her name several times during our conversation."

"That doesn't surprise me. He tells her everything, takes her opinion on everything. You may be certain that the moment you were out of his room he went and told her of the conversation."

"What are the Empress's present feelings towards Germany?"

"I expect I'll surprise you. She's fervently anti-German. She denies the Germans all honor, conscience or humanity.

Only the other day she said to me, 'They've lost the moral sense and all Christian feeling!' "

Wednesday, November 25, 1914

Petrograd is delighted. It is said, with a wealth of detail, that the Germans have been totally defeated between Lodz and Lowicz, and their troops are making a supreme effort to escape being surrounded. General Bielaiev, Chief of Staff, has told Sazonov that two or three German corps are surrounded already.

Thursday, November 26, 1914

Sazonov is delirious with joy.
"Our victory at Lodz is splendid, complete, and far more important than all our successes in Galicia. We're waiting for the fruits of our victory to be harvested before making it public."
From the Foreign Office I went to the General Staff building, which is opposite it on the other side of Winter Palace Square, where General Bielaiev confirmed what Sazonov has told me.
"We've won a victory, a great victory. But between Brzeziny and Strykov, the Germans are still making desperate efforts to cut their way through north. That is why in our communiqué we have confined ourselves to saying that the advantage is with our troops and the Germans are finding it very difficult to secure their retreat. Their losses, too, are

enormous, and three of their corps are almost completely surrounded. I've been working all night to arrange transport for 150,000 prisoners. Personally I build great hopes on the results of this victory."

In the city, the public delight is to be read on every face. Out of curiosity I stopped my car at the façade of Our Lady of Kazan. The faithful were simply streaming into the great national sanctuary which is one mass of gold and precious stones. The candle-sellers at the doors cannot meet the demand, and before the Sacred Portal the crowds throng impatiently to kiss the miraculous icon of the Virgin.

Friday, November 77, 1914

This morning Sazonov's face was not so radiant as yesterday. When I asked him certain details about the battle of Lodz, he was inclined to evade my questions.

"It's a victory for us," he said, "patently a victory. But we don't know the exact results yet. Besides, the battle is still continuing."

"What about the three German corps being surrounded?"

"I know nothing."

"Couldn't you telephone General Bielaiev?"

"I've just done so. He knows nothing either, except that in southern Poland the Austrian army, which is defending the approaches to Cracow, was driven back yesterday."

Saturday, November 28, 1914

The German corps, which were half-surrounded near Lodz, have succeeded in escaping at the cost of appalling losses. The Russian plan failed at the last moment through the fault of General Rennenkampf, who was lacking in vision and quickness of movement.

The general staff has published a communiqué in the following terms:

> *The rumors in circulation as to the magnitude of our victory between the Fistula and the Wartha originate in private correspondence, and must be accepted with reserve. There is no doubt that the German plan of surrounding the Russian army on the left bank of the Fistula has completely failed. The Germans have had to retreat in unfavorable conditions and suffering huge losses. The battle is developing in our favor, but the enemy continues his stubborn resistance.*

The public is grievously disappointed.

Sunday, November 29, 1914

Public opinion in Russia is certainly too nervy and imaginative – not practical enough. It is very natural that the public should be dissatisfied, or even irritated, at being misled about the results of the battle of Lodz, but in its disappointment it forgets that if the Germans have escaped a complete disaster, they have nonetheless suffered a heavy reverse. Everywhere I find nothing but pessimism and expressions of war-weariness or disillusionment.

What would it be if the Germans had won?

Monday, November 30, 1914

I am getting information from every quarter that Count Witte is tirelessly carrying on his campaign in favor of peace.

I had this confirmed this evening by Countess K....., with whom I and a few close friends were dining. She does not share Witte's opinions, but she often has occasion to see him and is also well informed as to what is going on behind the scenes at the palace.

"Witte's influence is very great at the moment," she told me. "His pronouncements are making a great impression. At Princess P.....'s yesterday he spent more than an hour arguing that we ought to make peace at once, otherwise he is certain that we are on the way to defeat and revolution. I have never seen him so pessimistic."

"Where do France and England come in in his argument? After all, it was not Russia who came to their assistance, but they who came to the assistance of Russia."

"That's exactly the reply he got, that we had no right to abandon our Allies. His answer was, 'But it is as much to France and England's interest not to persist in this stupid venture as it is to ours!' "

I expressed my astonishment that such things could be said with impunity by a member of the Council of Empire, one of His Majesty's Secretaries of State.

"It would be so easy to silence him!" I said.

"They daren't silence him."

And she told me that the Emperor hates Witte but is very much afraid of him, afraid of his intellect, his arrogance, his pointed, acid remarks, his epigrams and his intrigues. Besides, they have more than one secret between them, the revelation of which would be very awkward for Their Majesties.

"You know," she went on, "that when Witte was President of the Council and Minister of Finance, he was very much mixed up in the affairs of the famous Philippe, Rasputin's predecessor. You may remember, too, that the Emperor asked President Loubet to grant the magician the degree of doctor of medicine, and that Monsieur Loubet naturally evaded that absurd request. But Philippe was absolutely determined to be a Doctor of Medicine, and gave the Emperor no rest. Then Witte applied to the War Minister, General Kuropatkin, to have Philippe appointed medical officer on the Reserve, and he was also authorized to wear the uniform of a civil general!"

As the name of Philippe has thus cropped up, I will give a few details of his biography as I did earlier for Rasputin.

In February 1903, the Chief of the Russian Police abroad, Ratchkovsky, whose assistance had often been profitably utilized in the minor affairs of the Alliance, asked for an audience with Delcassé and expressed a desire for confidential information about the antecedents of the magician Philippe, a native of Lyons, who had been cutting a ridiculous figure at the Russian court for more than a year. "I'm afraid," he said, "that the eccentricities of this charlatan will end in some frightful scandal. The German party would certainly use him as a tool against the Alliance."

Delcassé put the matter in my hands. I give a summary of the information I obtained at once from the police.

Philppe Nizier-Vachod was born on April 25, 1849 at Loisieux in Savoy. His relatives were humble farmers. At thirteen, he came to live in Lyons with one of his uncles, who employed him in his butcher's business at la Croix-Rousse. The boy already revealed curious tastes, such as a love of solitude, a hankering after the mysterious, and a strong inclination for sorcerers, fortune-tellers, mesmerists and somnambulists. He soon tried his hand at occult medicine and succeeded straightaway.

In 1872, he left his uncle's butcher's shop and opened a consulting room at No. 4, Boulevard du Nord, where he treated his patients with psychic fluids and astral forces. Of medium height and heavily built, child-like in manner, and simple in his ways, with his gentle voice, high forehead under thick, dark hair, and limpid, fascinating and penetrating eyes, he had an amazing fund of sympathy and magnetism that seems to have powerfully affected everyone with whom he came into contact.

In September 1877, he married Jeanne Landar, one of his patients, whom he had cured. By her he soon had a daughter.

In 1887, the doctors of Lyons denounced him for the illegal practice of their profession. He was convicted and fined, but as always happens in such cases, his conviction increased his reputation. In 1890 and 1892 he again appeared before the courts and was fined on each occasion, but at each of these trials all the evidence had been favorable to the accused. All the witnesses, including those the magician had failed to cure, had emphasized his kindness, pity and unselfishness, the soothing and strengthening power of his presence, and the gentle balm that flowed from his slightest movement.

With a view to keeping on the right side of the law in future, Philippe employed a Polish physician named Steintzky, who possessed a genuine degree and countersigned his prescriptions. A few years later he took as his assistant a young French doctor, Lalande, who shortly after became his son-in-law.

Thereafter his consulting room, transferred to No. 35, Rue de la Tête-d'Or, was never empty. Artisans, shopkeepers, concierges and cooks always formed the backbone of his clientele, but after 1896 they were joined by society people, well-dressed women, magistrates, actresses, officers and priests. The woman who had kept the tobacco shop opposite and informed the police, said that she was amazed at the society folk she saw going in and out. One day she noticed a Russian prince, a tall, thin man whose name she had forgotten, and who had called several times with two fine ladies. Philippe's cook had also shown her, with great pride, a letter with large seals, bearing the Russian arms. The whole quarter had been talking about it.

Sometime before this letter arrived, two Russian ladies, Madame S….. and Madame P….., who were passing through Lyons, called to consult Philippe. They were astounded at his gift of divination and supernatural authority, so they gave him no rest until he agreed to accompany them to Cannes, where they introduced him to Grand Duke Peter Nicolaievitch, his wife Grand Duchess Militza, and her sister Princess Anastasia Romanovsky, Duchess Leuchtenberg, who subsequently married Grand Duke Nicholas as her second husband in 1907.

The information gathered by the police stopped there. Later on we shall see what happened afterwards.

How did the magician of Lyons get in touch with the Tsar and Tsaritsa? Manuilov, who was the intermediary, told me quite recently.

The meeting took place in September 1901, during the visit of the Russian sovereigns to France. At that time, Manuilov was in Paris, employed on a mission for the Okhrana and under the orders of the famous Ratchkovsky. Grand Duchess Militza had informed Philippe that the Emperor and Empress would be glad to have a talk with him at Compiègne. He arrived there on September 20. Manuilov was instructed to receive him at the doors of the palace and question him before conducting him to the imperial apartments.

"I had before me," he told me, "a heavily-built fellow with a big moustache. He was dressed in black and looked quiet and grave, rather like a schoolmaster in his Sunday best. His clothes were absolutely ordinary, but spotlessly clean. There was nothing remarkable about him except his eyes, blue eyes half-hidden by heavy eyelids, but every now and then a curious, soft light shone in them. Around his neck hung a small, black silk triangular bag. I asked him what it was. He offered mysterious excuses for his inability to answer me. When I saw him afterwards, this amulet was still on his breast. One evening I was in a railway carriage alone with him and he was asleep and snoring like a trooper. I tried to take off his talisman to see what was inside, but I'd no sooner touched him than he woke with a start."

From the first audience, Philippe hypnotized the sovereigns, who induced him on the spot to make his home in Russia. He went there almost at once. A house was got ready for him at Tsarskoe Selo.

He immediately won the full confidence of his imperial hosts, who highly appreciated his quiet manner and extreme discretion, as well as his attainments in magic. Once or twice a week he carried out experiments in hypnotism, prophecy, incarnation and necromancy in their presence. The Tsar's weak will was greatly fortified by these nocturnal séances. Innumerable decisions were communicated to him by the ghost of his father, Alexander III. In all questions of health, Philippe's advice was accepted implicitly.

Among the confidences exchanged between the imperial couple and Philippe was a matter between the three of them, a secret of the most intimate nature, but both a state and palace secret. The Tsaritsa was married on November 26, 1894, and had given birth to four daughters, the youngest of whom, Anastasia, was born on June 18, 1901. The Tsar, the Tsaritsa and the Russian nation were anxiously awaiting the appearance of a Tsarevitch. As all the mysteries of nature were an open book to Philippe he claimed that he could not only prognosticate the sex of unborn children but actually determine it. By combining the most transcendental practices of hermetic medicine, astronomy and psychurgy, the magician undertook to direct at will the evolution of the embryonic phenomena. A complicated method!

In the spring of 1902, Alexandra Feodorovna was expecting another child. She had no doubt that this time it would be a son. The Emperor was no less certain. Philippe encouraged them in their belief. But, on September 1, the Empress had a sudden pain and before any help could be given she saw all her hopes dashed to the ground.

It was a nasty blow to Philippe's reputation. An attempt was made to spread a rumor that the Empress had never really been pregnant and that the physiological disorders observed were entirely explained by her state of nerves, but the real facts soon came out and at court there was a loud outcry against the magician of Lyons.

Notwithstanding all this, the Emperor and Empress retained their loyal confidence in him, calmly accepted his explanation, and lost nothing of their belief in his magical powers.

Yet they did not disregard the secret warnings that reached them from religious circles. The Empress's confessor, Monsignor Theophanes, of whom they were exceedingly fond, succeeded in forcing them to grave reflections. Had not their faith in the occult arts carried them beyond the permitted limits? Was not the disappointment they had just suffered a warning from God?

They felt impelled to perform some solemn act of Christian devotion and humility.

For some considerable time, the Holy Synod had been leisurely considering the canonization of an obscure monk, the blessed Seraphin, who had died in the odor of sanctity in the monastery of Sarov, near Tambov, somewhere around 1820. No one was interested in the matter, and it dragged on through endless enquiries and adjournments. Also, the promoters of the canonization were faced with a formidable obstacle: the corpse of the ascetic had passed through all the normal stages of necrosis and putrefaction. Now, the Orthodox Church holds that the incorruptibility of the human corpse is an essential mark of sanctity.

However that may be, the Tsar and Tsaritsa suddenly intervened most enthusiastically for the canonization of the holy man. In his capacity as supreme guardian of the Church, Nicholas II furnished himself with a detailed account of the enquiry and ordered that there should be no further delay in bringing it to a conclusion. Henceforth the matter became an obsession with the sovereigns, and they held continual conferences with the metropolitans of St. Petersburg, Kiev and Moscow, the Procurator of the Holy Synod, the Bishop of

Tambov and the Abbot of Sarov. But what pleased them more than anything was the fact that their dear Philippe, who combined his attainments in magic with a childlike and generous piety, thoroughly approved their zealous endeavor.

It was all that was needed to disturb the slumbers of the Holy Synod, which immediately discovered in the life of the hermit Seraphin an unsuspected wealth of virtues, merits and miracles. As if by enchantment, all difficulties vanished, procrastination ceased, and objections were overruled.

On January 24, 1903, the Metropolitan of Moscow submitted to the Emperor a report recommending: (1) the admission of the Blessed Seraphin to the catalogue of saints; (2) the exhibition of his mortal remains as relics; (3) the preparation of a special service in his honor. The Tsar wrote at the foot of the report, "Read with a feeling of joy indescribable and the deepest emotion." The canonization decree received the imperial assent and was issued on February 11.

All that remained was to celebrate the pontifical ceremonies that definitively mark the elevation of a holy man to the rank of a saint, and the Emperor decided that they should be distinguished by unusual pomp. He would be present in person with the Empress and the whole imperial family.

The preparations took several months and the ceremonies began on July 30. For a whole week, Sarov had been the lodestar of all the higher clergy of the Empire, thousands of priests, monks and nuns, a crowd of officials and officers, not to mention a motley and gaping mob of one hundred thousand pilgrims. Their Majesties arrived in the evening and were received with the sound of anthems and the din of Church bells. A storm of cheering accompanied them. The whole night was taken up with the nocturnal mass for the dead.

The next day, July 31, began with morning mass and the sacrament. Their Majesties participated at the sacred table. In the afternoon there was another memorial service for the eternal repose of the soul which was to be glorified. In the evening, the remains of Seraphin were taken in procession through the churches and the monastery. The Emperor helped to carry the bier. About midnight, the precious relics were uncovered and exhibited for the first time for the veneration of the faithful. Then prayers, litanies and psalms followed each other uninterruptedly till morning.

On August 1, Monsignor Anthony, Metropolitan of St. Petersburg and President of the Holy Synod, celebrated the pontifical high mass for the canonization. It lasted nearly four hours. Towards evening, Seraphin's reliquary was again carried in procession through the town and the monastery. Sermons, eulogies, the chanting of hallelujahs and a whole series of minor services took up the following day. On August 3, by way of finale to these endless devotions, a church that had been recently built was consecrated to the new saint.

A year later, on July 30, 1904, the Empress gave birth to the present heir to the throne, the Tsarevitch Alexis, but by then Philippe had already lost imperial favor.

The mishap of September 1, 1902, had been strongly exploited against him, and foreseeing the decline of his fortunes, many of his partisans had hastened to disown him. Some went so far as to say that he had the evil eye, and even that he had the mark of the Antichrist upon him. Moreover, the prolonged intimacy between this foreigner and the sovereigns began to outrage national feeling. Puritan circles in Moscow were furious that the Emperor should allow his palace to be profaned by the black magic of this heretical charlatan. And again, although the magician professed to live in the non-material world and ignore the exigencies of politics, he had been more or less consciously a tool in many intrigues. Thus he had gradually become the object of implacable hatred.

In the spring of 1903 attacks upon him increased. From Paris, the Police Chief, Ratchkovsky supplied their authors with arguments. Armed with information he had obtained from the French police, he even sent a report directly to the Emperor, calling his attention to Philippe's three convictions.

Just at this time, the magician happened to have gone to Lyons on some family business and Ratchkovsky utilized his absence to affect the Tsar's mind still more adversely against him in the hope of preventing his return. But Philippe got wind of the plot against him and on April 19, 1903, he telegraphed to Grand Duke Nicholas, imploring him to see the Emperor at once on his behalf.

A fortnight had not passed before Ratchkovsky, a most important official in the imperial administration and the guardian of so many secrets, was dismissed out of hand. No compensation was given or promised him. He found himself, without means, on the streets of Paris.

Towards the end of 1903, however, diplomatic relations between Russia and Japan become more strained every day. War was patently on its way.

A rightful understanding of the drama about to be played out in the Far East was well beyond the intellect of the ex-butcher boy, yet he was bold enough to prophesy a swift and brilliant victory. He even indicated publicly the Commander-in-Chief, a Grand Duke, whom his intuitive genius told him the Tsar must select.

The Emperor is very jealous of his authority and at once realized that a court cabal was using the magician to influence him in the exercise of his sovereign powers. He immediately dismissed Philippe on some vague excuse, whilst loading him with flowers and gifts.

The magician sorrowfully turned his steps homewards. After the grandeur and luxury of Tsarskoe Selo, the Tête d'Or and its neighborhood seemed horribly vulgar. In returning to his dull consulting room and resuming relations with his lowly clientele of days gone by, he tasted all the bitterness of human misfortune. He soon became morose and harassed, imagining himself surrounded by enemies, watched by the police, and persecuted by mysterious and powerful persons. Then he lost his daughter, Madame Lalande, whom he dearly loved. Stricken with grief, he retired to his country place at Arbresle, where he died after a short illness on August 2, 1905.

Chapter 7

Tuesday, December 1, 1914

Hardly has Russian authority been established in Galicia than the officials introduce the worst practices of Russification as a sort of gift of welcome.

When entering Galician territory two months ago, Grand Duke Nicholas issued a proclamation couched in generous terms:

> *To you, the peoples of Austria and Hungary, Russia brings freedom and the realization of your national dreams. She desires that each of you may henceforth grow and prosper, retaining the precious heritage of its language and its religion.*

Of this fine program already nothing is left. Russian nationalism stalks triumphant throughout Galicia.

The administrative authority is concentrated in the hands of a governor-general, Count Vladimir Alexeievitch Bobrinsky. I know him well. He's an intelligent, honest and agreeable man, but perhaps the most reactionary of all the nationalists. The basis of his creed is hatred of the Uniat religion. Now, the Uniat Church has no less than 3,750,000 adherents in Galicia out of a total population of five million inhabitants.

Bobrinsky is in the habit of saying, "I recognize only three religions in Eastern Europe: the Orthodox, the Catholic and the Jewish. The Uniats are traitors to orthodoxy, renegades and apostates. We must bring them back into the true path by force."

Persecution began at once: The arrest of the Uniat Metropolitan, Monsignor Szeptycki; the expulsion of Basilian monks; the confiscation of ecclesiastical property; the destruction of Ruthene missals; the replacement of Uniat priests by Russian priests; the carrying off Ruthene children to Kiev or Kharkov to be brought up in the orthodox faith – such is the account for these last two months on the religious side. On the political side, we must add the suppression of all Ruthene papers, the closing of the University and the schools, the dismissal of all Galician officials and their replacement by a horde of Russian bureaucrats.

I spoke officially to Sazonov about this situation which prejudices the future of Russian influence in these Galician districts in which the Hapsburgs have made themselves very popular.

"I'll admit," he said, "that Bobrinsky's policy is often unfortunate and that our officials are heavy-handed. But don't expect me to take up the cudgels for the Uniats. I respect the Roman Catholics, although I regret they have fallen into error. But I hate and despise the Uniats because they are renegades."

The other day, Grand Duke Nicholas was complaining of the delay in the arrival of supplies for the army in Galicia. "I'm expecting trainloads of ammunition. They send me trainloads of priests!"

Wednesday, December 2, 1914

The situation of the Russian armies in Poland is becoming difficult. North of Lodz, the Germans have received reinforcements from the western front and are decidedly getting the upper hand.

General Rennenkampf has been relieved of his command as it was his slowness that caused the failure of the fine outflanking movement of November 25.

The Germans claim to have captured 80,000 unwounded Russians in the last fortnight.

Also the morale of Russia is far from improving. The pessimism I see about me is reported to be prevalent in Moscow. Kiev and Odessa also.

As one would expect, Count Witte exploits this to rail against the war. His line at the moment is to attribute to the "calculated inertia of the French army" the scale and violence of the offensive the Russians are now having to withstand in Poland. With his haughty scorn and sardonic sneer, he goes about saying, "The French are quite right not to fight anymore as the Russians are stupid enough to let themselves be killed instead."

I have had great difficulty in procuring the insertion in the press of several notes or articles setting out the great scale of our material and moral effort. Not one of the papers has had the honesty to reveal the fact that if the Russians have to deal with twenty-one German corps (not counting the Austro-Hungarians), the French and English are faced with no less than fifty-two.

Saturday, December 5, 1914

Between Lodz and Lowicz, stubborn fighting is still continuing; and the Russians are giving way.

Grand Duke Nicholas has had me informed that he is as determined as ever to pursue his advance on Silesia, but his Chief of Staff General Janushkevitch sees a fatal obstacle in the difficulty of transportation and the major losses. In the course of the last five weeks, the Russians have lost 530,000 men, 280,000 of them against the Germans.

Sunday, December 6, 1914

The Russians have evacuated Lodz; the Germans entered it at once.

It is no small loss to our Allies. Lodz has no less than 380,000 inhabitants, i.e. the populations of Lille and Roubaix combined. It is the center of the textile industry, the Manchester of Poland.

South-east of Cracow, the Austro-Hungarians are retreating.

Pope Benedict XV has asked the Russian Government if it will consent to a suspension of hostilities during Christmas Day. While thanking the Holy Father for this merciful thought, the Imperial Government has replied that it could not agree to an armistice, first because the orthodox Christmas does not coincide with the Catholic Christmas, and secondly because it could place no faith in any undertaking given by Germany.

When Sazonov told me of this answer, I was extremely sorry.

"The idea of a 'truce of God' was splendid. You ought to have accepted it. There's nothing in your point about the two calendars. You could have claimed a second armistice on your own Christmas Day, thirteen days later. And as for Germany violating the armistice, she'd have raised the conscience of the world against her and alienated all that moral force for which the Papacy still stands."

Sazonov replied in jerky, impatient tones.

"No, no, it was impossible, impossible!"

The discussion was evidently not to his liking. In his uncompromising attitude I recognized the ancient enmity between the Eastern Church and the Church of Rome. Besides, the Holy Synod must have intervened with all its routine intolerance against the suggestion made by the Pope.

All the same I ventured further.

"The Holy See can go much further along the lines it is asking us to make possible. If it utters a word of pity or reproof now and then, the war may possibly become less inhuman. Here's one example: Isn't it a terrible thing that the wounded who fall on the wire in front of the trenches cannot be assisted, and that their groans and cries for help are heard for days and days? And what about the fate of prisoners? And the bombardment of open towns? What a field of action this is for the mediation of the Holy See. We simply must not discourage it in its first initiative."

But I felt that I was speaking to no purpose.

Tuesday, December 8, 1914

I am getting reports from many quarters that the Russian army is running short of gun ammunition and rifles. I have been to General Sukhomlinov, the War Minister, to ask him for definite information on this matter.

He gave me a very friendly reception. Between his heavy eyelids, a winking smile made the little wrinkles on his brows contract. His whole personality breathes physical exhaustion and deceit.

I questioned him very closely.

He kept on answering, "Don't worry, I've prepared for everything," and he produced for me the most comforting of figures.

Then, taking me to a long table laden with maps, he described the operations in progress in Poland. With a fat, quivering finger he showed me all the fronts and pointed out all the objectives.

"You see," he said, "how the left wing of our armies is making rapid progress towards Upper Silesia, while leaving only a small force to contain the Austro-Hungarians in the south. Grand Duke Nicholas's plan is to develop his offensive by this left wing with the greatest possible intensity, even if the German thrust in the direction of Warsaw compels the right wing to dig in between the Vistula and the Warta. So, all's going well. I'm sure we shall hear some very good news before long."

As I took my leave he gave me a sly look I shall never forget.

Wednesday, December 9, 1914

The uncertainty shrouding the military operations in Poland, the only-too-justifiable presentiments of enormous losses suffered by the Russian armies, and, last but not least, the evacuation of Lodz, have led to a profound melancholy among the public. Everyone I meet is downhearted. The signs of depression are to be seen not merely in drawing rooms and clubs, but in public offices, shops and in the streets as well.

This afternoon I went into an antiquary's shop on the Liteiny. After a few minutes' bargaining over something or other, he asked me with a look of horror in his face, "When will this dreadful war end? Is it true that we have lost a million men around Lodz?"

"A million?" I exclaimed. "Who told you that? Your losses are serious, but I can assure you they are nowhere near that figure. Have you sons or relatives in the army?"

"No, thank God! But this war is too long, too terrible. Besides, we shall never beat the Germans. Then why not have done with it at once?"

I listened to his opinions to the best of my ability and assured him that we should certainly win if we held on.

He listened to me with a skeptical, frightened look, and when I stopped, he continued, "You French may be victorious, perhaps, but not we Russians. The game's lost. Then why in God's name let all these men be massacred? Why not have done with it at once?"

How many more Russians must be arguing like that at the present moment? What a strange mentality this nation has, a nation capable of such sublime sacrifices and yet so prone to despondency, self-desertion and anticipatory resignation to the worst misfortunes.

When I returned to the Embassy, I found old Baron von H….. who was a force in the political world some ten years ago, but since then has confined himself to the pleasures and trivialities of the social world.

He spoke about military events.

"Things are going very badly. There's no good in deluding ourselves. Grand Duke Nicholas is incompetent. The Battle of Lodz is madness, a disaster! Our losses are more than a million men. We shall never get the better of the Germans again. We must begin to think of peace."

I pointed out that the three Allied countries are bound to continue the war until the defeat of Germany, as nothing less than their independence and national integrity is at stake. I added that a humiliating peace would inevitably provoke a revolution in Russia, and what a revolution! I said that I also had unlimited confidence in the loyalty of the Emperor to our common cause.

H…. continued in a low voice, as if we might be overheard. "Oh, the Emperor … the Emperor …"

He stopped. I pressed him.

"What do you mean? Go on."

He resumed, looking very uncomfortable as he was treading on dangerous ground.

"At the moment, the Emperor is very angry with Germany, but he'll soon realize that he's leading Russia to destruction. He'll be made to realize it. I can hear that low hound Rasputin telling him, 'Well, how much longer are you going to spill the blood of your people? Don't you see that God is abandoning you? On that day, peace will be at hand, Monsieur l'Ambassadeur."

At this point I broke off our conversation in a sharp tone.

"It's all silly talk. The Emperor has sworn on the Holy Gospels and the icon of Our Lady of Kazan that he will never sign peace so long as there is a single enemy soldier on Russian soil. You'll never make me believe that he won't keep such an oath. Don't forget that, the day he swore it, he insisted on my being with him as witness and guarantor of his undertaking before God. On that point he will always be immovable. He would face death rather than break his word."

Thursday, December 10, 1914

The Serbians have inflicted a defeat on the Austro-Hungarians near Valievo. The enemy left 20,000 prisoners and fifty guns in the hands of the victors.

The French Government returned to Paris yesterday.

Saturday, December 12, 1914

General de Laguiche writes to me from General Headquarters, "Events are taking a favorable turn in the Cracow district. In the north, the status quo is maintained on the Ilno-Lowicz-Petrokov line, and I think that the positions contemplated have been reached there. Evidently operations will be less active there than on the Silesian side."

Monday, December 4, 1914

Has the Russian offensive towards Silesia already been checked? Yesterday they suffered a severe reverse south of the Vistula, near Limanova, that has freed Cracow and seems bound to have an effect on the whole South Poland front. Nothing is being said about this defeat.

At the present time, the Emperor is on a visit to the Caucasus front, where operations are developing successfully.

Tuesday, December 15, 1914

In Western Galicia, the Russians are falling back towards the Vistula along the whole line. This retreat means the end of the offensive against Silesia.

Prince von Bülow has been appointed Ambassador in Rome. The great game between Germany and Italy is about to begin.

Wednesday, December 16, 1914

The series of successes that the Germans have obtained in Masuria and Poland during the last four months have all been produced by railway strategy, that is the swift and secret transfer of a mass of soldiers to another part of the front for an unexpected blow. The great network of lines that run parallel to, and behind, the frontiers of Prussia, Posen and Silesia, enable these great lateral movements to be carried out in a few days, whereas the Russian General Staff needs several weeks for the slightest change in the redistribution of its troops on the line of battle.

Thursday, December 17, 1914

Grand Duke Nicholas has informed me, with great regret, that he has been obliged to discontinue his operations. The reason he gives for this decision is the excessive losses his troops have recently sustained and the fact, more serious still, that the artillery has used up all its ammunition.

    I have complained to Sazonov of the situation thus brought to my notice, and my tone was pretty sharp.

    "General Sukhomlinov has assured me a dozen times," I said, "that all precautions had been taken to secure that the Russian artillery should always have an abundant supply of ammunition. I have emphasized to him the enormous consumption that has become the normal scale of battles. He has vowed that he was in a position to satisfy all requirements and meet all eventualities. He even gave me written proof. Please mention the matter on my behalf to the Emperor.2

"I won't fail to tell His Majesty what you've just told me."

We left it at that. Sazonov's opinion of Sukhomlinov's character is a sufficient guarantee that he will make the most of my complaint.

Friday, December 18, 1914

I learned yesterday that the Russian artillery is short of ammunition; I learn this morning that the infantry is short of rifles!

I went at once to General Bielaiev, Army Chief of Staff at the Ministry for War, and asked him for an explanation.

A hard worker, and the soul of conscience and honor, he made a clean breast of everything.

"Our losses in men have been colossal, although if it were merely a matter of replacing those losses, we could soon do so as we have more than 800,000 men in our depots. But we're short of rifles to arm and train these men. Our original reserve was 5,600,000 rifles — at least we thought it was. Grand Duke Nicholas thought so; I thought so myself. We have been criminally deceived. Our magazines are nearly empty. Forgive me for giving no further explanation of a very painful matter. To make good the deficit, we are about to purchase a million rifles in Japan and America, and we hope to arrive at an output of one hundred thousand a month in our own factories. Perhaps France and England could also let us have a few hundred thousand. The position is hardly less difficult as regards gun ammunition. The consumption has surpassed all our calculations and anticipations. At the beginning of the war we had 5,200,000 rounds of 76 mm. shrapnel in our arsenal. Our entire reserve is exhausted. The armies need 45,000 rounds per day. Our maximum daily output is 13,000. We hope it will reach 20,000 about February 15. Until that date, the situation of our armies will not only be difficult but dangerous. In March, the deliveries on orders we have placed abroad will begin to arrive. I presume we shall thus have 27,000 rounds a day around April 15 and 40,000 after May 15. That is all I can tell you, Monsieur l'Ambassadeur. I have kept nothing from you."

I thanked him for his candor, made some, notes and withdrew.

Outside, under a dull grey, leaden sky, an icy wind viciously lashed the banks of the Neva, whirling the snowflakes before it. The wintry desolation of the great river, frozen as far as the eye could reach between its granite quays, had never before seemed so utterly inhuman. The landscape seemed the visual embodiment of all the tragedy, the element of implacable and remorseless destiny in the history of the Russian nation.

Saturday, December 19, 1914

Today is the Emperor's name day. A thanksgiving service has been held at Our Lady of Kazan. All the court dignitaries, ministers, high officials and the diplomatic corps have attended in full dress. The public thronged the far end of the nave between the two noble rows of columns in pairs.

In the dazzling blaze of the candelabra and candles, the glittering of the icons – one mass of gold and precious stones – the national sanctuary is a superb edifice. Throughout the service the anthems followed each other with a wealth of melody, perfection of execution, breadth and solemnity that attained the highest pitch of religious emotion.

Towards the end of the ceremony, I singled out Goremykin, the President of the Council, and drawing him behind a pillar, I taxed him with the inadequate military support given by Russia to our common cause. Buchanan and Sazonov were listening and joined in the conversation. In his slow, skeptical way Goremykin tried to defend Sukhomlinov:

"But there's the same shortage of munitions in France and England as well. Yet your industries are far better equipped than ours, and your machine-tool industry is on a far higher level. And how could anyone anticipate such a prodigal expenditure of ammunition?"

"I don't blame General Sukhomlinov," I protested, "for not having foreseen before the war that every battle would mean a perfect orgy of ammunition. Nor do I blame him for the delays inevitably involved in the backward state of your industries. But I do blame him for having done nothing to avert the present crisis in the three months since I told him, from General Joffre, that it was coming. And the shortage of rifles! Isn't that even more criminal? "

Goremykin made a formal protest in evasive language and weary gestures. Buchanan supported me vigorously. Sazonov acquiesced by his silence.

What a strange phenomenon was this discussion between allies in the church to which Field-Marshal Prince Kutusov came to pray before starting for the war of 1812, within two paces of his tomb and under the trophies abandoned by the French during the retreat from Russia.

Sunday, December 20, 1914

I hear from many quarters that in intellectual and liberal circles there is a good deal of criticism of France, criticism as malevolent as unjust and acrimonious.

Waves of Francophobia have swept over Russia four or five times since the last years of the Catherine the Great. French ideas, fashions and manners have periodically irritated the Russians. The last wave, to which the present symptoms are related, only affected the Intelligentsia who have never forgiven us for giving financial assistance to Tsarism and thus strengthening the autocratic regime.

In 1906 Maxim Gorky had the insolence to write:

> *This is what you have done, oh France, you, the mother of Liberty! Your venal hand has closed the highway to independence for a whole nation. But no! The day of our emancipation will not be postponed though it will cost us far more blood, through your fault. May that blood*

> *stain your flaccid, lying cheeks! As for me, I spit in your face, my loved one of yore!*

At the present time a silly charge is added to the grievance of the loans, that it is France that has dragged Russia into the war in order to recover Alsace-Lorraine for herself at the price of Russian lives.

I am doing what I can to counteract these tendencies, but my activities are necessarily limited and secret. If I have too much to do with liberal circles, I shall become an object of suspicion to the Government party and the Emperor. I shall also put a formidable weapon in the hands of the reactionaries of the Extreme Right and the gang around the Empress who are preaching that the alliance with republican France is a mortal peril to orthodox Tsarism, and that the only path to safety lies in a reconciliation with German Kaiserism.

Monday, December 21, 1914

During my call on Madame Goremykin, a kind old lady who looks very attractive under her crown of white hair, her husband came in to join us at tea.
I remarked in a tone of friendly reproach, "In Our Lady of Kazan yesterday you struck me as taking the military situation remarkably calmly."

He answered in his feeble, deceitful voice, "What do you expect? I'm so old! I ought to have been in my coffin long ago. I told the Emperor so only the other day, but His Majesty wouldn't listen to me. And perhaps, after all, it's as well as it is. At my age men don't try and change the order of things more than is necessary."

Thinking over this skeptical remark this evening, I wondered whether it were no less ill-timed than I thought at first and whether, if confined to the Russian Empire, it did not contain a substantial element of wisdom.

The words of Joseph de Maistre came to my mind: "Woe to bad governments! Triple woe to bad governments that desire to mend their ways!"

Tuesday, December 22, 1914

The public have now known for two days that the Russian operations have been stayed, and in the absence of official news the situation is supposed to be worse than it really is. For this reason General Headquarters decided today to issue the following communication:

> *The taking up of a shorter front by our armies is the result of the unfettered decision of the military authority. The movement is a natural one and the consequence of the concentration of very large German forces against us. This decision will also bring us further advantages. Unfortunately it is impossible to furnish public opinion with explanations of a military nature.*

This communiqué, with its clumsy wording, has produced an unfortunate effect. Everyone is thinking, 'Things must be going badly if that's all they can tell us!'

Wednesday, December 23, 1914

Madame P..... (Sister in charge of a front line hospital), who has just returned from Poland, tells me that the courage and poise of the Russian troops are altogether splendid. Yet no trial is spared them: furious and uninterrupted fighting; frightful losses from artillery fire; wearying marches in the snow; the ghastly sufferings of the wounded owing to the difficulty of transportation; and the terrible cold, &c.

She also gave me several curious examples of the gentleness displayed by the Russian soldier to Austrian and German prisoners.

It is a feature of the national temperament: the Russian has no bellicose instincts and a very warm heart. Contrasted with the German national epics, the Russian bylinas are very eloquent from this point of view. They never glorify war and their heroes, their *bogatyrs*, are always in the role of the defender. The Russian peasant is also naturally charitable. A *moujik* must be absolutely penniless to refuse alms to anyone asking him for them, "in the name of Christ"! And he is immediately stirred to the depths of his soul at the sight of poverty, of disease or of a prisoner.

It is this evangelical instinct that makes the Russian soldier so ready for reconciliation and fraternization with his foe. During the 1812 retreat, the French had a horrible taste of the savagery of the Cossacks and the cupidity of the Jews, but they almost invariably received sympathy and help from the regular soldiery and the peasants. There is plenty of evidence on this point. During the Crimean War also, invitations to fraternize came from the Russian trenches whenever there was the slightest suspension of hostilities.

Thursday, December 24, 1914

General de Laguiche, writing from Baranovici, has confirmed General Bielaiev's revelations. The reason for the suspension of the Russian operations is not the size of the German forces, but the total lack of gun ammunition and rifles. Grand Duke Nicholas is reduced to despair but is doing everything he can to remedy this grave situation.

Several thousand rifles have already been made available as the result of stringent orders. The output of the national factories is to be raised. Meanwhile, military operations are to be continued so far as practicable. The invasion of Germany is still the objective.

Saturday, December 26, 1914

On his return from the Caucasus, the Emperor has stayed in Moscow. He had a most enthusiastic reception and had a chance of seeing for himself the fine spirit with which all grades of Moscow society are inspired.

All the Moscow papers have fastened onto the occasion to affirm that the war must be fought out until the defeat of

Teutonism. Several have remarked, very happily, that to attain that end, a "flash of enthusiasm" is not enough. What is needed is stubbornness of will, inexhaustible patience, and a determination to face and accept immense sacrifices.

The Emperor has several times said to those around him, "I feel I'm really at the heart of my people here. The atmosphere is as wholesome and bracing as at the front."

Sunday, December 27, 1914

Everyone who spoke to the Emperor in Moscow, talked of Constantinople, and all in the same vein:

"The acquisition of the Straits is of vital interest to the Empire, far more important than all the territorial advantages Russia may obtain at the expense of Germany or Austria. The neutralization of the Bosphorus and the Dardanelles would be an imperfect, hybrid compromise, fraught with peril for the future. Constantinople must be a Russian city. The Black Sea must become a Russian lake."

A French manufacturer, who has come from Kharkov and Odessa, tells me that the same thing is being said there. But whereas the historical, political, and mystical aspects inspire Moscow, it is the commercial argument that appeals to southern Russia. The corn of the *tchernoziom* and the Donetz coal basin are responsible for the cry for the Mediterranean.

Monday, December 28, 1914

It is becoming ever clearer that there are two currents in Russian public opinion: one flowing on towards bright horizons and beckoning conquests – Constantinople, Thrace, Armenia, Trebizond, Persia; the other beating against the invincible obstacle of the Teutonic cliff and ebbing back to gloomy prospects, ending in pessimism, a feeling of impotence, and resignation.

The really curious point is that these two currents run side by side – or, at any rate, frequently alternate – in the same individual, as if they both satisfied the two outstanding propensities of the Russian soul, dreams and disillusionment.

Tuesday, December 29, 1914

What a curious person Madame Anna Alexandrovna Vyrubova is. She is not titled, holds no office, receives no salary, and appears at no ceremonies. This perpetual self-effacement and utter disinterestedness are her whole capital with the sovereigns, so accustomed to the importunity of place-hunters and self-seekers. She is the daughter of Taneiev, Director of the Emperor's Privy Seal Office, and has practically no money. It is all that the Empress can do to get her occasionally to accept some cheap jewel, or a dress, or cloak.

Physically, she is coarse and heavily-built, with a round head, fleshy lips, limpid eyes devoid of expression, a full figure and a high color. She is thirty-two years of age. She dresses with a thoroughly provincial plainness and is very devout, but unintelligent. I have met her twice at the house of her mother, Madame Taneiev (née Tolstoy), who, by contrast, is well-informed and distinguished. We had a long talk together. Anna Alexandrovna struck me as unattractive and very dull-witted. As a girl, she was maid-of-honor to the Empress who arranged her marriage with a naval officer, Lieutenant Vyrubova. After a few days of married life came divorce.

At the present time, Madame Vyrubova lives at Tsarskoe Selo in a very modest villa at the corner of the Sredniaya and the Zerkovnaya, 200 meters from the Imperial Palace. In spite of all the decrees of etiquette, the Empress frequently pays prolonged calls on her friend. She has even reserved a room for her in the palace itself. The result is that the two women are nearly always together. In any case, Madame Vyrubova regularly spends the evenings with the sovereigns and their children. No one else ever enters the family circle. They play draughts and patience, do puzzles, and occasionally play a little music. Highly proper novels – English novels, for preference – are read aloud. When the children have gone to bed, Madame Vyrubova stays with the sovereigns until midnight and thus takes part in all their conversations, always on Alexandra Feodorovna's side. As the Emperor never ventures to decide anything without his wife's opinion, or rather approval, the net result is that it is the Empress and Madame Vyrubova who really govern Russia.

Princess R… said to me when I was discussing the imperial court with her recently, "Isn't it grievous to think that the masters of Russia live in such an atmosphere? It's as if they lived in rooms that are never aired. Just think, no one, I mean no one, ever sees them alone, or lunches with them, or goes for a walk with them, or dines with them, or spends an evening with them, not a soul, except Anna Vyrubova! When I remember what my parents told me of the courts of Alexander II and Alexander III, it makes me want to cry. No doubt they had their intrigues, feuds, favoritisms, and even scandals, as all courts have, but at any rate there was some life about them. The monarchs were approachable. You could talk quite freely with them so that they learned a good deal. In turn, you got to know and like them. But now, what a contrast, what a lapse!"

How can one place Madame Vyrubova? What is the hidden motive for her behavior? What is her object? What are her hopes? The favorite description of her is that she is an intriguer. But it's a curious sort of intriguer who despises honors and refuses reward. Before I met her, I thought her character must have some resemblance to that of the Princesse des Ursins. I was very wide of the mark and owe a humble apology to the memory of the famous *camerera mayor*. She directed the married life of Philip V and Marie Louise, of course. But Saint-Simon has written of her "that she had an air of noble dignity that attracted rather than repelled," and even if she may be charged with great ambitions, they were, at any rate, "vast ambitions, far higher than those of her sex." Lastly, she combined a genius for political intrigue with the highest and most brilliant qualities of mind, not to mention a charm of manner that survived to her old age. Compared to that splendid specimen of womanhood, Vyrubova cuts a very poor figure. To account for her position and importance in the imperial palace perhaps it is enough to refer to her personal devotion to the Empress, the devotion of a servile and inferior being to a royal lady who is always ailing, weighed down by her own power, a lady who is prey to all sorts of terrors and feels that some horrible fate is forever hanging over her.

Wednesday, December 30, 1914

Nicholas Maklakov, the Minister of the Interior, has told me of something that happened to him when he was travelling recently, an incident that brings out a curious side of Russian mentality.

"I was coming back in a *troika* from Jaroslavl," he said. "I was alone and barely a dozen versts from my destination, when I was caught in a snowstorm. You couldn't see two paces ahead. That didn't prevent my coachman from whipping up his horses to try and reach the town before nightfall. Before long he had lost his way. He hesitated and turned to the right, then to the left. I was beginning to get uneasy, particularly as the storm was getting very much worse. Suddenly the vehicle stopped. My man crossed himself vigorously three times and muttered a prayer. Then, throwing his reins over the shafts, he yelled at his horses, 'Gee up! Gee up! Come on, lads! Come on, little brothers!' The three horses pricked up their ears, snorted, shook their heads this way and that, and then galloped off through the blinding snowflakes. My driver turned round to me and said, 'see, *barin*, when you've lost your way, the best thing to do is to trust to your beasts and the grace of God!' An hour later I was in Jaroslavl."

I replied to Maklakov, "Your fable's very poetic, but I'll admit I should have liked it better in peace time."

Thursday, December 31, 1914

In an hour's time, 1914 will be over.

The exile's melancholy lot!

Since this war first turned the world upside down, events have already so often upset the most rational calculations and mocked at the most prudent expectations, that one cannot venture into prophecy except within the limits of near horizons and immediate contingencies.

This afternoon, however, I have had a long and frank talk with the Swiss Minister, Odier. The exchange of information, interchange of ideas, and difference in our points of view, have widened my horizons somewhat. Odier has a lucid and accurate mind, and he combines a strong sense of reality with a wealth of experience. We came to the conclusion that Germany made a serious mistake in thinking she could finish the war straight off; that it will be a very, very long struggle; and that victory will ultimately rest with the most tenacious of the combatants.

The war will thus become a war of attrition, and the attrition, alas, must be complete, involving the exhaustion of food supplies, industrial machinery and products, man power and morale. And it is plain that it is the morale that will bring about the decision in the last desperate hour.

Looked at from this point of view, the problem cannot be regarded as other than an anxious one for Russia. Russia is so prone to lose heart, to fluctuate in her desires, and grow weary of her dreams. Notwithstanding its splendid gifts of heart and mind, no nation records so many bankruptcies and miscarriages in its moral life as the Russian. One of the types that crops up most frequently in Russian literature is the desperate man, the man resigned to anything and everything, the 'failure.' I was recently reading a moving passage in a book of Chekov's, the novelist who, next to Tolstoy and Dostoievsky, has given the best analysis of the Russian soul.

> *Why do we tire so soon? How is it that after squandering so much fervor, passion and faith we almost always go to ruin before the age of thirty. And when we fall, how is it that we never try to rise again?*

Chapter 8

Friday, January 1, 1915

Sazonov, Buchanan and I have been amicably discussing the problems we three shall have to face in the year of 1915. None of us has any illusion about the immense effort required of us by the war, an effort we have neither the opportunity nor the right to shirk, as nothing less than the independence of our national life is at stake.

"The military experiences of the last few months," I said, "particularly of the last few weeks, embody a valuable lesson, I think, that we should be wrong not to take into account."

"What lesson?" asked Sazonov.

After warning them that I was expressing a purely personal opinion, I continued. "As the German bloc is such a hard nut to crack, we should endeavor to detach Austria-Hungary from the Teutonic coalition by any and every method of force or persuasion. I believe we should succeed in a very short time. The Emperor Franz Joseph is very old. We know he bitterly regrets this war and only asks to be allowed to die in peace. You have beaten his armies in Galicia again and again; the Serbs have just won a brilliant victory at Valievo; Rumania threatens; and Italy is doubtful. The Hapsburg Monarchy was in no greater peril in 1859 and 1866, yet the same Franz Joseph then accepted serious territorial sacrifices to save his crown. Quite between ourselves, my dear Minister, if the Vienna Cabinet agreed to cede Galicia to you, and Bosnia-Herzegovina to Serbia, would not that seem to you an adequate return for making a separate peace with Austria-Hungary?"

Sazonov pulled a face and replied drily, "What about Bohemia? And Croatia? Would you leave them under the present system? It's impossible."

"As I'm speaking to you personally, forgive me for saying that, in this terrible hour of trial for France, the Czech and Yugoslav problems seem to me secondary."

Sazonov peevishly shook his head.

"No, Austria-Hungary must be dismembered."

I then resumed my original arguments and developed them. I showed that the defection of Austria-Hungary would have important consequences from the strategic and moral points of view, that Russia would be the first to derive benefit from them, that it was in our obvious interest and our plain duty to concentrate the whole of our offensive power and destructive forces against Germany, and if the Vienna Cabinet offered us reasonable terms of peace, we should commit a grave error if we rejected them *a priori*. If necessary, we could require that a generous measure of self-government should be granted to the Czechs and Croats. That alone would be a resounding victory for Slavism.

Sazonov seemed moved by my persistence.

"It wants thinking about," he said.

The moment I got back to the embassy, I sent a report of this conversation to Delcassé, reminding him of the unquestionable advantage to France of the preservation of a great political system in the Danube basin.

Tuesday, January 5, 1915

The street is always an instructive sight. I often notice what a vague, preoccupied and absent-minded creature the passing *moujik* looks.

Here is a phenomenon one may observe at an any time, a phenomenon that sometimes thrusts itself upon one's notice even without looking for it:

Two sleighs approach from opposite directions. They are still twenty meters apart and exactly in line with each other. Typically, the drivers casually let the reins lie loosely on their horses' backs. They look about them in an inattentive, unseeing way. The vehicles are now no more than ten meters apart. The *izvochtchiks* merely begin to realize that they will collide if they do not change direction. They slowly fumble for the reins, but the presence of the obstacle immediately ahead has not entirely dawned upon them even then. When the horses' noses are all but touching, there is a pull at the bridle and they swerve sharply to the right, unless the two sleighs are not already upside down in the snow.

Several times I have amused myself calculating the time that elapses between the moment at which it is plain that the two sleighs are in the same track and the moment at which the *izvochtchiks* pull the reins to avert a collision. I have found it to be from four to eight seconds by my watch. The Paris and London driver would make up his mind at the first glance and act accordingly in less than a second.

Is the inference that the *moujik* is slow-witted and stupid? Certainly not! But his mind is always wandering. In his brain, fitful and disordered impressions chase one another continuously; they seem to have no relation to reality. His usual state of mind oscillates between reverie and mental dispersion.

Wednesday, January 6, 1915

The Russians have just inflicted a defeat on the Turks near Sarykamish, on the Kars-Erzerum road.

This success is a particularly fine piece of work as our Ally's offensive is in a region of mountains as high as the Alps, intersected by precipices and with passes often over 2,500 meters in height. It is appallingly cold at this season of the year, and there are incessant snowstorms. There are no roads and the whole region is laid waste.

The army of the Caucasus is performing prodigies of valor every day.

Thursday, January 7, 1915

During the last nine days, there has been heavy fighting on the left bank of the Vistula, in the sector between the Bzura and the Ravka. On January 2, the Germans succeeded in carrying the important Borjymov position. Their front is thus no more than sixty kilometers from Warsaw.

This situation comes in for very strong comment in Moscow, if I am to credit the information given to me by an English journalist who was dining in the Slaviansky Bazar only yesterday.

"In all the drawing rooms and clubs in Moscow," he said, "there is great irritation at the turn military events are taking. No one can understand this suspension of all our attacks and these continuous retreats that look as if they would never end. But it is not Grand Duke Nicholas who gets the blame but the Emperor, and still more the Empress. The most absurd stories are told about Alexandra Feodorovna. Rasputin is accused of being in German pay, and the Tsaritsa is simply called the *'Niemka'* [the German woman]."

Several times before have I heard the Empress charged with having retained sympathies, preferences and a warm corner in her heart for Germany. The unfortunate woman in no way deserves these strictures. She knows all about them and they give her great pain.

Alexandra Feodorovna is German neither in mind nor spirit, and has never been so. Of course, she is a German by birth, at any rate on the paternal side, as her father was Louis IV, Grand Duke of Hesse and the Rhine. But she is English through her mother, Princess Alice, a daughter of Queen Victoria. In 1878, at the age of six, she lost her mother and thenceforward resided habitually at the court of England. Her upbringing, education and mental and moral development were thus quite English. She is still English in her outward appearance, her deportment, a certain strain of inflexibility and Puritanism, the uncompromising and militant austerity of her conscience, and last, but not least, in many of her personal habits. That is all that is left of her Western origin.

In her innermost being, she has become entirely Russian. In the first place, I have no doubt of her patriotism, notwithstanding the legend I see growing up around her. Her love for Russia is deep and true. And why should she not be devoted to her adopted country which stands for everything dear to her as woman, wife, sovereign and mother? When she ascended the throne in 1894 she knew already that she did not like Germany, and particularly Prussia. In recent years she has taken a personal dislike to Emperor Wilhelm, and he it is whom she holds exclusively responsible for the war, this "wicked war that makes Christ's heart bleed every day." When she heard of the burning in Louvain, she cried out, "I blush to have been a German!"

But her moral naturalization has gone even further. By a curious process of mental contagion, she has gradually absorbed the most ancient and characteristic elements of the Russian soul, all those obscure, emotional and visionary elements that find their highest expression in religious mysticism.

I have already referred to the morbid proclivities she inherits from her mother's side and which betray themselves in her sister Elizabeth as a kind of charitable exaltation, and in her brother the Grand Duke of Hesse as a taste for the freakish. These hereditary tendencies, which would have been more or less checked if she had continued to live in the practical and balanced West, have found in Russia the atmosphere most favorable to their perfect development. Are not all those symptoms – moral unrest, chronic melancholy, vague sorrows, the see-saw between elation and despondency, the haunting obsession of the invisible and the life beyond, and superstitious credulity – that are outstanding features of the Empress's personality, traditional and endemic in the Russian people?

Alexandra Feodorovna's submissive acceptance of Rasputin's ascendency is no less significant. She is behaving exactly like one of the old Tsaritsas of Moscow when she sees in Rasputin a *Bojy tchelloviek*, 'a man of God,' 'a saint persecuted (as Christ was) by the Pharisees,' or when she endows him with the gifts of prophecy, miracle-working and exorcism, or allows the success of a political step or a military operation to depend upon his blessing.

She carries us back to the times of Ivan the Terrible or Michael Feodorovitch, and takes her place, so to speak, in the Byzantine setting of archaic Russia.

Friday, January 8, 1915

Towards three o'clock this afternoon, as the last relics of day were already submerging in a desolate darkness, I walked along the Kronversky Prospekt on my way to the French Hospital which is at the far end of Vassili Island.

On my left, the Fortress of St. Peter and St. Paul thrust forth its angular bastions under a shroud of snow from which the flat roof of the state prison barely protruded. A dense, leaden mist hung heavy over the cupola of the cathedral in which are the tombs of the Romanovs, and the gilded spire above it was lost in the somber sky. Ahead of me, I had glimpses of the motionless sheet of the Neva, studded with great blocks of ice, through the leafless trees of a bare and deserted park.

To heighten the sinister setting of the hour and the place, the corner of a lonely avenue I passed on my right was marked by a low building with yellowing walls and barred windows, a building of secret and shameful aspect. Two police officers came out of it together. It was the Okhrana.

This fearsome institution dates from the days of Peter the Great, who created it in 1697 under the name of the Preobrajensky Prikaz. Its historical origins must be sought much earlier on, however. They are to be found in Byzantine traditions and Tartar methods of rule. Its first Chief was Prince Romodanovsky, and it immediately acquired a terrible reputation. From that time, espionage, secret denunciation, torture, and secret execution were the normal and regular instruments of Russian policy. From the start, the Preobrajensky Prikaz applied the true principles of a State Inquisition, mystery, arbitrary action and ferocity. In the reigns of Peter II, Anna Tvanovna, and Elizabeth Petrovna, the institution lost something of its native vigor, but the Empress Catherine II, 'the friend of philosophers,' lost no time in restoring its secret authority and implacable character. Alexander II kept it at that high level.

It needed the genius for despotism of Nicholas I to discover that a State service which already had so many exploits to its credit was defective and inadequate. Immediately after the Decembrist conspiracy, he entirely reorganized the Okhrana, which was thenceforward known as the Third Section of His Imperial Majesty's private Chancellery. In all these reforms could be observed the influence of Prussian methods and a tendency to imitate Prussian bureaucracy and Prussian militarism.

The direction of the department was entrusted to a general of German origin, Count Alexander Benckendorff, and no autocrat ever had a more potent weapon of inquisition and coercion. After a few years of this regime, Russia was essentially a Police State.

In the disorganization which succeeded the Crimean War, Alexander II felt the necessity of modernizing the administrative legislation of the Empire to a certain extent. The judicial system, which offered no guarantee of justice whatever, was recast on lines more in keeping with western ideas, but the Third Section still retained its extravagant privileges. To realize its place in the State organization and its reputation in society, it is enough to remember that three of its successive Directors were Count Orlov, Prince Dolgoruky and Count Shuvalov.

The assassination of Alexander II in 1881, and the spread of the Nihilist movement, gave the opponents of liberal reforms the chance of their life. Throughout his life, the 'Most Pious' Alexander III conscientiously devoted himself to extirpating the evil germ of modernism and bringing Russia back to the theocratic ideal of the Muscovite Tsars. The police, of course, took the lead in this work of reaction, but since August, 1880, it had ceased to be attached to the Private Chancellery of His Imperial Majesty, being rather under the Ministry of the Interior, where it formed a special department with its own police corps.

Under the direction of General Tcherevin, a personal friend of Alexander III, it was as powerful as in the days of Nicholas I. Shrouded in mystery, thrusting its tentacles into every part of the Empire and even abroad, outside the jurisdiction of the courts, disposing of huge funds and free of all supervision, it frequently imposed its decrees on the ministers and even the Emperor himself.

The superstitious reverence of Nicholas II for the memory and opinions of his father safeguarded him from making any changes in a service animated by such matchless loyalty and so zealous for the safety of the dynasty. His decrees of May 23, 1896m and December 13, 1897, confirmed and increased the powers of the police.

Those powers were well illustrated during the revolutionary troubles of 1905, when the Okhrana fomented strikes, attempts at assassination, and pogroms in all quarters, mobilized General Bogdanovitch's 'Black Bands,' and tried to rouse the fanaticism of the rural masses in favor of orthodox Tsarism. The debate in the Duma during June 1906, the revelations of Prince Urussov, the proceedings that were subsequently taken against the ex-Chief of Police Lopoukhin, and the confessions or silences of the police officers Guerassimov and Ratchkovsky, brought to light the shocking part played by *agents provocateurs* like Azev, Gapon, Harting, Tchiguelsky and Mikhailov in the anarchist plots over the last few years. It was even thought that their handiwork could be traced in the assassinations of Plevhe, the Minister of the Interior, and Grand Duke Sergius.

What is the Okhrana contemplating now? What plot is it weaving? I am told that its present Chief, General Globatchev, is not altogether deaf to reason, but in times of crisis the spirit of an institution will always prevail against the personality of its chief.

Nor can I forget that the Police Department at the Ministry of the Interior is in the hands of Bieletzky, a man entirely lacking in scruples, bold and deceitful, a tool of Rasputin and all his gang.

The Police Department at the Ministry of the Interior and its annex, the Okhrana, function over the general police of the Empire, the administrative, judicial, and political police. But in addition to these two great public services, there is a complicated mechanism attached to the Minister of the Court's department, the duty of which is to ensure the personal safety of Their Majesties. I cannot find any monarchical state in modern history in which the safety of the sovereigns has appeared to require such active and painstaking vigilance and such a rampart of open or secret precautions.

The task is accomplished in the following way: All the military and administrative organs employed in the protection of the sovereigns are under the orders of the Governor of the Imperial Palaces. His post is greatly coveted because it confers on its holder immense power, and entitles him to approach the Tsar at any time. The present holder is General Vladimir Nicolaievitch Voyeikov, formerly Commander of the Regiment of Guard Hussars, son-in-law of Count Fredericks, Minister of the Court. His predecessor was

General Diedulin, who succeeded the famous General Trepov.

In the first place, General Voyeikov has under his orders the Cossack Escort Regiment of four squadrons, with a total strength of 650 men. The Officer Commanding the Regiment is General Count Alexander Grabbé. These Cossacks are selected from the strongest and most active in the Empire, and are posted to observation, patrol and escort duty outside the palace. These are the men to be seen galloping at intervals of fifty meters day and night in the avenue that surrounds Tsarskoe Selo Park.

Then comes His Majesty's Regiment, four battalions with a total strength of 5,000 men. The commander of the regiment is General Ressin. Recruited with the greatest care from all the corps of the guard, and remarkably smart in their plain uniforms, these hand-picked infantry men supply the guards for the palace gate and the sentries scattered about the park. It also furnishes some thirty guards distributed about the halls, corridors, staircases, kitchens, domestic offices and cellars of the imperial residence.

In addition to these cavalry and infantry contingents, General Voyeikov has at his disposal a special unit, His Majesty's Railway Regiment, comprising two battalions with a total strength of 1,000 men. This regiment is commanded by General Label and is in charge of the management of the imperial trains and responsible for the inspection of the route Their Majesties are travelling. This work is of the highest importance, as to blow up the Tsar's train is one of the ideas that obsess Russian anarchists. Not so long ago one of them succeeded in concealing himself by clinging to the undercarriage of one of the coaches with a bomb in his pocket.

The protection given by these military forces is supplemented by that given by two administrative organs, appropriately equipped, the Police of the Imperial Court and His Majesty the Emperor's Personal Police.

The Police of the Imperial Court, under the direction of General of Police Ghérardi, has a strength of 250 police officers, and duplicates to a certain extent the guards and sentries posted at the gates and in the palace buildings. It watches the entrances and exits, inspects the servants, tradesmen, workmen, gardeners, visitors, &c. It observes and records everything that goes on among the entourage of the sovereigns. It spies, eavesdrops, pries into everything and gets everywhere. In the execution of its task, it never makes the slightest exception.

On that point, I can give personal testimony. Every time I was received by the Emperor at Tsarskoe Selo and Peterhof (and on each occasion I was in full uniform, in a court carriage and with a Master of Ceremonies at my side), I had to go through the usual process. The police officer on duty at the great gates put his head inside the carriage and was handed the regulation pass by the groom.

I once expressed my surprise at such strictness to Evreinov, the Director of Ceremonies. "We can't be too careful, Ambassador," he replied. "Don't forget that towards the end of Alexander II's time the Nihilists blew up the dining-room at the Winter Palace within a few feet of the bedroom in which poor Empress Marie lay dying. Our revolutionaries are no less bold and ingenious now. They've tried to kill Nicholas II seven or eight times already."

His Majesty the Emperor's Personal Police has even wider functions. It is a kind of branch of the great Okhrana, but responsible solely and directly to the Governor of the Imperial Palaces. Its Commanding Officer is General of Police Spiridovitch, who has under his orders 300 police officers who have all gone through an apprenticeship in the ranks of the judicial or political police. General Spiridovitch's main task is to see to the safety of the sovereigns when they are outside their palace. The moment the Tsar or Tsaritsa have left the Dvoretz, he is responsible for their lives. It is a particularly grave responsibility as Nicholas II is a thoroughgoing fatalist, piously convinced that he will not die before the hour decreed by God, and therefore allows only well-screened measures for his personal safety and in particular no conspicuous deployment of police officers.

To do its work thoroughly and well, the Personal Police has to have an intimate knowledge of the organization, designs, schemes, plots, all the audacious, unceasing and subterranean activities of subversive elements. For this purpose, General Spiridovitch is furnished with all the information acquired by the Police Department and the Okhrana. The high importance of his duties also gives him the right to enter any of the administrative departments at any time and insist upon any inquiry he thinks fit. The Chief of the Personal Police is thus able to furnish his immediate superior, the Governor of the Imperial Palaces, with a formidable weapon for political and social espionage.

Saturday, January 9, 1915

Delcassé has just replied to my telegram of January 1, in which I reported my conversation with Sazonov about the possibility of inducing the Vienna Cabinet to make a separate peace. He gives me strict orders not to say a word that might lead the Russian Government to think that we will not hand over Austria-Hungary to Russia *in toto*.

When my Councillor, Doulcet, had read the telegram through, I said to him, "You might just as well have read out the news of a military defeat. I shouldn't have been a bit more flabbergasted."

Are the Russian people as religious as is commonly asserted? It is a question I have often turned over in my mind, and my answers have been pretty indefinite.

Yesterday, I was reading some of Merejkovsky's suggestive pages in 'religion and Revolution,' and the question presented itself to my mind once more.

Merejkovsky says that, somewhere around 1902, a number of Russians, who were uneasy in their highly devout minds, arranged in St. Petersburg a series of conferences in which priests sat with laymen under the chairmanship of a bishop, Monsignor Sergei, Rector of the Theological College.

"For the first time," he writes, "the Russian Church found itself face-to-face with the lay world, lay culture and society, not for the purpose of forcing a superficial fusion, but to strive for a free and intimate communion. For the first time questions were put that had never been raised with the same searching of conscience and real torture of mind since the ascetic separation of Christianity and the world. The walls of the room seemed to open and reveal boundless horizons. This tiny assembly seemed, as it were, the threshold of an ecumenical council. Speeches were made that were more like prayers and prophecies. An atmosphere of enthusiasm was created in which everything seemed possible, even a miracle. A tribute must be paid to the heads of the Russian clergy: They met us more than halfway with an open mind, a holy humility, a desire to understand, to help, to save the victim of error, but the line of demarcation between the two camps was deeper than we at first thought. Between ourselves and them we discovered a great abyss that it proved impossible to bridge. We made tunnels towards each other but we could not meet, for we were digging at different levels. For the Church to respond, something more than reform would have been required. What was needed was a revolution, a new revelation rather than a new interpretation; not the sequel to the Second Testament but the beginning of the Third; not a return to the Christ of the first coming but an impulse towards the Christ of the second. A hopeless misunderstanding was the result. To us, religion was worship; to these priests it was routine. The sacred words of the scriptures, in which we heard the voices of the seven thunders, to them were just as the sentences of the catechism learned by heart. We thought of the face of Christ as of the sun shining in his splendor; they were satisfied with a dark smudge on the halo of an old icon."

There lies the great religious drama of the Russian conscience. The nation is more sincere, or at any rate more Christian, than its own Church. In the simple faith of the masses, there is more spirituality, mysticism and evangelism than in the orthodox theology and ordinances. The official Church is daily losing its hold over men's hearts by allowing itself to become the tool of autocracy and an administrative institution and police force.

Fifteen years ago, Tolstoy's dramatic and famous break with canonical orthodoxy revealed the full gravity of the moral crisis with which Russia is afflicted. When the Holy Synod launched its excommunication, messages of approval and admiration poured into Yasnaia Poliana. Even priests raised their voices against the terrible sentence. Theological students went on strike and indignation was so general that the Metropolitan of St. Petersburg thought it necessary to send an open letter to Countess Tolstoy in which he characterized the verdict of the Holy Synod as an "act of love and charity" towards her apostate husband.

The Russian people are deeply evangelical. The Sermon on the Mount practically sums up their religion. What appeals to them most in the Christian revelation is the mystery of love, which, emanating from God, has redeemed the world. The essential articles of their Credo are the words of the sermon in Galilee: Love one another; love your enemies; do good to them that hate you; pray for those who spitefully use you; I ask not for sacrifice, but love.

Hence the *moujik's* infinite pity for the poor, the unfortunate, the oppressed, the humbled, and all to whom fate has been unkind. It is this that gives Dostoievsky's work such a ring of national truth; it seems wholly inspired by the word of Christ. "Come unto Me all ye that are heavily laden." Alms, good works and hospitality take an enormous place in the life of the lowly. I have travelled over the world and never found any other race so charitable.

Besides, the *moujik* himself feeds on the sympathy he lavishes on others. His face is a study in fervor and sincerity when he murmurs the eternal response of the orthodox liturgy to the accompaniment of vigorous signs of the cross: *"Gospodi, pomiloui!"* [Lord have mercy on me!]

Next to sympathy for the afflicted, the religious sentiment that strikes me as most active in the popular conscience is the admission of sin. Here again we can see the influence of the Galilean teaching. The Russian seems haunted by the idea of sin and repentance. Along with the publican of the sacred parable, he is always saying, "Oh God, have mercy upon me, poor sinner." To him, Christ is primarily He who said, "The Son of Man is come to save the souls in peril," and who also said, "I am not come to call the just but the sinners."

The *moujik* is never tired of listening to the Gospel of Saint Luke, which is *par excellence* the gospel of forgiveness. What moves him to the depths of his soul is the privilege of forgiveness and the preference bestowed by the divine Master on those who hate their sins: "There is more joy in Heaven for one sinner that repenteth than for ninety and nine just men that need no repentance." He never tires of hearing the parables of the prodigal son and of the strayed sheep, the healing of the Samaritan leper and the promise of the Kingdom of God to the crucified thief.

Thus, contrary to common report, the Russian is very far from attaching importance to formal rites exclusively. Of course, the form of worship, services, sacraments, blessings, icons, relics, scapularies, candles, anthems, the practice of crossing himself, and genuflexions play a great part in his devotions. His lively imagination makes him very susceptible to outward pomp. But the moving force within him, and by a long way the most potent, is implicit faith, pure Christianity, without an element of metaphysics, the ever-present thought of the Savior, a deliberate contemplation of suffering and death and vague meditation on the supernatural world beyond our ken and on the mystery by which we are surrounded.

In many respects it is this evangelical idealism that accounts for the multitude of sects in Russia. There is no doubt that the discredit into which the official church had fallen owing to its subservience to the autocracy has contributed to the development of the spirit of sect, but the multiplicity of schisms is due to a more intimate need of the Russian soul.

Innumerable indeed are the religious communities that have broken away from the orthodox church or sprung into being outside it. First comes the most ancient, as also the largest and most austere of them, the Raskol, which has some points of resemblance to our Jansenism. Then there are the Doukhobors, who admit only one source of inspiration — spiritual intuition — and refuse to perform military service on the ground that they cannot shed blood; the Beglopopovtsy, abjuring priests who flee the satanical servitude of the official church; the Molokanes, "milk drinkers," who strive to live the Galilean life in its simple purity; the Stranniki, "Wanderers," who wander at their own sweet will through the steppes and the icy forests of Siberia in the hope of escaping from the kingdom of Antichrist; the Chtoundists, who preach agrarian communism "to put an end to the reign of the Pharaohs"; the Khlysty, who feel Christ born within them in their erotic ecstasies, and whose most brilliant representative at the moment is Rasputin; the Skoptzy, who practice castration to escape the allurements of the flesh; the Bialoritzy, who dress in white, "like the angels in Heaven," and go from village to village teaching innocence; the Pomortsy, who renounce the baptism they have received in infancy, because "Antichrist reigns over the Church," and repeat the baptismal sacrament with their own hands; the Nikoudichniky, bitter enemies of the social order, who seek the true Kingdom of Christ on earth "further on, ever further on," where sin is impossible; the Douchitely, "stranglers," who cut short the tortured last hours of the dying by choking them, from motives of human pity and retrospective sympathy for the sufferer of Calvary. And how many more!

All these sects trace their origin from the same principle: They all reveal the idea of a creed founded solely on purity of heart and the brotherhood of man, the necessity of direct communication between the soul and its God, the impossibility of believing that the clergy are an indispensable mediator between the Heavenly Father and His flock, the personal inspiration that refuses to accept the chains of the Church, and, lastly and mostly, the anarchy inherent in the Russian nature. The domestic activities of these communities reveal all the forms, excesses and varieties of religious emotion, the highest spirituality and the lowest materialism, the exaltation of the spirit and the mutilation of the flesh, fanaticism and belief in miracles, illuminism and divination, ecstasy and hysteria, asceticism and lust.

The faith of the Russian people being approximately as I have just described, one is faced with a very vexing dilemma. How is it that the *moujik* with so evangelical a spirit allows himself to be guilty of such appalling atrocities when his anger is roused? The murders, tortures, burnings and looting that marked the troubles of 1905 show us that he is capable of the same horrors as in the days of Pugatchev, or Ivan the Terrible, or any other period of his history.

It seems to me the reason is twofold: In the first place, the great majority of Russians have remained primitive, that is hardly beyond the stage of instinct; they are still the slaves of their impulses. Christianity has only penetrated certain parts of their nature; it in no way reaches their reason, and appeals less to their consciences than to their imaginations and emotions. It must be admitted, too, that when the *moujik's* rage has subsided, he at once recovers all his Christian gentleness and humility. He weeps over his victims and says masses for the repose of their souls. He confesses his crimes publicly, beats his bosom and sits in sackcloth and ashes. He revels in repentance and excels in the art of making it impressive.

The second reason is that the Gospels contain numerous precepts from which inferences can be drawn subversive of the modern state as we conceive it. The parable of the rich man who burns in Hell merely because he is rich, while Lazarus rests in Abraham's bosom, is a dangerous subject of meditation for the simple minds of the Russian proletariat and peasantry. In the same way, when life is very hard and they feel the wretchedness of their social condition very deeply, they like to think that it was Christ who said, "The first shall be last and the last first." Nor are they ignorant of the terrible words, "I am come to bring fire on the earth." Lastly, the tendency to communism, that lurks deep down in every *moujik*, finds more than one argument in its favor in the Galilean program.

Tolstoy has eloquently interpreted the Gospels "in the Russian sense," and he does not hesitate to say that private property is inconsistent with Christian doctrine, that every man has as much right to the fruits of the glebe as he has to the rays of the sun, and that the land should belong exclusively to those who cultivate it.

Tuesday, January 12, 1915

In the endless succession of foggy and icy days that make up winter in Petrograd, it is a depressing business to visit the Hermitage Museum.

The Italian galleries are encountered even before the last steps of the majestic staircase leading from the vestibule have been mounted. As if from the unfolding of a landscape, one sees the Titians, Veroneses, Tiepolos, Tintorettos, Canalettos, Guardis and Sciavones, the whole Venetian school, with here and there a few canvases of Guercino, Caravaggio and Salvator Rosa, hardly distinguishable in the gloom. From the windows in the roof descends a yellowish, dirty light that might have been filtered through some thin material. Through this wan veil, all these works of the Venetian masters, all these scenes of a luxurious life with its pomp and pageantry, seem to be suffering from intolerable homesickness. Tiepolo's 'Cleopatra' and Titian's 'Danae' fill one with pity. Dante's lines came to my mind: *"O settentrional vedovo sito!"* [O land of the North, unhappy widow who knows not the splendors of the South!].

There is the same air of melancholy in the French rooms, where the art of the seventeenth and eighteenth centuries is superbly represented by Poussin, Claude Lorrain, Mignard, Lenain, Largillière, Van Loo, Lemoyne, de Tory, Watteau, Chardin, Pater, Greuze, Boucher, Lancret, Fragonard, Hubert, Robert, &c. It is a unique collection and several of its canvases may be reckoned among the most exquisite and radiant creations of the French genius. But in the livid atmosphere of today, all these pictures lose their vivid color, their freshness, their brilliance, their spirit and their soul. The colors fade, the spell of harmonies is broken, the vibrations cease, the luminous glow is dimmed, the skies grow dark, the relief vanishes, the faces disappear. The long silent gallery seems like a cemetery.

Yet there is one part of the Hermitage where it is a treat to linger, even on dark days: I mean the four rooms devoted to Rembrandt.

The tawny half-light falling from the windows seems but an extension of the amber vapor in which the pictures are bathed. In the dim and golden fluid flowing through the gallery, the art of the great visionary attains a phenomenal power of calling dead things to life. Each face seems to glow with a strange, profound, remote and boundless vitality. The external world ceases to exist; the very depths of the life of the spirit are reached; the insoluble mystery of the soul and human destiny is touched. After a prolonged contemplation of masterpieces such as 'Pallas,' 'The Danae,' 'Abraham and the Angels,' 'The Sacrifice of Isaac,' 'The Reconciliation of David and Absalom,' 'The Fall of Aman,' 'The Parable of the Vineyard,' 'The Denial of St. Peter,' 'The Descent from the Cross,' 'The Unbelief of St. Thomas,' 'The Jewish Bride,' 'The Old Man of the Ghetto,' &c., it is easier to understand Carlyle's great thought: "History is a grandiose drama, played on the stage of the infinite, with the stars for lights and eternity as the background."

Thursday, January 14, 1915

According to the Gregorian Calendar, the year 1915 begins today. At two o'clock, under a wan sun and pearl-gray sky, which here and there cast silvery shadows on the snow, the

Diplomatic Corps called at Tsarskoe Selo to wish the Emperor a Happy New Year.

As usual, the ceremony is marked by the full display of pageantry, luxury of setting and that inimitable exhibition of pomp and power in which the Russian court has no rival.

The carriages drew up at the foot of the steps of the immense palace that Empress Elizabeth had built in her ambition to eclipse the court of Louis XV. We were taken into the Hall of Mirrors, a mass of gilding and glass, and a blaze of light. The various missions lined up in order of seniority, each ambassador or minister having his staff behind him.

Almost at once the Emperor entered, followed by his brilliant suite. He looked very well and his face was smiling and calm.

He conversed for a few minutes with each mission.

When he reached me, I offered him my congratulations, appending the words of encouragement and good cheer that General Joffre had asked me to convey to Grand Duke Nicholas. I added that in its recent declaration to the Chambers, the Government of the Republic had solemnly affirmed its determination to continue the war to the bitter end and that that determination is a guarantee of final victory.

The Emperor answered, "I have read that pronouncement of your Government and my whole heart goes with it. My own determination is no less. I shall continue this war as long as is necessary to secure a complete victory. You know I have just been visiting my army. I found it animated by splendid ardor and enthusiasm. All it asks is to be allowed to fight. It is confident of victory. Unfortunately, our operations are held up by the lack of munitions. We shall have to be patient for a time. But it is only a temporary suspension and Grand Duke Nicholas's general plan of campaign will in no way be changed. At the earliest possible moment my army will resume the offensive and the struggle will be continued until our enemies sue for peace. My recent journey all over Russia has shown me that I and my people are one on this point."

I thanked him for these words.

After a moment's reflection, he drew himself up and said in a thrilling voice that stressed each word.

"I should also tell you, Ambassador, that I am not unaware of certain attempts that have been made, even in Petrograd, to spread a notion that I am discouraged, that I see no possibility of crushing Germany, and that I am even thinking of making peace. Those who spread such rumors are vile creatures, German agents, but all their intrigues and inventions are beneath contempt. It is my will alone that counts, and you may be sure that I shall not change."

"The Government of the Republic has absolute confidence in the feelings that inspire Your Majesty," I said, "and has therefore ignored the miserable intrigues to which Your Majesty is good enough to refer. It will appreciate the more highly the declarations I shall convey to it in the name of Your Majesty."

He shook my hand and continued. "And please accept my very best wishes for yourself, my dear Ambassador."

Friday, January 15, 1915

A bright, sunny day, such a rare delight in these interminable winters! Although it is extremely cold, I went for a walk on the Islands where the northern sun was displaying all its magic over the icy expanse of the Gulf of Finland. A few clouds, shot through with flame, dotted the silvery blue of the sky. The northern lights played over the horizon. The hoar frost on the trees and the dazzling carpet of snow on the ground sparkled at intervals as if diamond dust had been scattered with a lavish hand.

I reflected upon what the Emperor had said to me yesterday, words that once more engraved on my mind the splendid moral resolution that has been his attitude since the war began. His idea of duty is certainly as high and grand as possible because it is perpetually nourished, vitalized and illuminated by his religion. But otherwise I should say that, as regards the exact science and the practical use of power, he is patently not equal to his task. I hasten to add that there is no one who could cope with such a task; it is quite *ultra vires*, beyond human power.

Does autocracy still meet the needs of the Russian character and the present stage of Russian civilization? It is a problem on which even the best minds hesitate to deliver an opinion, but what cannot be doubted is that autocracy is no longer compatible with the territorial expansion of Russia, the diversity of its races, and the development of its economic resources.

Compared with the present Empire of no less than 180,000,000 people spread over an area Of 22,000,000 square kilometers, what was the Russia of Ivan the Terrible, Peter the Great, Catherine II, or even Nicholas I? A genius no less than Napoleon's would be required to govern a state that has reached such colossal dimensions, to control all the energies and cogwheels of such a huge machine, and to unite and secure the smooth working of such complex elements.

Whatever may be the intrinsic virtues of autocratic Tsarism, it is a geographical anachronism.

Saturday, January 16, 1915

Yesterday, Madame Vyrubova was the victim of a railway accident outside Tsarskoe Selo. She was picked up with a fractured thigh, a dislocated shoulder, and severe contusions on the head. She was taken to the Empress's military hospital, and the Tsaritsa went at once to her friend's bedside.

The injured lady was in such a state of exhaustion and shock that the surgeons considered it impossible to operate at all until she had recovered her strength. They have decided to let her rest until today and simply applied temporary measures of relief.

Meanwhile, on the Empress's orders, Rasputin was at once sent for while he was dining with some lady friends in Petrograd. A special train brought him to Tsarskoe Selo an hour later.

When he was taken into Madame Vyrubova's room, she was still quite unconscious. He surveyed her calmly, just like any doctor. Then he resolutely touched the poor patient's forehead, murmuring a short prayer, after which he called out three times, "Annushka! Annushka! Annushka!"

At the third time she was seen to open her eyes.

Then, in an even more imperious tone he ordered, "Now, wake up and rise!"

She opened her eyes wide.

He repeated, "Rise!"

With her free arm she made an effort to get up.

He continued, but in a gentle voice. "Speak to me!"

She spoke to him in a feeble voice that grew stronger with every word.

Sunday, January 17, 1915

Major Langlois, who is liaison officer between the French G.H.Q. and the Russian G.H.Q., has arrived from Baranovici and leaves tomorrow for Paris via Sweden.

He has left Grand Duke Nicholas "full of enthusiasm and determined to resume the offensive the moment his army has received its munitions." The moral of the troops is good but their strength is weakened by recent losses.

Monday, January 18, 1915

I have been discussing the Russian peasant with Countess P....., who spends a large part of every year on her estates, nobly doing her duty as a barina. As a matter of fact, her moral inclination and a certain instinct for equity and good works make her prefer the society of the lowly.

"In the West," she told me, "no one understands our *moujiks*. Because a very large number of them cannot read or write, they are supposed to be defective in intelligence, stupid, if not barbarous. It's a tremendous mistake! They are ignorant, that is they have no knowledge; they lack positive notions; their education is very limited, and often non-existent. But though they may be untutored, their intelligence is nonetheless remarkable for its range, elasticity, and also its activity."

"Activity?"

"Certainly. Their minds are always at work. The *moujik* does not talk much, but he is always thinking, reflecting, turning things over in his mind, and dreaming."

"What does he think and dream about?"

"Primarily his material interests, his harvests, his cattle, the poverty that grinds him down or threatens to do so, the price of clothes and tea, the burden of taxation and forced labor, the next agrarian reform, and so on. But thoughts of a much more lofty nature obsess him also and echo into the very depths of his soul. That is particularly true in winter, in the long evenings in the *isba*, and the monotonous walks in the snow. A slow and melancholy reverie then claims him entirely. He thinks of human destiny, the meaning of life, the parables in the Gospels, the duty of generosity, the redemption of sin by suffering, the ultimate triumph of justice on God's earth. You can have no idea what a passion for reflection and a feeling for poetry are often to be found in the souls of our *moujiks*. I should add, too, that they use their intelligence very cleverly. They are splendid in discussion; they argue with much skill and subtlety. They often give you most witty replies, and display a talent for waggish insinuations and a fine sense of irony."

Tuesday, January 19, 1915

The Minister of Justice, Stcheglovitov, leader of the Extreme Right in the Council of Empire, and the most fervent and uncompromising of the reactionaries, has just called on me to thank me for some slight service I was able to do him.

We talked about the war, and I warned him it would be a very long one

"Illusions," I said, "cannot be tolerated any longer. The real test, the nature of which is becoming clear, has hardly begun, and it will be more and more severe. We must arm ourselves with an ample supply of moral and material forces, just as a ship is equipped for a long and dangerous voyage."

"Of course we must! The trial that it has pleased Providence to inflict upon us promises to be a terrible one, and we are obviously only at the beginning. But with God's aid, and the help of our good Allies, we shall come through triumphant. I have no doubt about our ultimate victory. But forgive me, Ambassador, if I lay stress on something you have just said. You think, and rightly, that we must equip ourselves with moral forces as much as with guns, rifles, and shells, as it is plain that this war has dreadful suffering and terrible sacrifices in store for us. I shiver at the thought. But so far as Russia is concerned, the problem of moral forces is comparatively simple. If the faith of the Russian people in monarchy is not troubled, they will face any trial and accomplish miracles of heroism and self-effacement. Never forget that in the eyes of Russians, I mean true Russians, His Majesty the Emperor personifies not only supreme authority but religion and the Fatherland itself. Believe me, outside Tsarism there is no salvation because there would be no more Russia." With a warmth in which I detected the thrill of rage as well as patriotism, he added, "The Tsar is the Anointed of the Lord, sent by God to be the supreme guardian of the Church and the all-powerful ruler of the Empire. In popular belief, he is even the image of Christ upon earth. As he receives his power from God, it is to God alone that he must account for it. The essential divinity of his authority has the second result that autocracy and nationalism are inseparable. Then, down with the fools who dare to assail these dogmas! Constitutional liberalism is a heresy as well as a stupid chimera. There is no national life except within the framework of autocracy and orthodoxy. If political reforms are necessary, they must be carried out only in the spirit of autocracy and orthodoxy."

I replied, "The main point that impresses me in what Your Excellency has just said is that the essential element of the strength of Russia is a close and intimate union between the Emperor and his people. For reasons different to yours, I come to the same conclusion. I shall never cease to advocate that union."

When he had gone, I reflected that I had just heard an exposition of the doctrine of pure Tsarism as taught twenty years ago by the famous procurator of the Holy Synod, Pobiedonostsev, to his young pupil Nicholas II, the same doctrine that the great writer Merejovsky once defined in a study on the insurrectionary troubles of 1905, a masterly work in which these bold words may be found:

> In the house of the Romanovs, as in that of the Atrides, a mysterious curse descends from generation to generation. Murders and adultery, blood and mud, 'the fifth act of a tragedy played in a brothel.' Peter I kills his son; Alexander I kills his father; Catherine II kills her husband. And beside these great and famous victims there are the mean, unknown, and unhappy abortions of the autocracy, such as Ivan Antonovitch, suffocated like mice in dark corners, in the cells of the Schlusselburg. The block, the rope, and poison, these are the true emblems of Russian autocracy. God's unction on the brows of the Tsars has become the brand and curse of Cain.

Wednesday, January 20, 1915

Yesterday Rasputin was run over on the Nevsky Prospekt by a *troika* going at full speed. He was picked up with a slight wound to the head.

After the accident to Madame Vyrubova five days ago, this fresh warning from Heaven is only too eloquent: The war is displeasing God more than ever!

Thursday, January 21, 1915

The pacifist propaganda with which Germany is so busy in Petrograd is also at work in the armies at the front. At several points, proclamations in Russian have been seized inciting the soldiers to stop fighting and declaring that Emperor Nicholas, with his fatherly heart, has already been won over to the idea of peace. Grand Duke Nicholas has thought it advisable to protest against these allusions to the Tsar. In an Army Order he has denounced this insidious scheme of the enemy as a vile crime. The Order ends thus: "All faithful subjects know that in Russia everyone, from the Commander-in-Chief to the private soldier, obeys, and obeys only, the sacred and august will of the Anointed of God, our deeply revered Emperor, who alone has the power to begin and end a war."

Monday, January 25, 1915

This afternoon, some shopping took me to Vassily Ostrov, the island that is the center of the intellectual life of Petrograd, as it is the quarter of the Academy of Sciences, the Academy of Fine Arts, the School of Mines, the Naval School, the Zoological Museum, the Historical and Philological Institutes, several schools, the physical and chemical laboratories, and all the great scholastic establishments.

As the weather cleared up a little, I left my car there and went for a stroll in the streets. I passed students at every step. How different they looked from the students one sees in the Latin Quarter in Paris, or the streets of Oxford and Cambridge. The faces, gestures, and voices, in fact the whole personality, of French students are the personification of youth, vitality, and a happy-go-lucky enthusiasm in the work and play of life. Even the eyes of those who look tired seem to sparkle with clear and frank intelligence. The outstanding characteristic of the English students, with their healthy complexion and loose limbs, is their air of determination, instinct for the practical, and cold, resolute, and well-balanced intellects.

Nothing of the kind is to be seen here. In the first place, Russian students are usually a sorry spectacle, with their haggard faces, drawn features, hollow cheeks, frail figures, thin arms, and pronounced stoops. These emaciated bodies in worn-out and tattered clothing are a living witness of the wretched condition of the university proletariat in Russia. Many students have no more than twenty-five rubles (60 francs) a month to live on, i.e. one-third of the bare minimum required to support a normal existence in this bleak climate. The result of this defective physiological replacement is not merely a debilitated organism. Combined with the strain of an active brain and mental anxieties, it involves the nervous system in a condition of permanent irritation. Hence these melancholy, or fevered, anxious, and haggard faces, these fanatical or prematurely aged looks, these features of ascetics, visionaries, and anarchists. I could not help thinking of the remark in 'Crime and Punishment' put into Judge Porphyre's mouth by Dostoievsky. "Raskolnikov's crime is the work of a mind over-excited by theories."

The women students, of whom there is a large number, repay observation no less. I happened to notice one coming out of a café in the company of four young men. They stopped on the pavement outside to resume an argument. The tall, pretty girl with bright, hard eyes under her astrakhan cap, was laying down the law. Two more students soon came out of the *traktir* and joined the group around her. Here, before my eyes, I had perhaps one of the most original types of Russian womanhood, a missionary of the revolutionary gospel.

Russian novelists, particularly Turgeniev, have often said that the women of their country greatly excel the men in strength of character, decision, and the temper of their wills. In the matter of love-making, it is almost always the woman who takes and retains the offensive, arouses and worries her partner, lays down the law, and decides everything; it is the woman whose orders are accepted and whose will prevails.

Russian women are just the same in a very different department of their activities, the domain of revolutionary political action.

In the faraway era of Nihilism, women, and particularly young girls, immediately won a high place among the most formidable protagonists in the heroic epoch of the *Narodnaia*

Volia. They had no rivals in their tragic work. In their first exploits they proved themselves wonderful Emmenides.

On January 24, 1878, Vera Zassulitch opened the series by firing point blank at General Trepov, the Prefect of the Saint Petersburg police. On March 13, 1881, Sophie Perovsky played an active part in the assassination of Alexander II. The following year, Vera Figner fomented a military revolt at Kharkov. In 1887, Sophie Gunsburg organized an attempt on the life of Alexander III. A little later, Catherine Brechkovsky embarked with Tchernov upon that untiring propaganda campaign that familiarized the humblest of the *moujiks* with the mirages of the Socialist gospel. In 1897, the lovely Marie Vietrov, imprisoned in the Fortress of Saint Peter and Saint Paul, and violated in her cell by a police officer, poured the oil of her lamp over herself and burnt herself to death. In 1901, Dora Brilliant joined with Guerchuny, Savinkov and Bourtzev to found the *Boievaia Organizatsya*, the "Fighting Organization," and on February 17, 1905, she kept watch at the Kremlin in Moscow in order that her comrade, Kalaiev, should be undisturbed in throwing the bomb that blew Grand Duke Sergius to pieces.

It is, of course, very difficult to find out anything about the counter-measures of the Russian police and judicial authorities in political affairs. The trials of which the public hears from time to time are always kept very quiet. They are always held *in camera* and the censorship only allows a short notice in the press. But I can give the names of, at any rate, twenty women who have played a part in plots and attempted assassinations over the last few years: Sophie

Ragozinnikov, Tatiana Leontiev, Marie Spiridonov, Seraphima Klitchoglou, Zynaida Konopliannikov, Lydia Stoure, Nathalie Klimov, Marussia Benevsky, Lydia Ezersky, Sophie Venediktov, Catherine Ismailovitch, Helene Ivanov, Anastasis Bitzenko, Marie Chkolnik, &c.

The share of women in terrorist plots is thus very important and often decisive.

What is the explanation of the fascination that revolutionary action has for Russian women? They obviously find in it something that satisfies the strongest instincts of their soul and temperament: their craving for excitement; their pity for the sufferings of the lowly; their genius for devotion and sacrifice; their excessive admiration of heroic deeds; their scorn of danger; their thirst for strong emotions; their hunger for independence; their taste for mystery and adventure, and a fevered, extravagant and rebellious existence.

Tuesday, January 26, 1915

I lunched at the Winter Palace with the Grand Mistress of the Court, the worthy Madame Narishkin. The other guests were Prince Kurakin, Princess Juri Troubetzkoy, Prince and Princess Shakhovskoy, Count Dimitri Tolstoy (Director of the Hermitage), Count Apraxin, &c.

The only subject of conversation was the war, which was discussed in very cautious language. All were agreed that it will be a very long war, that it still has many painful shocks in store for us, but that we are obliged to continue it to victory or perish forever.

In a tête-à-tête with Madame Narishkin I asked her what were the Emperor's views.

"He's splendid," she said. "Not the slightest sign of discouragement. Still calm, still resolute. Always ready with an encouraging word. Always the same absolute confidence in victory."

"What about Her Majesty the Empress?"

Referring to Madame Vyrubova's recent accident, Madame Narishkin replied, "You know that Her Majesty the Empress has had a sore trial over the last few days, and as she is very susceptible to emotional influences, her health has suffered. But she is just as determined as the Emperor, and only yesterday she said to me, 'We did everything we could to avert this war, and we may thus be certain that God will give us victory.' "

B…., who is greatly interested in the lowly and has passed a good deal of his time in the country, quoted to me today some expressive remarks made by a peasant he met some time ago.

> "It was at the great Lavra at Kiev," he said, "one of the pilgrims' days. In front of the Sacred Door I spied an old woman who must have been at least eighty. She was bent double, a bundle of bones, and could hardly drag herself along. I gave her a few kopecks to make her talkative,

and asked her, 'You look very tired, my poor friend. Where have you come from?'

'I'm from Tabinsjk, away in the Urals.'

'What a long way!'

'Yes, a very long way.'

'But you came by train, I suppose.'

'No, I can't afford a railway fare. I've walked.'

'Walked, from the Urals to Kiev? How long has it taken you?'

'several months. I don't know exactly.'

'I suppose you had someone with you.'

'No, I came alone.'

'Alone?" I looked at her in amazement. She continued. 'Yes, alone ... with my soul.'

I slipped a twenty-ruble note into her hand. It was a lot of money for her, but her remark was worth far more."

Wednesday, January 27, 1915

I have been calling on the venerable and attractive Koulomzin, Secretary of State, Member of the Council of Empire, Chevalier of the Distinguished Order of Saint Andrew, as I wanted to thank him for sending me a pamphlet. He is nearly eighty, and though he has grown old in the performance of his high duties, his mind is as clear as ever it was. I like talking to him, as he has a wealth of experience, good sense, and kindness of heart.

On the subject of the war he was very encouraging.

"Whatever our difficulties at the moment, may be it is an obligation of honor for Russia to overcome them. She owes it to her Allies and herself to continue the struggle, at any cost, until the complete defeat of Germany. But our Allies must be patient. In any case, the continuance of the war depends on His Majesty alone, and you know what his views are."

Then we talked about domestic politics. I did not conceal from him that I am uneasy about the discontent observable in all quarters and in all ranks of society.

He admitted that he, too, was concerned at the state of public opinion, and that reforms were required, but he added in a determined tone that impressed me, "The reforms I am contemplating, it would take too long to describe them in detail, have nothing in common with those advocated by our Constitutional Democrats in the Duma, and still less – forgive my plain speaking – with those so fervently recommended by certain Western publicists. Russia is not a Western country and never will be. Our whole national temperament is averse to your political methods. The reforms I have in mind are inspired by the two principles that are the pillars of our present system, and must be retained at any cost: autocracy and orthodoxy. Never forget that the Emperor has received his authority from God Himself in the sacrament of coronation, and that he is not only the head of the Russian State but the supreme guardian of the Orthodox Church, the supreme judge of the Holy Synod. The separation of civil and religious authority that seems so natural to you in France is impossible with us: it runs counter to our whole historic evolution. Tsarism and Orthodoxy are linked together by an indissoluble bond, the bond of divine right. The Tsar is no more free to renounce absolutism than to abjure the orthodox faith. Outside autocracy and orthodoxy, there is room for nought save revolution, and by revolution I mean anarchy, the total subversion of Russia. With us, revolution can only be destructive and anarchist. Look what happened to Tolstoy. As the climax to his aberrations, he renounces orthodoxy. He at once falls into anarchy. His break with the Church inevitably led him to deny the authority of the State."

"If I understand you rightly," I said, "political reform must be accompanied, perhaps even preceded, by ecclesiastical reform,-the suppression of the Holy Synod and the restoration of the Patriarchate, for example."

In obvious embarrassment, he replied, "You touch on a difficult question, Ambassador, a question on which the best minds are unhappily divided. But much can be done along those lines."

After a few remarks by way of digression, he turned the conversation to the eternal Russian problem in which all the others are involved, the agrarian problem. There is no one more competent to discuss this grave question than he, as, in 1861, he took an active part in the emancipation of the serfs and has been concerned in all the successive reforms since that date. He is said to have been one of the first to discover that the original idea was a mistake and to admit that the *moujik* should have been given personal ownership, the full and unrestricted proprietorship of his plot of land. The conveyance of the land to the *mir* has had the result of imbuing the Russian peasant with the essentially communist notion that the land belongs legally to those who cultivate it. The famous ordinances issued by Stolypin in 1906, and inspired by so liberal a spirit, had no more zealous advocate than Koulomzin.

He concluded as follows.

"In my view, the whole future of Russia depends upon the transfer to the peasantry of as much land as possible and the establishment of peasant proprietorship among the rural masses. The effects produced by the reform of 1906 are already very substantial. If God keeps us from absurd adventures, I believe that in fifteen or twenty years the system of private property will have completely ousted that of communal ownership among the peasantry."

Friday, January 29, 1915

As I was passing Tauride Gardens this afternoon, I met four soldiers on prison duty, who, sword in hand, were accompanying some wretched *moujik*, a ragged, haggard figure with a contrite and resigned expression, who could hardly drag his worn-out boots through the snow. The little procession was making for Chpalernaia Prison.

On the way, a woman stopped to gaze at it, a woman of the people, half-concealed in a great cloak of greenish wool lined with fur. She took off her gloves, unhooked her *pelisse*, rummaged in her thick skirts, drew out a purse, took a small coin from it, and gave it to the prisoner, simultaneously making the sign of the cross. The soldiers walked more slowly and stood aside to let her do so.

Before my eyes I had the scene from 'resurrection' in which Tolstoy shows us Maslova being taken from prison to the court between two policemen and receiving alms from a *moujik* who approaches her and makes the sign of the cross in the same way.

Sympathy with prisoners, convicts, and all who fall into the formidable clutches of the law, is inherent in the Russian people. In the eyes of the *moujik*, a breach of the penal code is not a crime, much less a moral wrong; it is a misfortune, a piece of ill-luck, a fatality that may happen to anyone if God so decrees.

Saturday, January 30, 1915

In a heart-to-heart talk with Sazonov, I have returned to the Polish question.

"I've no hesitation in mentioning it," I said, "as I know you're as anxious as I am to see the Kingdom of Poland restored."

"Under the scepter of the Romanovs," he broke in abruptly.

"That's what I mean. You know my point of view. To me, Poland, reconstituted in its national integrity and restored as an autonomous kingdom, is the necessary advanced guard of Slavism against Teutonism. Whereas if all the political ties between Poland and Russia were severed, she would inevitably fall into the orbit of Germany. Poland would thus resume her historic mission on the frontiers of Eastern Europe, the mission she performed in olden times when she fought against the Teutonic knights. At the same time it would mean a final rupture, a decree absolute of divorce between Germany and Russia."

"I agree with everything you've said and that's why our Germanophiles hate me so. But what do I care for their hatred, as I'm advocating one of the Emperor's pet ideas?"

"I think, too. The resurrection of Poland under the scepter of the Romanovs would be of very great advantage to the internal evolution of the Russian State. I'm not speaking as an Ally now, but rather as a friend of Russia, and, to a great extent, a political theorist. What I mean is this: one of the things that has struck me most in the year I have been with you, something that is hardly noticeable at all abroad, is the importance of the non-Russian populations within the Empire. Not their numerical importance alone, but rather their moral importance, their high notion of their ethnical individualism and their claim to stake out a national life distinct from that of the Russian mass. All your subject peoples – Poles, Lithuanians, Letts, Balts, Esthonians, Georgians, Armenians, Tartars and so on – are suffering from your administrative centralization, particularly as your bureaucracy has a heavy hand. Sooner or later you'll be compelled to introduce regional autonomy. If you don't, you'll have to be on your guard against separatism. From this point of view, the establishment of an autonomous Poland would be a very helpful innovation."

"You touch on the most ticklish and complex problem in domestic politics now. In theory I'd go a long way in the direction you suggest, but if we got down to practical solutions, you'd see how difficult they are to reconcile with Tsarism. Yet, to me, there's no Russia without Tsarism."

Sunday, January 31, 1915

'The Official Messenger of Petrograd' publishes the text of a telegram dated July 29 last, in which the Tsar Nicholas proposed to Emperor Wilhelm that the Austro-Serbian dispute should be referred to the Hague Tribunal.

The document reads as follows:

> *I thank you for your conciliatory and friendly telegram, whereas the communications of your Ambassador to my Minister today have been in a very different tone. Please clear up this difference. The Austro-Serbian problem must be submitted to the Hague Conference. I trust to your wisdom and friendship.*
>
> *Nicholas.*

The German Government omitted to publish this telegram in the series of messages passing directly between the two sovereigns in the critical days preceding the war.

I asked Sazonov, "How is it that neither Buchanan nor I knew of so important a document?"

"I didn't know of it myself. The Emperor sent it on his own initiative, without consulting anyone. In his mind it was a direct and personal appeal to the confidence and friendship of Emperor Wilhelm. He would have put forward his proposal again, and through official channels, if the Kaiser's answer had been favorable. As a matter of fact the Kaiser never replied at all. The minute of the telegram was discovered the other day when His Majesty's papers were being arranged. I got the Telegraph Service to confirm that the message had actually reached Berlin."

"It's alarming to think that our governments knew nothing of this telegram. It would have made an immense impression on public opinion in all countries. Just remember, July 29 was the time when the Triple Entente was leaving no stone unturned to save the cause of peace."

"Yes, it's most alarming."

"And think of Emperor Wilhelm's frightful responsibility for letting Emperor Nicholas's proposal go without a word in reply!"

"The only reply to such a proposal would have been acceptance. He did not reply because he wanted war."

"That is what History will say, for it is now clear that on July 29 Emperor Nicholas offered to submit the Austro-Serbian dispute to international arbitration, and that on the same day Emperor Franz Joseph fired the train by ordering the bombardment of Belgrade, and Emperor Wilhelm presided at the famous Potsdam Council that decided upon a general war."

Monday, February 1, 1915

On the left bank of the Vistula, in the region of Sochaczev, the Russians are engaged in a series of partial, short attacks that correspond closely with what Grand Duke Nicholas has called "as active a defense as possible."

In the Bukovina, they are slowly retreating owing to the shortage of ammunition.

Friday, February 5, 1915

I have just had a call from the Minister of Agriculture, Krivoshein. Of all the members of Goremykin's Cabinet, he and Sazonov are the most Liberal and the most devoted to the Alliance.

The Department of Agriculture is of vital importance in Russia; it may be said that it governs all economic and social life. In the performance of his huge task, Krivoshein displays qualities very rare among Russians — a clear and methodical head, a taste for precise and accurate information, a notion of leading principles and broad outlines, and the spirit of enterprise, persistence, and organization. His colonizing work in Siberia, Turkestan, Ferghana, Outer Mongolia, and the Kirghiz Steppe, is showing surprising results every year.

I asked him what were his impressions of G.H.Q., from which he has recently returned.

"Splendid," he said, "splendid! Grand Duke Nicholas is most confident and enthusiastic. The moment his artillery gets ammunition, he will take the offensive again. He is as determined as ever to march on Berlin."

He then spoke to me of the declaration to be read by the Government at the reopening of the Duma next Tuesday.

"I hope this declaration will have a great effect in Germany and Austria. It is certainly no less vigorous and uncompromising than that recently made by your Government to the Chambers. I can assure you that henceforth no one will wonder whether Russia is determined to continue the war to victory or not."

Then he told me that the day before yesterday the Emperor detailed to him at great length his ideas of the broad principles of the future peace, and several times declared his intention of doing away with the German

Empire. "I will not have," the Tsar said in a determined tone, "I'll never have, another ambassador of the German Emperor at my court."

Taking advantage of the friendly frankness of our relations, I asked Krivoshein if he were not afraid that the conduct of operations might soon be hampered, if not actually paralyzed, by internal difficulties.

After a moment's hesitation he replied, "I can trust you, Ambassador, and I'll tell you candidly what I think. I haven't the slightest doubt about the victory of our armies, on one condition – that there's the closest co-operation between the Government and public opinion. That co-operation was perfect at the beginning of the war, but I must admit, unfortunately, that it is threatened now. I spoke about it to the Emperor the day before yesterday. Unhappily this question is nothing new. The antagonism between the imperial authority and civil society is the greatest scourge of our political life. I have been watching it regretfully for a long time. A few years ago, I expressed all my resentment at it in a phrase that became rather celebrated at the time. I said, 'The future of Russia will remain precarious so long as the Government and society continue to regard each other as two hostile camps and refer to each other as *they* instead of using the word *us* to designate the Russian nation. Whose fault is it? Nobody's and everybody's, as usual. You're uneasy about the abuses and anachronisms of Tsarism. You're right. But can any substantial reform be ventured upon during the course of a war? Certainly not! For even if Tsarism has grave faults, it also has some of the highest qualities, qualities for which there is no substitute. It is the potent link between all the heterogeneous elements that the work of centuries has gradually grouped around ancient Muscovy. It is Tsarism alone that constitutes our national unity. Cast away that life-giving principle and you'll see Russia at once fall apart and dissolve. To whose advantage? Certainly not to that of France. One of the strongest reasons for my advocacy of Tsarism is that I believe it capable of evolution. It has been through so much evolution already. The institution of the Duma is a fact of enormous importance that has changed all our political psychology. I hold that further restriction of the imperial power is still necessary, and that the control of the Duma over the administration must be extended: I also think that there must be extensive decentralization in all our public services. But, once more, Ambassador, this can only take place after the war. For the moment, as I said to His Majesty the other day, the plain duty of Ministers is to remove the causes of friction that has been observable for several months between the Government and public opinion. It is a *sine qua non* of victory."

Tuesday, February 9, 1915

Much excitement today at the Tauride Palace, where the new session of the Duma has begun.

The Government pronouncement is all that Krivoshein had said. I could not ask for a tone of greater resolution. There was a thunder of applause when Goremykin said as loudly as his feeble voice would let him, "Turkey has joined our enemies, but her military forces are already shaken by our glorious Caucasian troops, and ever clearer before our eyes rises the radiant future of Russia on the shores of the sea that washes the walls of Constantinople."

This was followed by a moving speech by Sazonov, who very wisely made but a passing reference to the question of the Straits.

"The day is at hand which will see the solution of the economic and political problems now raised by the necessity of securing Russia access to the open sea."

The orators who followed him on the tribune voiced the aspirations of the nation.

Evgraf Kovalevsky, the Deputy for Voronej, declared that the war must put an end to the age-old struggle between Russia and Turkey, and he was cheered to the skies as he said, "The Straits are the key of our house. They must pass into our keeping with the territories on their shores."

In the same way Miliukov, the leader of the "Cadets," roused his audience to the highest pitch of enthusiasm when he thanked Sazonov for his words. "We are glad to know that the realization of our national task is making good progress. We can now be certain that Constantinople and the Straits will become ours at the opportune moment through diplomatic and military measures."

During a kind of interval, I had a talk with the President, Rodzianko, and several deputies – Miliukov, Shingariev, Protopopov, Kovalevsky, Basil Maklakov, Prince Boris Galitzin, Tchikhatchov and others. They all brought the same impression from their provinces. All of them told me that the national conscience had been stirred to the depths, and that the Russian nation would rise as one man against a peace that was not a peace of victory and did not give Constantinople to Russia.

Shingariev took me on one side and said, "What you have been seeing and hearing, Ambassador, is the real Russia, and I'll guarantee that, in her, France has a loyal ally, an ally who is prepared to give her last man and her last kopeck to the cause of victory. But it is true that Russia must not be betrayed by certain secret cabals that are becoming dangerous. You are in a better position than we ourselves, Ambassador, to see many things that we can only suspect. You cannot be too vigilant."

Shingariev, the Deputy for Petrograd, member of the "Cadet" Party, and a doctor by profession, is a distinguished and honest man. He was interpreting very accurately what all the soundest elements of the Russian public are thinking today.

Wednesday, February 10, 1915

When the war broke out, many Russian Socialists felt that it was their duty to co-operate with the other forces in the country in resistance to German aggression. They thought, too, that the universal brotherhood of the popular masses would be strengthened on the field of battle, and that the domestic emancipation of Russia would be the fruit of victory.

None of them was more convinced of this than one of the revolutionaries, Bourtzev, who had taken refuge in Paris and who made a name for himself in showing up the *agents provocateurs* of the Okhrana and denouncing the infamous methods of the imperial police. He was also very much impressed by the lofty tone of the proclamation to the Russian people issued by the Emperor on August 2:

> *In the dreadful hour of trial, let all intestine strife be forgotten, the bonds between the Tsar and his people be strengthened; and may Russia rise as one man to repel the attack of the insolent foe!*

A fortnight later, the publication of the proclamation to the Poles fortified him in his views. Without in any way renouncing his doctrines, or his hopes, he bravely advocated to his comrades in exile the necessity of a temporary reconciliation with Tsarism. To prove his trust in the new spirit of the Imperial Government, he then returned to Russia, believing that he could be more usefully employed in his own country.

He had hardly crossed the frontier before he was arrested. He was thrown into prison, and detained, pending trial. At length he was tried for certain of his former writings, and without receiving any credit for his conduct since the beginning of the war he was condemned to penal servitude for life in Siberia for the crime of high treason. He was immediately sent to Turukansk on the Jenissei, in the Polar Circle.

This morning I received from Viviani, Minister of Justice, a telegram describing the deplorable effect Bourtzev's sentence has had on the Socialists of France, and asking me to do everything in my power, but with due circumspection, to obtain a pardon for Bourtzev.

Apart from the patriotic attitude displayed by Bourtzev at the beginning of the war, his biography gives me no argument I can use in his favor with the imperial authorities who utterly detest him.

Vladimir Lvovitch Bourtzev, a scion of the small landed nobility, was born at Fort Alexandrovsk in 1862. At the age of twenty, he was imprisoned for his revolutionary propaganda. Released a month later, he was arrested again in 1885, and this time sentenced to seven years' detention in Siberia. A year later he succeeded in escaping from the penal settlement, and took refuge in Geneva, and subsequently in London.

Although English traditions as regards hospitality to political refugees are extremely liberal, he soon found himself in conflict with the law having published in his review, 'Narodno Voletz' (The Will of the People), a series of articles exhorting the youth of Russia "to imitate the glorious assassins of Alexander II." This incitement to regicide cost him eighteen months' hard labor.

On the expiration of his sentence, he returned to Switzerland, where his first act was to publish a pamphlet,

'Down with the Tsar,' that was quite enough to justify the sentence of the English judge.

By way of occupying his spare time, he edited a very interesting review, 'Byloie' (The Past), devoted to the history of liberal ideas and seditious movements in Russia.

But his hatred of Tsarism, the lust of battle, his romantic taste for secret and spectacular action, would not let him rest for long. In December 1901, he joined with Guerchouny, Azev, Tchernov, Dora Brilliant and Savinkov in starting a 'Fighting Organization' that was to concentrate and direct all the militant energies of the Socialist Party. A plan of campaign was drawn up.

Three victims of high station were selected: first, the Procurator of the Holy Synod, the fanatical theorist of autocracy, Pobiedonostsev; then General Prince Obolensky, Governor of Kharkov; and, lastly, the Minister of the Interior, Sipiaguin.

The attempt on Pobiedonostsev's life failed owing to the work of an informer. Prince Obolensky was only slightly wounded, but on April 15, 1902, Sipiaguin was shot through the heart and died instantly. Thereafter terrorist exploits multiplied apace.

At the end of 1903, the Russian Government protested to the Swiss Government against the facilities obtained by the revolutionaries on Swiss territory for the preparation of their plots. The information accompanying this protest was only too convincing. Bourtzev and his accomplices were accordingly expelled. They took refuge in Paris. Bourtzev took up his residence in a small house in the Boulevard Arago, where he professed to live a peaceful life devoted exclusively to historic research; but secretly and by degrees he transferred there the whole 'Fighting Organization' with its archives, secret meetings, and store of explosives.

At that time I was Director of the Russian Department at the Foreign Office, and it was thus that the name and activities of Bourtzev became known to me. Rataiev, the agent of the Okhrana in Paris, was not slow to discover the mysterious meeting place in the Boulevard Arago. On April 20, 1914, the Russian Embassy asked us to expel Bourtzev, denouncing him as one of the most dangerous revolutionaries, irreconcilable, and fanatical. The note given to us by the Ambassador, Nelidov, ended thus: "Bourtzev possesses a remarkable faculty for exciting the pernicious instincts of the revolutionary youth and turning them in a very short space of time into fanatics committed to crimes of violence."

It was this last sentence that particularly struck me. Its tone was different from that of the ordinary notes we were always receiving on the subject of Russian refugees. It described an uncommon character, and suggested an individual of marked originality.

The file also enclosed a photograph with a view to facilitating the task of our police. I saw a man who was still young, a man of frail appearance with a hollow chest and narrow shoulders. His face made a strong impression upon me – a haggard, ill-looking, ascetic face, brightened – or rather lit up – by his eyes that fascinated me with their gentle ardor. I at once understood this man's influence, his power to inspire and sweep others along, the strange magnetism that made him such a wonderful creator of energy in others, and so formidable an apostle of the gospel of revolution.

On the back of the photograph I read this dedication:

> *Never forget the great names of Jelabov, Sophie Perovskaia, Khalturin and Grinevitsky! Their names are our standard. They died in the firm conviction that we shall follow in their glorious tracks.*

On April 26, the Prefecture of Police notified Bourtzev of the decree of expulsion. However, since he had settled in Paris, he had made friends with the leaders of French Socialism, whose admiration and sympathy he had quickly gained by all that he had gone through and the fervor of his democratic mysticism, his persuasive eloquence, and the shy and moving gentleness of his frank eyes. He implored them to save him from a fresh migration.

Those were the days of the Combes Ministry, which submitted passively to the dictation of the Socialists in order to preserve its majority with the Left. Delcassé was Minister for Foreign Affairs, but on all questions of domestic policy he differed from his colleagues and jealously confined himself to his diplomatic duties, in which he consulted no one. Hence his amazement and rage when Nelidov told him in June that Bourtzev was still at large in Paris. An urgent appeal by Jaurès to Combes had prevented the decree of expulsion from being carried into effect.

Bourtzev, of course, made good use of the unfettered liberty he enjoyed in Paris. He brought the 'Fighting Organization' to the highest pitch of perfection. On July 28, in one of the busiest streets of Saint Petersburg, the Ismailovsky Prospekt, the Minister of the Interior, Plehve, was killed on the spot by a bomb.

Once more, and with greater insistence, the Russian Ambassador demanded the deportation of Bourtzev. Delcassé brought the matter up before the Council of Ministers, sent me several times to Police Headquarters, and spoke to Combes personally. It was in vain. The all-powerful protection of Jaurès shielded the terrorist once more, and the decree of expulsion was annulled.

These recollections of the 'Bourtzev Case' did not exactly encourage me to open the negotiations Viviani has imposed upon me. To whom should I apply? How, and in what form, was the discussion to be opened? The problem was all the more ticklish as questions of pardon appertain to the Minister of Justice's department. The present holder of that office is Stcheglovitov, the fiercest of all the reactionaries, the most jealous upholder of autocratic prerogatives, and a man who alleges that the alliance of Russia with the Western democracies means the inevitable downfall of Tsarism.

In my difficulty, I had a friendly talk with Sazonov.

He almost jumped out of his skin at first.

"A pardon for Bourtzev? You're not thinking of that! However carefully you may put it, you'll give Stcheglovitov and all our wild men of the Extreme Right a terrific argument against the Alliance. It's not the right moment either, indeed it isn't!"

But I reasoned with him and argued that a pardon for Bourtzev would be interpreted in all quarters as an act of national solidarity. I added that the French Socialist Ministers, such as Guesde, Sembat, and Albert Thomas, who were helping most patriotically in the war, needed assistance and encouragement in their task, and that an exhibition of clemency in favor of Bourtzev would do a good deal to strengthen their position with the advanced section of their party, in which all the old prejudices against Russia were still alive. I ended up by begging Sazonov to see if he could not lay my request before the Emperor personally without sending it up through Stcheglovitov:

"It's not a legal matter. It's a diplomatic affair of the first rank because it touches the moral relations of the two allied countries. My Government has no desire whatever to intervene in your domestic affairs. All it asks me to do is to suggest to you a step that will do the Russian cause a great deal of good in France. So I'm certain the Emperor will approve my appeal directly to himself. When the matter is brought to his notice in that way, I'm quite certain what his reply will be."

"I'll look into it, and think it over. I'll mention the matter again in a day or two."

After a few moments of gloomy silence Sazonov resumed as if some fresh objection had struck him.

"If you knew what infamous lies Bourtzev had the audacity to publish against the Emperor and Empress, you'd realize how dangerous your request is."

"I can trust to His Majesty's great judgment."

Friday, February 12, 1915

The repeated attacks to which the Russians have been treated in covering Warsaw on the Bzura line during the last ten days are only a feint. All indications point to the fact that the Germans have concentrated in East Prussia everything necessary for a very violent offensive, under the pressure of which the Russian line is already wavering.

Saturday, February 13, 1915

This morning Sazonov received me with a broad smile.

"I've good news for you. Guess!"

"What do you mean? Bourtzev's pardon?"

"Yes. I was received by the Emperor yesterday evening and put your request to him. I didn't get through without a struggle. His Majesty said: "Does Monsieur Paléologue know all the infamous things Bourtzev has written about the Empress and myself?' But I persevered, and the Emperor is so kind and has such a lofty conception of his sovereign mission, that he replied practically at once, 'All right. Tell the French Ambassador that I give him the wretch's pardon.' His Majesty could not resist the temptation to add, 'I don't seem to remember my Ambassador in Paris ever intervening to secure a pardon for any French political criminal.' "

I asked Sazonov to convey to the Emperor the expression of my deepest gratitude, and thanked him warmly personally for having pleaded my cause so effectively.

"You may be certain," I said, "that you and I have just rendered the Alliance a great service."

Chapter 9

Sunday, February 14, 1915

From the Tilsit region on the Lower Niemen, to Plotzk on the Vistula, the Russian army is on the retreat on a front of 450 kilometers. It has lost its entrenchments on the Angerapp and all the defiles between the Masurian Lakes that are so favorable for defense. It is retiring hastily on Kovno, Grodno, Osowiec and the Narev.

This series of reverses gives Rasputin his chance of gratifying his implacable hatred of Grand Duke Nicholas.

In his early days in St. Petersburg, in 1906, the *staretz* had no warmer patrons than Grand Dukes Nicholas and Peter Nicolaevitch and their Montenegrin wives, Grand Duchesses Anastasia and Militza. But one fine day, Grand Duke Nicholas realized his mistake, and, as a man of courage, did his best to repair it. He begged and prayed the Emperor to send the infamous *moujik* away. He returned to the charge several times, but nothing came of it. Rasputin has been hatching his revenge ever since.

So I am not surprised to hear that he is always railing against the Commander-in-Chief to the sovereigns. With his usual flair, he has at once discovered the arguments to which they are most susceptible. On the one hand, he is accusing the Grand Duke of resorting to all sorts of hypocritical methods of winning popularity with the soldiery and creating a political following in the army. On the other, he is always saying, "Nikolatcha can never succeed in any of his operations because God will never bless them. How could God possibly bless the actions of a man who has betrayed me, the *Bojy tchelloviek*, the 'Man of God'?"

Monday, February 15, 1915

I have been discussing Poland with Count R....., who is a raving Nationalist.

"You must admit," I said, "that the Poles have some ground for not loving Russia."

"That's true enough. We've sometimes been pretty hard on Poland. But Poland has fairly paid us back."

"In what way?"

"By giving us the Jews."

It is perfectly true that there was no Jewish question in Russia before the partitions of Poland.

Before that epoch, the only policy pursued by Tsarism towards the Jews was to deport or kill them off. These summary methods had to be dropped when the fate of the great Israelite communities in the annexed territories had to be determined. They were assigned a zone of residence on the western borders of the Empire and subjected to certain police regulations that were not unduly vexatious.

But during the preparations for the second partition, Catherine II suddenly introduced the regime of penalties and servitude from which they are not yet freed. By a decree dated December 23, 1791, she restricted their residential zone, she forbade them to take part in agriculture, she confined them to the towns and their ghettoes, and she enunciated the abominable doctrine, that prevails even today, that anything that is not expressly permitted is forbidden to a Jew.

This exhibition of despotism and iniquity might seem surprising in the philosopher-Empress who was the friend of Voltaire, d'Alembert, and Diderot, and the sovereign who claimed to draw her political inspiration from the Esprit des Lois. But there was a potent, though indirect, grievance that was responsible for her anger with the Jews. She loathed the Revolution, expended all her hatred and invective on it, and regarded it as a terrible menace to all thrones, and a criminal and diabolical affair. On September 27, 1791, the Constituent Assembly had emancipated the Jews and granted them equal civil rights. Catherine II replied with her decree of December 23, the evil effect of which was intensified by subsequent measures.

Thus, by an ironic repercussion of fate, the generous initiative of the French Revolution opened an era of persecutions at the other end of Europe, persecutions that were destined to be as prolonged and grievous as any Israel has known through the ages.

Tuesday, February 16, 1915

The 9th Army is having great difficulty in extricating itself from the forest region that stretches east of Augustovo and Suvalki. At Kolno, on the Lomza road further south, one of its columns has been surrounded and destroyed. The communiqués of the Stavka are confined to an announcement that, under the pressure of large forces, the Russian troops are retiring to the fortified line of the Niemen.

But the public understands.

This afternoon, I passed the Church of the Resurrection as I was driving through the industrial Kolomna quarter. A funeral stopped there at the same moment. The procession was a long one composed solely of workmen and *moujiks*.

I had my car stopped at the corner of the Torgovaia, and under the scandalized eyes of my footman, I mingled with the humble group following the bier.

Many and many a time have I watched such a crowd. Nowhere are Russian faces so expressive as in church. The mysterious darkness of the nave, the glittering candles, the play of light on icons and reliquaries, the smell of incense, the moving beauty of the singing, the imposing display of priestly robes, the magnificence of the whole liturgical apparatus, and the very length of the services, have a sort of enchantment that gives life to dead souls and brings them before our eyes.

In the faces before me, two expressions could soon be distinguished – faith and resignation: a simple, contemplative and sentimental faith, a dumb, passive and sorrowful resignation.

Fatalism and piety are the very essence of all Russian souls. To the great majority of them, God is only the theological synonym for fate.

Thursday, February 18, 1915

The 10th Army has not yet succeeded in completely escaping the German clutches. With a strength of four corps, perhaps twelve divisions, it is said to have already left 50,000 prisoners and 60 guns in the enemy's hands.

I have been dining privately at Tsarskoe Selo with Grand Duke Paul.

The Grand Duke questioned me anxiously about the operations that have just resulted in the loss to Russia of the invaluable pledge of East Prussia.

Every detail I gave him drew a deep sigh from his lips.

"What does it all mean, in God's name?" Then, recovering himself with a fine air of determination, he continued, "It doesn't matter! We shall go through with it. If we have to retreat further, we shall retreat. But I'll promise you we shall continue the war to victory. As a matter of fact, I'm only repeating to you what the Emperor and Empress said to me the day before yesterday. They're fortitude itself, both of them. Not a word of complaint or discouragement. They simply help each other to bear up. Not a soul about them, not a soul, I tell you, ever dares mention peace now."

Friday, February 19, 1915

The three corps of the 10th Army that were in danger of being surrounded in Augustovo Forest have at last succeeded in retiring to the line of the Bobr, where reinforcements have reached them. The communiqué of the Stavka simply reads: "Between the Niemen and the Fistula, our troops are gradually leaving the scene of the recent actions."

Saturday, February 20, 1915

Yesterday, the Anglo-French fleet bombarded the forts that command the entrance to the Dardanelles. It is the prelude to a landing on the Gallipoli Peninsula.

As I had to call on Sazonov this afternoon, I brought him away in my car. As we were crossing the Champ-de-Mars, we noticed several companies of infantry who were drilling. The men had difficulty in marching in the snow. The yellow fog that hung over the great parade ground gave the whole scene a most gloomy and funereal aspect.

Sazonov remarked with a sigh, "Look! There's a sad sight for you. I suppose there's about a thousand men there, and they're not conscripts being put through their paces, but trained men who are no doubt leaving for the front in a few days. And there's not a rifle among them! Isn't it dreadful? For Heaven's sake, Ambassador, stir up your Government to come to the rescue. If they don't, where shall we be?"

I promised him to press them again, and with the greatest vigor, to accelerate the dispatch of the rifles expected from France, for the sight of these poor *moujiks* on their way to the slaughterhouse tore my heart apart.

As we were continuing our drive in silence, a scene from Shakespeare came to my mind, a scene in which the great dramatist seems to have concentrated all the ironic pity with which the spectacle of human follies filled him. It is at the beginning of Henry IV: The merry Falstaff is presenting to Prince Henry of Lancaster a troop he has just recruited, a gang that is simply a collection of ragged beggars without arms.

"I never did see such pitiful rascals!" cries the Prince.

"Tut, tut!" cries Falstaff. "Food for powder, food for powder. They'll fill a pit as well as better. Tush, man! Mortal men, mortal men!"

Sunday, February 21, 1915

The communiqué of the Stavka announces the evacuation of East Prussia, and explains it without concealing too much. What impresses the public most is the insistence of the Russian General Staff on the advantage the enemy derives from his railway system. So the pessimists are going about saying, "That's why we shall never beat the Germans."

At the beginning of this month, the Duc de Guise (son of the late Duc de Chartres) arrived incognito in Sophia. He had fallen in with Delcassé's suggestion that he should use his influence with Tsar Ferdinand to persuade him to throw in his lot with us.

Ferdinand showed no anxiety to receive his nephew and on various excuses he did not receive him until he had made him wait six days. When at length he was taken to the palace, the Duc de Guise strongly insisted on the political reasons for Bulgaria's joining our coalition. With even greater fervor, he employed the family arguments that impose on the grandson of King Louis Philippe the duty of helping France.

The Tsar Ferdinand heard him out with his most attentive and amiable expression, but told him point blank that he meant to retain a completely free hand. And then, quite suddenly and with that evil smile I have so often seen on his face, he continued, "Now that you've done what you were sent to do, be my nephew once more."

And after that he talked commonplaces all the time.

The Duc de Guise was received at the palace three times over the next few days, but he never succeeded in bringing back the conversation to political matters.

On February 13, he left for Salonica.

The failure of his mission is significant.

Tuesday, February 23, 1915

The Germans continue to make progress between the Niemen and the Vistula.

With a reference to the weariness of his troops and the exhaustion of his ammunition supply, Grand Duke Nicholas had me discreetly informed a few days ago that he would be glad to see the French Army take the offensive with a view to preventing the transfer of German forces to the Eastern front.

In acquainting the French Government with his desire, I took care to remind them that Grand Duke Nicholas had not hesitated to sacrifice Samsonov's army on August 29 last in answer to our appeal for help.

The reply has been exactly what I expected. General Joffre has just ordered a vigorous attack in Champagne.

Wednesday, February 24, 1915

This afternoon as I was calling on Madame O…., who takes a very active part in Red Cross work, the door of the room suddenly flew open. A tall man, dressed in top boots and the long black caftan that well-to-do *moujiks* wear on holidays, strode towards Madame O….. and gave her a resounding kiss on the hand.

It was Rasputin.

With a swift glance at me he enquired, "Who is it?"

Madame O….. introduced me.

He continued. "Oh, yes, the French Ambassador! I'm pleased to meet him. He's the very man I want to see."

He began to rattle along, so much so that Madame O…., who acted as interpreter, had not even time to translate.

Thus I had a chance of taking stock of him. Dark, long, and ill-kempt hair, stiff black beard, high forehead, broad, aquiline nose. But the whole expression of the face was concentrated in the eyes – light-blue eyes with a curious sparkle, depth and fascination. His gaze was at once penetrating and caressing, naive and cunning, direct and yet remote. When he was excited it seemed as if his pupils became magnetic.

In short, jerky phrases, and with a wealth of gesticulation, he gave me a pathetic picture of the sufferings inflicted on the Russian people by the war.

"There are too many dead and wounded, too many widows and orphans, nothing but ruin and tears. Think of all the poor fellows who'll never come back, and remember that each of them has left behind him five, six, ten persons who can only weep. I know of villages where everybody's in mourning. And what about those who do come back? What are they like? Legless, armless, blind. It's terrible! For more than twenty years we shall harvest nothing but sorrow on Russian soil."

"Yes, indeed, it's terrible enough," I said, "but it would be far worse if all these sacrifices were to be in vain. A peace that was no peace, a peace that was the result of war-weariness, would be not merely a crime against our dead, it would bring with it internal crises from which our countries might never recover."

"You're right. We must fight on to victory."

"I'm glad to hear you say so, as I know several people in high places who are relying on you to persuade the Emperor not to continue the war."

He gave me a suspicious glance and scratched his beard. Then he shot out, "There are fools everywhere."

"Yes, but the bad thing is that these fools are believed in Berlin. Emperor Wilhelm is convinced that your friends, and you yourself, are using all your influence for peace."

"The Emperor Wilhelm? Why, don't you know he's inspired by the Devil? All he says and does is what the Devil tells him to. I know what I'm saying. It is the Devil alone who helps him. But one fine day the Devil will suddenly leave him, because God has so decreed. And Wilhelm will fall flat like an old shirt thrown on a dunghill."

"Then our victory is a certainty. It's obvious that the Devil cannot win."

"Yes, we shall be the victors. But I don't know when. God chooses the hour that seems good to Him for His miracles. We are not at the end of our trials. Much more blood and many more tears must flow."

He returned to his first topic, the necessity of alleviating the sufferings of the masses.

"It will cost enormous sums, millions and millions of rubles, but there must be no consideration of expense. When the people suffer too much, they get bad, you see. They may become dangerous. They may even sometimes go so far as to talk of a republic. You must tell the Emperor all this."

"You can't expect me to talk evil of a republic to the Emperor."

"Of course not, but you can tell him that you can't pay too much for the happiness of the people, and that France will give him all the money he needs. France is so rich!"

"France is rich because she works hard and saves hard. Quite recently she advanced large sums to Russia."

"Advanced large sums? What sums? I'm sure it was a case of more money for the *tchinovniks*. The peasants wouldn't get a kopeck of it. Take my word for it. No, speak to the Emperor as I told you."

"Speak to him yourself. You see him far more often than I."

He did not like my obstinacy. Raising his head and pressing his lips, he replied, in a tone that was all but insolent.

"That's not my business at all. I'm not the Emperor's Finance Minister. I'm the Minister of his soul!"

"All right, then. I'll speak to the Emperor, as you suggest, the next time I see him."

"Thank you! Thank you! Just one word more: Is Russia going to have Constantinople?"

"Yes, if we win."

"Is it certain?"

"I firmly believe so."

"Then the Russian people won't regret having suffered so much and will be willing to suffer more."

Thereupon he embraced Madame O....., clasped me in his arms, and strode out, banging the door behind him.

Saturday, February 27, 1915

The Anglo-French fleet is continuing its attack on the Dardanelles with the greatest vigor. All the outer forts are already silenced. The result is great public excitement in Russia, which expects to see the Allied ships off the Golden Horn any day now.

The Byzantine mirage mesmerizes public opinion more and more, and, indeed to such a pitch as to leave it almost indifferent to the loss of East Prussia, as if the defeat of Germany were not a condition precedent to the fulfilment of the Byzantine dream.

Sunday, February 28, 1915

The German advance in Poland and Lithuania has been stayed, and near Prasnyez, eighty kilometers north of Warsaw, they have even suffered a serious reverse.

Monday, March 1, 1915

This morning, Sazonov called the attention of Buchanan and myself to the excitement that the Constantinople question is rousing in all ranks of Russian society.

"A few weeks ago," he said, "I could still think that the opening of the Straits did not necessarily involve the definite occupation of Constantinople. Today I have to admit that the whole country demands that radical solution. Hitherto, Sir Edward Grey has confined himself to informing us that the question of the Straits must be settled in conformity with Russia's wishes. It is true that King George has gone further and said to our Ambassador, Benckendorff that Constantinople must be ours.

But the hour for plain speaking has come. The Russian people are now entitled to know that they can count on their Allies in the realization of their national task. England and France should say openly that they agree to the annexation of Constantinople by Russia when the day for peace arrives.

General Pau, who commanded the army in Alsace at the beginning of the war and captured Mulhausen, has reached Petrograd via Salonica, Sofia, and Bucharest. His mission is to convey French decorations to the Russian army. The impressions of France he brings are excellent.

I gave a dinner in his honor this evening. He communicated the confidence which his every word and look inspire to all present.

Wednesday, March 3, 1915

I presented General Pau to the Emperor today. General de Laguiche was with us.

At ten minutes to one, Count Benckendorff, Grand Marshal of the Court, took us to His Majesty in one of the small drawing rooms of Tsarskoe Selo. The Emperor was his natural and kindly self, as usual, but his questions to General Pau about our army, supplies, and operations were as obvious and casual as ever. As a matter of fact, the four young Grand Duchesses and the Tsarevitch came in with the Mistress of the Robes, Madame Narishkin. After the introductions we went straight in to luncheon.

In accordance with old Russian tradition, there is no dining room in the Alexander Palace. Meals are served sometimes in one room, sometimes in another, according to circumstances. Today the table, a round, old-fashioned family table, was laid in the library, where the sun, sparkling reflections of the snow and bright views down the garden created a light-hearted atmosphere.

I was on the Empress's right and General Pau on her left. Madame Narishkin was on the Emperor's right and General de Laguiche on his left. On my right, I had the eldest of the

Grand Duchesses, Olga Nicolaievna, who is nineteen-and-a-half. Her three sisters, the Tsarevitch and Count Benckendorff were the other members of the party.

The conversation was quite free and natural, but nevertheless dragged a little.

The Empress looked very well. She was obviously making a special effort to be gracious and smiling. She returned several times to the same subject Rasputin discussed so warmly with me, the endless chain of suffering the war means for the poor, and the political and moral duty of helping them.

The Tsarevitch found the meal long, and every now and then started playing pranks, to the despair of his sisters who frowned at him. The Emperor and Empress smiled and pretended not to notice him.

General Pau made an excellent impression with his natural dignity, his fine face – the face of an honest soldier – and his reputation for military talent, honor, and religious fervor.

The moment we rose from the table, the Emperor drew me to the end of the room and said in a serious tone, "You may remember the talk I had with you last November. My views have not changed since then, but there is one point on which events compel me to be more precise: I mean Constantinople. The question of the Straits is preoccupying public opinion in Russia to the highest degree. It is a current that flows more strongly every day. I could not admit my right to impose on my people the terrible sacrifices of this war if I did not reward them with the realization of their time-honored ambition. My mind is therefore made up, Ambassador. I shall adopt the radical solution of the problem of Constantinople and the Straits. The solution I outlined to you in December is the only possible and practical one. The City of Constantinople and southern Thrace must be incorporated in my Empire. Of course, I should be prepared to allow the city to be administered on special principles designed to safeguard foreign interests. You know that England has already expressed her approval. King George told my Ambassador quite recently, 'Constantinople must be yours.' That pronouncement is a guarantee of England's goodwill, but if any misunderstanding on questions of detail should arise, I shall count on the help of your Government in settling it."

"May I tell my Government, Sire, that Your Majesty's views on the problems that interest France directly have not changed either?"

"Certainly. I want France to emerge from this war as great and strong as possible. I agree beforehand to everything your Government wishes. Take the left bank of the Rhine, take Coblentz. Go even further, if you think it wise."

Then he took me back to the Empress, who was talking to General Pau and General de Laguiche. Five minutes later the sovereigns withdrew.

Monday, March 8, 1915

In accordance with instructions in a telegram from Delcassé this evening, I have told Sazonov that he may rely on the goodwill of the French Government as regards the questions of Constantinople and the Straits being solved in the manner desired by Russia.

Sazonov thanked me most warmly.

"Your Government," he said, "has just rendered the Alliance an invaluable service. Perhaps you yourself do not know how valuable."

Tuesday, March 9, 1915

The Emperor is extremely jealous of his authority. As is so often the case with weak characters, his jealousy is of the silent and suspicious, obstinate and resentful, variety.

Count Kokovtsov has given me a curious illustration of it.

"You may remember," he said, "that after the assassination of Stolypin in Kiev, in September 1911, the Emperor appointed me President of the Council. The moment my appointment was decided upon, I left His Majesty, who was just going to the Crimea, and returned straight to Petersburg. I took up my duties as soon as possible, and after three weeks or so I went to make my report to the Emperor, who was still at Yalta. As you may imagine, I had some pretty grave matters to put before him. He received me most kindly. 'I'm very pleased with you, Vladimir Nicolaievitch,' he said with a friendly smile. 'I know you've gathered good men around you and are working in the right spirit. I feel that you won't treat me as your predecessor, Peter Arkadievitch, did.' Speaking personally, Stolypin was not a friend of mine. There was plenty of mutual respect, but little sympathy between us. But I couldn't help answering, 'Peter Arkadievitch died for Your Majesty, Sire!' 'He died in my service, true, but he was always so anxious to keep me in the background. Do you suppose I liked always reading in the papers that the President of the Council has done this, the President of the Council has done that? Don't I count? Am I nobody?' "

Friday, March 12, 1915

As the price of its consent to Russia's designs on Constantinople and the Straits, the British Government has asked the Imperial Government to agree that the neutral zone in Persia (i.e. all the central part of Iran, including the Ispahan region) shall be incorporated into the English zone.
　Sazonov immediately replied to Buchanan, "Certainly!"
　Thus the Persian question, which has been a bone of contention between England and Russia for two centuries, has been settled in one minute!

Saturday, March 13, 1915

Count Witte died more or less suddenly from a cerebral tumor this morning. He was nearly sixty-seven.
　When telegraphing the news to Delcassé, I added, "With him a regular hotbed of intrigue has gone."

Sunday, March 14, 1915

It is now a week since I began to receive hints of a case of treachery on which the military authorities have preserved strict silence. I know now how serious it was.

A senior police officer, Lieutenant-Colonel Miassoyedov, who was formerly employed in the counterespionage police and was attached to the Intelligence Service of the 10th Army at the beginning of the war, has been arrested at Vilna on a charge of having communication with Germany.

The first information was given by a Russian officer, a prisoner-of-war whom the German General staff offered to set at liberty if he would agree to work in Germany's interest on his return to his own country. The officer pretended to agree, and his pretense was so convincing that he was given the name of the person to whom he was to apply for instructions as to the direction of his enquiries and the transmission of his correspondence. When he reached Petrograd, he immediately denounced Lieutenant Colonel Miassoyedov.

General Bielaiev, the Chief of the General Staff, was in no way surprised at receiving this information.

Around 1908, Miassoyedov, who was then in command of the police at the frontier station of Wirballen, had been implicated in an ugly case of smuggling. He had had to be placed on the retired list. He did not stay there long. His wife, a Jewish adventuress whom he had met at Carlsbad, had become a very close friend of Madame Sukhomlinov. The

Minister of War yielded to his wife's entreaties and took the unfaithful officer onto his personal staff.

Miassoyedov took advantage of his new post to extend his dealings with Germany and Austria, but notwithstanding all his cunning and the facilities given him by his official functions, he became the subject of very scandalous rumors and the most serious insinuations.

In 1911, Gutchkov, the leader of the Octobrist Party in the Duma, one day accused him publicly of being in the pay of the German General Staff. General Sukhomlinov covered his subordinate, and Miassoyedov then demanded, and obtained, satisfaction from Gutchkov. The duel was with pistols, and took place on one of the islands in the Neva. The conditions were very stringent, the distance between the duelists being fifteen paces only. Gutchkov a man of great courage and a splendid shot, placidly let his opponent fire first. When he heard the bullet whistle past his ear, he scornfully threw his weapon down and withdrew without so much as a look at the astonished Miassoyedov.

When Gutchkov's seconds asked him why he had spared the traitor's life he replied, "Because I don't want to save him from his natural death – hanging."

Thereafter Miassoyedov continued his intrigues in complete secrecy. Every day he has unlimited access to the Minister of War and Madame Sukhomlinov, to whom he acted as a sort of retriever and commission broker.

In August 1914, he was put in charge of the intelligence service of the 10th Army.

After securing certain subordinate officials and a flying officer as his accomplices, he sent the German General Staff reports on the movements of the Russian army, its condition as regards supplies, the state of public opinion, &c. The flying officer transmitted these reports when flying over the German lines at agreed times. There can be no doubt that these detailed and continuous reports have had a good deal to do with the series of reverses that have just compelled the Russians to evacuate East Prussia.

Before the Warsaw Court Martial, Miassoyedov protested his innocence, but the evidence against him seems to have been overwhelming. He was condemned to death and hanged on March 10.

The trial of his accomplices is not yet over.

Monday, March 15, 1915

The French Government has been considering the terms of peace to be imposed on Turkey by the Allies, and has instructed me to inform the Russian Government of the compensation France expects to receive in Syria.

The Emperor is now at G.H.Q., but he has asked me to go there to discuss the matter with him. Sazonov is invited also.

Tuesday, March 16, 1915

I left Petrograd yesterday evening in an imperial carriage attached to the Warsaw express, and this morning woke up in Vilna, from which place a special train conveyed me to

Baranovici. Until half-past twelve, we were traversing vast and almost deserted plains, stretching their rolling snowfields like an ermine carpet as far as the eye could reach.

Baranovici is a miserable little country town on the railway which connects Warsaw and Moscow via Brest-Litovsk, Minsk and Smolensk.

General Headquarters is established several versts from the town in a clearing in a forest of pines and birches. The various Staff departments are housed in a dozen trains standing fan-wise among the trees. Here and there between them, a number of military barracks and a few Cossack and gendarmerie posts can be seen.

I was taken straight to the imperial train, an endless line of huge saloons with the imperial arms in gold, under the sunlit foliage.

The Emperor received me immediately in his drawing-room car.

"I'm glad to see you here," he said, "at the General Headquarters of my armies. It will be another memory we shall have in common, my dear Ambassador."

"I already owe Your Majesty the unforgettable memory of Moscow. I cannot be in your presence here, at the heart of your armies, and remain unmoved."

"Let's have luncheon first. We can talk after. You must be very hungry."

We passed into the next car, comprising a smoking room and a long dining room. Luncheon had been laid for twenty guests. Grand Duke Nicholas Nicolaievitch sat on the Emperor's right, Grand Duke Peter Nicolaievitch on his left.

The place opposite His Majesty was occupied, as etiquette decrees, by Prince Dolgorukov, Marshal of the Court. I was on his right and had General Janushkevitch, Chief of Staff to the Commander-in-Chief, on my right. The table was narrow enough for conversation to be general.

We talked freely, and there was no lack of animation, no feeling of restraint. The Emperor was in high spirits and asked me about my journey, the success the French have just gained in the Argonne, the operations of the Allied squadrons off the Dardanelles, and so forth.

Then, with a sudden gleam of ironic satisfaction in his eyes, he said, "And we haven't said a word about poor Count Witte! I hope his death hasn't distressed you too much, Ambassador."

"No, indeed, Sire. When I reported his death to my Government, my funeral oration over him was confined to the words, 'With him a great hotbed of intrigue has gone.' "

"But that's exactly what I think. Listen, gentlemen …" He repeated my phrase twice. Then with a grave and solemn air, he remarked, "Count Witte's death has been a great relief to me. I also regard it as a sign from God."

His words revealed his fear and distrust of Witte.

As soon as luncheon was over, the Emperor took me into his study. It is a rectangular compartment, occupying the full width of the saloon, and filled with plain furniture and large leather chairs.

On a table there was a great pile of huge envelopes.

"Look at that," said the Emperor. "It's my daily task. I've got to get through all that today."

I know from Sazonov that he never misses this daily task, and is scrupulously careful to do the work – and it is heavy work – his position imposes.

He made me sit by him and with a kind smile gave me his whole attention.

"Now, I'm ready."

I described in detail the full program of civilizing work France intends to undertake in Syria, Cilicia and Palestine.

He made me carefully point out on the map the regions that would thus come under French influence and declared, "I agree to all you ask."

Our discussion on political topics was over. The Emperor then rose and took me to the other end of his study, where maps of Poland and Galicia were spread out on a long table.

He showed me the general distribution of his armies, and said, "In the Narev and Niemen regions, the danger is averted, but I attach even greater importance to the operations that have begun in the Carpathians. If our successes continue, we shall soon be masters of the main passes, which will enable us to break into the Hungarian plains. When that stage is reached, our operations will proceed more rapidly. By advancing along the southern slopes of the Carpathians, we shall reach the banks of the Oder and the Neisse. From there we shall penetrate into Silesia."

With these cheering words the Emperor released me.

"I know you're going back tonight, but we must meet again at tea. If you've nothing better to do, I'll take you to see some cinematograph films of our operations in Armenia. They're very interesting."

It was half-past two when I left the Emperor.

After a short talk with Sazonov, I called on the Commander-in-Chief, whose train was drawn up a few meters away.

The Grand Duke received me in a roomy and comfortable apartment spread with bearskins and eastern rugs.

In his customary frank and decided manner, he said, "I've some serious matters I want to talk to you about. It's not Grand Duke Nicholas talking to Monsieur Paléologue, it's the Commander-in-Chief of the Russian armies speaking officially to the French Ambassador. In that capacity, it's my duty to tell you that the immediate co-operation of Italy and Rumania is a matter of the greatest urgency. But please don't interpret these words as a cry of distress. I still think that, with God's help, victory will be ours. At the same time, without the immediate co-operation of France and Italy, the war will be prolonged for many months more and we shall run terrible risks."

I replied that the French Government had never ceased to intensify its efforts to gain allies. "Japan, Greece, Bulgaria, Rumania, Italy – Monsieur Delcassé has knocked at all their doors. At this very moment he is racking his brains as to how to get the Rumanian and Italian governments into line. But I cannot hide from you that Russia's claim to Constantinople and the Straits may perhaps make it impossible for these two governments to join our alliance."

"Oh, that's the business of diplomacy. It's outside my line altogether. Now let's talk as private individuals." He offered me a cigarette, made me sit beside him on a settee, and asked me innumerable questions about France. Twice he said to me, "I can't find words to express my admiration for France."

The course of conversation brought us to the question of operations. I told the Grand Duke what the Emperor had just told me about the plan of a general offensive in the direction of Silesia by the banks of the Oder and the Neisse:

"I confess I find it somewhat difficult to reconcile this plan with the disturbing prospects your statements open up."

The Grand Duke's face suddenly clouded over.

"I never discuss an opinion of His Majesty's except when he does me the honor to ask my advice."

Someone came in to say that the Emperor was waiting to have tea with us.

The Grand Duke took me with him. On our way, he showed me his saloon, which is fitted up most ingeniously and comfortably. His bedroom gets its light from four windows on one side of the carriage and is very simply furnished, but the walls are completely covered with icons. There must be at least two hundred of them!

After tea, the Emperor took me to a cinematograph improvised in a hut. We had a long series of picturesque scenes from the recent operations of the Russian army in the region of Tchorokh and Aghri Dagh.

As I gazed on the gigantic walls of Eastern Armenia, that chaos of huge mountains with their knife-edged crests slashed by ravines, I could realize all the valor the Russian soldiers must have displayed in advancing over such country in thirty degrees of frost and perpetual snowstorms.

When the show was over, the Emperor took me back to his saloon, where we parted.

At half-past seven, I left for Petrograd with Sazonov.

Friday, March 19, 1915

The Allied squadrons met with a reverse yesterday during a general attack on the forts that command the entrance to the Dardanelles. The French cruiser Bouvet struck a floating mine, the battleship Gaulois was put out of action, and two English battleships, Irresistible and Ocean, were sunk.

Saturday, March 20, 1915

The news of Miassoyedov's treachery is beginning to leak out in spite of the silence of the press. As usual, imagination joins in and searches for accomplices even amongst the greatest of the great at court. There is much excitement.

I have been shown in confidence a letter that the Labour Socialist Deputy, Kerensky, recently wrote to President Rodzianko, asking him to secure an immediate session of the Duma with a view to questions being put about the Miassoyedov affair.

"The center of all this treachery," he wrote, "is the Ministry of the Interior. Russian society knows well enough that those in charge of that department are bent solely on the restoration, at the earliest possible moment, of those old and close relations with the Prussian monarchy that were an indispensable support to our reactionary forces at home. The Duma must protect the country against these stabs in the back. In the name of my constituents, I beg you, Mr. President, to insist upon an immediate meeting of the Duma so that it may perform its duty of bringing the Executive to book at so grave a moment."

Of course, Rodzianko was unable to do anything.

Sunday, March 21, 1915

Feeling somewhat perturbed in mind as the result of my recent conversation with Grand Duke Nicholas, I have been to see General Bielaiev, Chief of the General Staff, and questioned him about the supply of ammunition for the Russian artillery.

This is the gist of his reply:

> *(1) The daily output of field-gun ammunition is at most 20,000 rounds at the moment;*

> *(2) If the orders placed abroad are executed by contract time, by the end of May the Russian artillery will have 65,000 rounds a day (of which 26,000 are expected from England and America). This figure will rise to 85,000 by the end of September;*

(3) *If the methods applied by the French munitions industry are adopted, our output could be increased by 10,000 after July. But if that result is to be obtained, the whole organization of Russian industry must be fundamentally changed.*

I am making urgent representations to Paris for the dispatch of a body of technical instructors.

Monday, March 22, 1915

After a Russian siege of four-and-a-half months, the fortress of Przemysl capitulated this morning.

From the strategic point of view, the incident is of very slight importance, but morally it steadies Russian public opinion a little at an opportune moment.

Tuesday, March 23, 1915

This evening I dined with Countess Marie Shuvalov, née Komarov, widow of Count Paul Andreievitch, who was Ambassador in Berlin and Governor-General of Poland. In addition to myself, she had invited Grand Duchess Marie Pavlovna, Maklakov (the Minister of the Interior), Prince Radziwill Tcharykov (formerly Ambassador to Constantinople), and others.

After dinner I had a long talk with Maklakov, who asked me about my recent audience with the Emperor. I enjoyed telling him of all the proofs the Emperor had given me of his determination to continue the war.

Maklakov kept on saying, "I'm very glad to hear you say so. Of course, we must go through with the war to the bitter end, yes, to the bitter end. I'm quite confident now that God will give us the victory."

But his face was deadly pale, his features were haggard, and he looked particularly downcast. For a long time he covered for Lieutenant Colonel Miassoyedov, and now he feels that the Emperor is angry with him and that the hour of his downfall is at hand.

Grand Duchess Marie Pavlovna was no less inquisitive about the impressions I had brought away with me from Baranovici. When I had told her what I thought, she said, ""I'm always easy in my mind when the Emperor is away from the Empress. It is she who makes him go wrong." Then she added, "I want to ask you an indiscreet question."

"With pleasure, Madame."

"Is it true that Miassoyedov's treachery was discovered by the French police, and that the reason the Emperor summoned you to Baranovici was to talk to you about it? And is it also true that Count Witte committed suicide when he found out that you had proof of his dealings with Germany in your possession?"

"I heard of the Miassoyedov affair only three or four days before his conviction and from a Russian officer. And as for Count Witte, I know for certain that he died quite suddenly of a cerebral tumor."

"I believe you. But the public will prefer my romance to your reality."

Wednesday, March 24, 1915

Interesting as the Russian novel is as an expression of the national mind and soul, illuminating as is the work of a Turgueniev, Tolstoy, Dostoievsky, Tchekov, Korolenko or Gorky from that point of view, Russian music carries us even further into the depths of the national conscience and emotions.

Renan has said of Turgueniev, "No man has ever been such an incarnation of a whole race. A world lived in him and spoke by his lips. Generations of ancestors, lost in the sleep of centuries, came to life and speech through him." Is that not even truer of Borodin, Moussorgsky, Rimsky-Korsakov, Tchaikovsky, Glazounov, Balakirev, or Liadov? Songs, operas, ballets, symphonies, orchestral and piano pieces, each work bears the imprint of the land and the race. Here one finds in the most seductive, fascinating and convincing forms the whole character and temperament of the Russians: their perpetual unrest, hasty and irresistible impulses, vague and sorrowful, impotent and conflicting aspirations; their tendency to melancholy, obsession by mystery and death, love of self-revelation and reverie, susceptibility to emotional extravagances; their bondage to their own passions, whether the most tender and refined or the most frenzied: their capacity for suffering and resignation on the one hand, fury and savagery on the other; their sensitiveness to the appeal of Nature and her still small voices and soothing or terrifying magic; and their vague realization of the atmosphere of fatality, gloom, tragedy, and enormity that shrouds the soil, the soul, and the history of Russia.

This afternoon I was deeply impressed by all this when I called on Madame S...., who for two hours sang me excerpts from Moussorgsky's works, Eremushka's 'Cradle Song,' 'The Elegy,' 'Hopak,' 'The Intermezzo,' 'The Dances of Death,' and so on, works throbbing with realism and emotional vitality. The power of musical evocation, the full force of suggestion through rhythm and melody, seem to reach their highest point in these songs.

Yet Moussorgsky has gone even further as an interpreter of the national conscience. His two lyrical dramas, 'Boris Godounov' and 'Khovantchina,' with their wondrous beauty, are first-hand authorities for a true understanding of the Russian soul.

A few days ago, I was present at a performance of 'Khovantchina.' The action takes place at the end of the seventeenth century and summarizes the remorseless struggle that Peter the Great maintained throughout his reign against the old Muscovite spirit, the barbarous, gloomy, and fanatical Russia of the boyars and monks, Raskolniks and Streltsy.

All the passions of that dark era appear successively on the canvas with the most lifelike relief. As in 'Boris Godounov,' the real hero, the protagonist in the drama, is the people. The national life is passing through one of its great crises, and from that point of view the last act has a grandeur that is nothing less than sublime.

Pursued by the Tsar's soldiery, the Raskolniks, or "Old Believers," have taken refuge in an *isba* buried in the heart of the woods. Their leader, the aged Dositheus, exhorts them to die rather than abjure their faith: he extols the virtue of death by fire, the "Red Death." After a number of enthusiastic or heartrending episodes, all the Raskolniks – men, women, girls, and children – agree to commit suicide; all of them long for martyrdom. They make a funeral pyre in a barn. The aged Dositheus recites the gospel. Hymns of triumph reply. Suddenly the pile of faggots blazes up and the doors of the *isba* are closed. Clouds of smoke seem to waft the dying anthems to the skies. The soldiers of the Tsar rush in just as the roof collapses on a heap of corpses.

For more than a century, suicide by burning, the "Red Death," was the fashion in the sect of the Raskol, and cost thousands and thousands of victims. The first apostle of this terrible doctrine was a simple *moujik*, Basil Volosaty, who was born about 1630 at Sokolsk, near Vladimir. He went about saying, "The Antichrist reigns on the earth, and the priests of the Church shamefully submit to his sway. To receive any sacrament from them, whether baptism, communion, marriage, or extreme unction, is to receive the mark of the Antichrist. The sins of him who bears that mark will never be forgiven. Then how shall he win salvation? By suicide. There is no other way. And if we think about it, how can we hesitate? By throwing ourselves into the flames, we immediately escape the power of the Antichrist. We get rid of all that is gross in us. We die with an unsullied faith and a purified soul. In exchange for a few moments of suffering we gain eternal bliss. We are immediately received in the company of saints."

The *Volosatovchtchina* spread with tremendous rapidity all over Russia. It made its greatest headway among the peasants and monks. Its principal centers were Vladimir, Kostroma, Suzdal, Yaroslavl, Novgorod, Onega, Viatka, Perm, and Western Siberia. Every year there were thousands of victims. At Potchekonie, in 1685, a single auto-da-fé accounted for seven hundred people. It needed all the ferocious energy of Peter the Great to check this madness.

But the same extraordinary phenomena have reappeared occasionally since. In the province of Olonetz, in 1860, there was a sudden epidemic of suicide by burning. The imperial police had to act with ruthless severity to suppress it.

Even in our own times, the annals of the Russian sects have had to record several cases of voluntary and wholesale auto-da-fé. In 1897, the Raskolnik village of Tarnov on the Dniester was terrorized by the preaching of a demented old woman, Vitalia, who announced the coming of the Antichrist. She saw him approaching in the curious form of the general census that the administrative authorities were then carrying out. When the census officials appeared in Tarnov, they found all the streets deserted and all the doors barricaded. Through a half-opened window a hand was thrust, in which was the following protest:

We are true Christians. The work on which you have come here would sever us from Christ who is our heavenly Fatherland, our only Fatherland. So we will not obey your orders; we will not give you our names. We would rather die for Christ.

The officials withdrew, saying they would shortly return with the police.

All the *moujiks* of the village immediately assembled in Vitalia's house and took counsel. The census, which was nothing but eternal damnation, must be avoided at any cost. After a brief discussion, the whole company, men and women, decided to bury themselves alive with their children. With a glowing and gloomy ardor, they feverishly dug four subterranean tunnels. Then, arrayed in shrouds and holding candles, they read their own burial service. For the last time Vitalia addressed them, without in any way hiding the ghastly sufferings that awaited them and yet would open the gates of heaven to them. Then, with songs of triumph, they all jumped into the pits, which they walled up from the inside.

When the authorities were informed and proceeded to exhume the bodies, it was found that the death agonies of the "martyrs" had lasted more than a day.

These tragic episodes are rare, but the religious sects that swarm in the shadow of orthodoxy are continually producing examples of collective "exaltation." Sometimes an epidemic of demonic possession breaks out in a village and spreads far and wide. Sometimes a hermitage or monastery becomes the center of a prophetic movement. Sometimes, again, a wave of idealist or sensual mysticism sweeps a whole district off its feet.

One of the most extraordinary manifestations that have been observed of recent years was the outbreak in the neighborhood of Kiev among the sect of the Maliovanists, which took the form of aberrations of the sense of smell. In their emotional fits, the faithful, simple peasants, thought they suddenly perceived smells of indescribable sweetness. With radiant faces they ran about smelling and blessing each other, convinced that what they noticed was the "odor of the Holy Spirit."

Facts of this kind, which are innumerable in the domestic history of Russia, emphasize one of the most characteristic features of the national temperament. No race is so susceptible to religious oratory and new ideas. In no other country, except, perhaps, the Mohammedan East, are the masses so excitable, so incapable of resisting mental contagion. Nowhere do psychic waves spread so rapidly and go so far. Every stage of the evolution of the Russian people is thus marked by a religious, moral or political epidemic.

In that respect the anarchist troubles of 1905 provide a most eloquent and formidable piece of evidence. The bloody mutinies in the fleet and army, the exploits of the "Black Band," the destruction in the Baltic Provinces, the pogroms of Armenians and Jews, were really nothing but epidemics of massacre, pillage and arson. In each of these tragic occurrences the mental contamination of the actors was practically immediate. By his susceptibility to every form of propaganda and the feebleness of his personal reactions, the *moujik* showed once more how backward he is, how near to nature, and how much the slave of his own instincts.

Saturday, March 27, 1915

In the whole realm of the Russian novel there are no feminine figures more appealing and seductive, or animated by a deeper and truer vitality, than the heroines of 'Smoke' and 'Anna Karenina,' yet Turgueniev and Tolstoy both went to life itself for their models.

The Irene of 'Smoke' reveals part of her secret herself. When that splendid creature, at once feminine and open-hearted, egotistical and passionate, tries to win back the man she was once to have married, but sacrificed to a calculation of personal advantage, the excuse she makes is that her ruined parents speculated infamously in her beauty in that she was taken to court and there attracted a very high personage who married her to a fat, tame general in order to make her his mistress. At the memory of this humiliation she lowers her eyes and murmurs, "It's a strange and melancholy story!" That young girl was the Princess Alexandra Sergueievna Dolgoruky, and the high personage who fell in love with her was none other than Emperor Alexander II. Around 1860, her influence with her imperial lover, the favors he heaped upon her, her quick intellect, charm of mind, and dignified manners, won her the nickname of *"La Grande Mademoiselle."* Before long, the Tsar married her to General Albedinsky, to whom a totally unexpected career was thus opened. He was Governor of Poland when he died.

Up to the last, Alexandra Sergueievna remained the friend and confidante of Alexander II. Her brother, Prince Alexander Dolgoruky, became Grand Marshal of the Imperial Court in the reign of Alexander III. One of her sisters married the present Grand Marshal, Count Paul Benckendorff.

Anna Karenina's adventure was also the result of observation from life. The character of Alexis Karenina, the main characteristics of Anna herself, and the moral struggle of the husband and wife, were suggested to Tolstoy by the secret drama that has just occurred in the family circle of the very worthy and pious Constantine Pobiedonostsev, the famous Procurator of the Holy Synod.

Sunday, March 28, 1915

Yesterday, the Emperor showed Sazonov a letter he had just received from Prince Gottfried von Hohenlohe, who is now the Austro-Hungarian Ambassador in Berlin after twelve years' service as a military attaché at the Royal and Imperial Embassy in Russia.

Recalling the friendly spirit the Emperor has always shown him, Prince Hohenlohe says he is prepared to answer for the pacific views of the court of Vienna. He has therefore suggested to the Tsar that a confidential envoy should be sent to Switzerland to confer with an emissary from Emperor Franz Joseph. He has no doubt that the basis of an honorable peace could easily be found.

"This letter," said Sazonov, "shows that the morale of Austria is very low, but no reply will be sent. Old Franz Joseph is not yet tired enough of the war to accept the terms we should impose."

I said nothing, as Delcassé has instructed me never to utter a word that might induce Russia to think that we will not abandon Austria to her *in toto*. But how, and by what mental aberration, is it that our people will not realize the enormous importance to us of detaching the Hapsburgs from the Teutonic coalition? Is our military situation so favorable as all that? Can the doubtful help we are expecting from Italy ever be worth as much as the immediate and irreparable loss to Germany that the defection of Austria would entail?

Tuesday, March 30, 1915

Ever since the war began, the Jews of Poland and Lithuania have been passing through the most terrible trials. In August, they were compelled to leave the frontier zone *en masse* and given no time to remove any of their belongings. After a short respite, the expulsions have begun again in the most summary, hasty, and brutal manner. All the Israelite inhabitants of Grodno, Lomza, Plotsk, Kutno, Lodz, Pietrokov, Kielce, Radom and Lublin have successively been driven into the interior in the direction of Podolia and Volhynia. Everywhere the process of departure has been marked by scenes of violence and pillage under the complacent eye of the authorities. Hundreds of thousands of these poor people have been seen wandering over the snows, driven like cattle by platoons of Cossacks, abandoned in the greatest distress at the stations, camping in the open around the towns, and dying of hunger, weariness and cold.

And to fortify their courage, these pitiful multitudes have everywhere encountered the same feelings of hatred and scorn, the same suspicion of espionage and treason. In its long and grievous history, Israel has never known more tragic migrations.

And yet there are 240,000 Jewish soldiers fighting, and fighting well, in the ranks of the Russian army!

Wednesday, March 31, 1915

Another lively discussion with Sazonov on the subject of the territorial claims that the Italian Government is making in Dalmatia.

"Italy's claims," he said, "are a challenge to the Slav conscience. Remember that Saint Isaac of Dalmatia is one of the greatest saints in the orthodox calendar."

I replied somewhat sharply, "We have taken up arms to save Serbia because the ruin of Serbia would have signified the final hegemony of the Teutonic powers, but we are not fighting to realize the chimeric dreams of Slavism. The sacrifice of Constantinople is quite enough."

"The days of Tsarisin are numbered. It is lost, lost beyond hope. But Tsarism is the very framework of Russia and the sole bond of unity for the nation. Revolution is now inevitable. It is only waiting for a favorable opportunity. Such an opportunity will come with some military defeat, a famine in the provinces, a strike in Petrograd, a riot in Moscow, some scandal or tragedy at the palace; it doesn't matter how. In any case, the revolution isn't the worst peril threatening Russia. What is a revolution, strictly speaking? It is the substitution of one political system for another by violence. A revolution may be a great benefit to a nation if it can reconstruct after having been destroyed. From that point of view, the English and French Revolutions strike me as having been rather salutary. But with us, revolution can only be destructive because the educated class is only a tiny minority, without organization, political experience, or contact with the masses. To my mind that is the greatest crime of Tsarism. It will not tolerate any center of political life and activity outside its own bureaucracy. Its success in that way has been so great that the day the *tchinovniks* disappear, the whole Russian State will dissolve. No doubt it will be the bourgeois, intellectuals, "Cadets" who give the signal for the revolution, thinking that they're saving Russia. But from the bourgeois revolution we shall at once descend to the working class revolution, and soon after that to the peasant revolution. And then will begin the most frightful anarchy, interminable anarchy. Ten years of anarchy! We shall see the days of Pugatchev again, and perhaps worse."

End of Volume 1

Printed in Great Britain
by Amazon